THE
TAVISTOCK AND ...
RAILWAY

BY

ANTHONY R. KINGDOM

This lovely 1930's scene 'Day Trip', depicted here by the railway artist Don Breckon, is typical of the Launceston Branch, particularly between Tavistock South and Lydford. It is reproduced from a print published by Solomon & Whitehead Ltd, signed and presented by Don Breckon to the author for use in this book.

Printed by   Western Litho Company of Plymouth,
              Heather House, Gibbon Lane, Plymouth
              Tel: (0752) 667241. Fax: (0752) 223855

ISBN 1 873029 00 4

Typical scene on the Launceston branch as No 5531 heads its train through sylvan beauty of a Dartmoor valley.

Devon Library Services

Bound by   Hartnolls Limited
              Bodmin
              Cornwall

Published by ARK Publications
              Newton Ferrers
              Devon

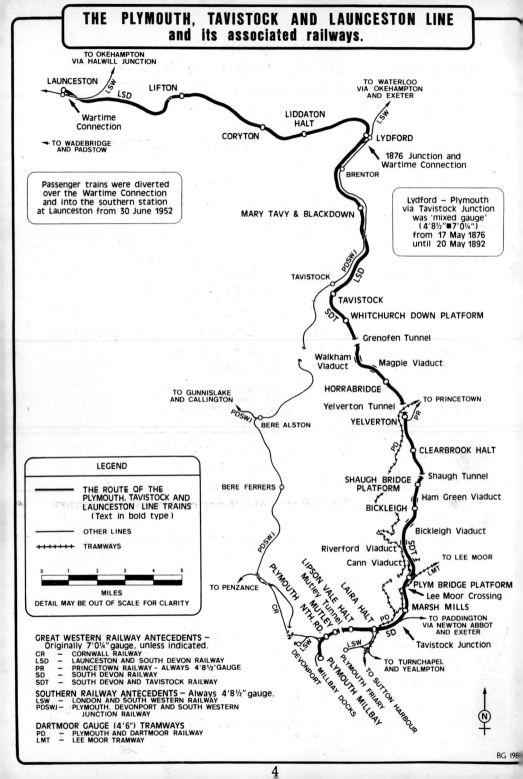

THE PLYMOUTH, TAVISTOCK AND LAUNCESTON LINE
and its associated railways.

TO OKEHAMPTON
VIA HALWILL JUNCTION

LAUNCESTON

LIFTON

Wartime
Connection

TO WADEBRIDGE
AND PADSTOW

LSW
LSD

CORYTON

LIDDATON
HALT

TO WATERLOO
VIA OKEHAMPTON
AND EXETER

LSW

LYDFORD

1876 Junction and
Wartime Connection

BRENTOR

Passenger trains were diverted
over the Wartime Connection
and into the southern station
at Launceston from 30 June 1952

MARY TAVY & BLACKDOWN

Lydford – Plymouth
via Tavistock Junction
was 'mixed gauge'
(4'8½" ■ 7'0¼")
from 17 May 1876
until 20 May 1892

PDSWJ
LSD

TAVISTOCK

TAVISTOCK

SDT

WHITCHURCH DOWN PLATFORM

Grenofen Tunnel

Walkham
Viaduct

Magpie Viaduct

TO GUNNISLAKE
AND CALLINGTON

HORRABRIDGE

Yelverton Tunnel

TO PRINCETOWN

PDSWJ

BERE ALSTON

YELVERTON

PR

PD

CLEARBROOK HALT

BERE FERRERS

Shaugh Tunnel

SHAUGH BRIDGE
PLATFORM

Ham Green Viaduct

BICKLEIGH

Bickleigh Viaduct

Riverford Viaduct

Cann Viaduct

SDT

TO LEE MOOR

LMT

LEGEND

━━━ THE ROUTE OF THE
PLYMOUTH, TAVISTOCK AND
LAUNCESTON LINE TRAINS
(Text in bold type)

──── OTHER LINES

+++++ TRAMWAYS

PLYM BRIDGE PLATFORM
Lee Moor Crossing

MARSH MILLS

0 1 2 3 4 5
MILES
DETAIL MAY BE OUT OF SCALE FOR CLARITY

TO PENZANCE

CR

PLYMOUTH NTH. RD.

LIPSON VALE HALT

Mutley Tunnel

MUTLEY

LAIRA HALT

PD

SD

TO PADDINGTON
VIA NEWTON ABBOT
AND EXETER

Tavistock Junction

DEVONPORT

LSW

LSW

Millbay Docks

PLYMOUTH MILLBAY

PLYMOUTH FRIARY

TO SUTTON HARBOUR

TO TURNCHAPEL
AND YEALMPTON

GREAT WESTERN RAILWAY ANTECEDENTS –
Originally 7'0¼" gauge, unless indicated.
CR — CORNWALL RAILWAY
LSD — LAUNCESTON AND SOUTH DEVON RAILWAY
PR — PRINCETOWN RAILWAY – ALWAYS 4'8½" GAUGE
SD — SOUTH DEVON RAILWAY
SDT — SOUTH DEVON AND TAVISTOCK RAILWAY

SOUTHERN RAILWAY ANTECEDENTS – Always 4'8½" gauge.
LSW — LONDON AND SOUTH WESTERN RAILWAY
PDSWJ– PLYMOUTH, DEVONPORT AND SOUTH WESTERN
JUNCTION RAILWAY

DARTMOOR GAUGE (4'6") TRAMWAYS
PD — PLYMOUTH AND DARTMOOR RAILWAY
LMT — LEE MOOR TRAMWAY

N

BG 198

Bibliography

Double Headed by G & D St John Thomas (David & Charles)

Go Great Western by T W E Roche MA (Branch Line Handbooks)

Historical Survey of Great Western Engine Sheds by
    E Lyons C Eng, MI Strc E (OPC)

Historical Survey of Great Western Engine Sheds 1837-1947 by
    E Lyons (OPC)

Historical Survey of Great Western Stations Vol 2 by R H Clark (OPC)

History of the Great Western Railway by E T MacDermot/C R Clinker
    (Ian Allan)

History of the Southern Railway by C F Dendy Marshall/R W Kidner
    (Ian Allan)

Launceston Castle by T L Jones MA (HMSO)

Locomotives of the GWR Parts 2, 4, 5, 6, 7, 9 & 11 (RCTS)

LSWR Locomotives 1873-1922 by F Brutt (Ian Allan)

Plymouth & Launceston by T W E Roche MA (Branch Line Handbooks)

Regional Histories of the Railways of Great Britain by
    D St John Thomas (David & Charles)

The Branch by B Mills (Plym Valley Railway Co Ltd)

The Gauge Conversion by C R Clinker (Avon Anglia)

The Lee Moor Tramway by R M S Hall (Oakwood Press)

The Plymouth & Dartmoor Railway by H G Kendall (Oakwood Press)

The Tavistock, Launceston & Princetown Railways by
    G H Anthony MICT (Oakwood Press)

The Withered Arm by T W E Roche MA (Branch Line & West Country
    Handbooks)

Through Western Windows by A S Caswell & T W E Roche MA (Town &
    Country Press)

Track Layout Diagrams of the GWR/BR by R A Cooke

Front cover: A striking study of Tavistock South during a pleasant summer evening on 8 August 1961. No 5569 pauses with the 5.30 pm Launceston to Plymouth train before setting off on the remaining 13 miles journey south.   Hugh Ballantyne

Front cover lower: See page 68 top

Rear Cover: Yelverton station at its busyest during a rainy day on 20 December 1955. Left to right, 4568 arrives bunker first with the 12.08 pm ex Princetown; 1408 waits in the up loop with the 12.50 pm Tavistock to Plymouth auto train; and 5567 waits on the down line with the 12.49 pm Plymouth to Launceston train.   Hugh Ballantyne

Acknowledgements

The author extends his sincere thanks to the following for their assistance, courtesy and time, generously given in the furtherance of the book.

Special thanks are due to Mr G H Anthony, MICT for permission to quote and refer to his notes. The late Mr T W E Roche, MA for his early works on the branch. The late J B N Ashford for his personal broad gauge notes and photographs. Mr E J Thomas and Mr L Crosier, both former signalmen on the branch, whose local knowledge has been a tremendous support. Mr Crosier was also responsible for the technical proof reading of the manuscript. Messrs M Wyatt and B Kohring for the loan of their tickets etc and Miss E Massey for the exacting job of typing the script on a word processor.

Photographs are acknowledged individually except those taken by the author or those from his private collection. Photographic work by R Elliff & Co Ltd, Photorail of Doncaster.

1   British Railways Board
2   Cornwall County Library
3   GWR Magazine
4   Great Western Society, South West Group
5   Launceston & Devon Post
6   Launceston Railway Circle
7   Ordnance Survey Office
8   Plymouth City Library
9   Public Records Office, Kew
10   Railway Magazine
11   Railway World
12   Signalling Records Society
13   South Devon Times
14   Tavistock Gazette
15   Tavistock Times
16   Trains Illustrated
17   West Devon Records Office
18   Western Independent
19   Western Evening Herald
20   Western Morning News

S. Ash;   D. Butler;   C. Barrett;
S. Blackmore;   A.L. Clamp;   A. Coombe;
D. Cullum;   A. Fairclough;   C. Fenneymore;
H. Frost;   B. Gibson;   L. Goodman;
P. Hayward;   J. Heseltine;   C.G. Lennox-Jones;
B. Lucas: R. Lumber;   D. Measey;
J.P. Morris;   R.K. Mulligan;   P.M. Pollinger;
P.J. Powell;   Col R. Spencer;   R. Taylor;
S. Taylor;   G. Thorne;   C. Winsor;
G. Wright;

Introduction

The Launceston branch had a complex and colourful history and a demise to match. It consisted of two formally independent railways which were joined together at Tavistock. They were the South Devon & Tavistock Railway which opened in 1859, and the Launceston & South Devon Railway which opened in 1865. They were in the forefront of the gauge war between the LSWR and the GWR and as such, they had the distinction of being mixed gauge between Lidford and Tavistock Junction on the branch and thence to Plymouth North Road on the main line. However with the advent of the LSWR main line from Lidford (as originally spelt) to Devonport, Kings Road during 1890, the branch returned to broad gauge passenger working. The demise of the broad gauge in May 1892 saw the removal of the 'third rail' as the branch became 'narrow' or more accurately, 4' 8^1/$_2$" standard gauge.

It was 36 miles long between its two terminii, and as its final demise was as late as 1966, it must surely qualify as a contestant for being one of the longest GWR branches both geographically and historically.

The second World War saw the bombing of Millbay and the consequent cessation of passenger services from there during 1941, whereupon all passenger services commenced and terminated at North Road. The description of the journey over the main line from Millbay to Lipson Junction is covered in 'The Yealmpton Branch' published by the OPC during 1974. From Lipson Junction the main line followed the course of the river Plym alongside its northern tidal bank after passing through the site of the former Laira Halt, with its famous motive power depot alongside. Still following the tidal Plym, the branch crosses it just west of Tavistock Junction and before they both swing northwards. From Marsh Mills the line was single throughout except for passing places at Bickleigh; Yelverton; Horrabridge; Tavistock; Lydford; Lifton and Launceston. It lost the use of its Launceston terminus in 1952 when branch trains were diverted into the Southern Railway station. World War 2 was also responsible for the connection of the branch to the SR main line at Lydford and Launceston prior to the build up for 'D' Day during 1943. The connections remained until closure and lifting which finally took place during 1966.

The 'Beeching Axe' was responsible for its complete closure, all protestations from local bodies were ignored by British Railway's whose pre-emptory attitude at that time was unshakeable. When closure did arrive it made railway history again, for it happened during the blizzard which started during late December 1962.

Copious chapters in many and varying publications have recorded this event in great detail therefore only a brief reference is made within the history chapter following.

Since closure, much of the trackbed had disappeared under a mantle of nature, but in the more urban areas, it has been built upon. Much of the moorland and river valleys over which the line ran are now conticent and empty. Only one station has survived with its building more or less intact, Coryton. This little country station is now a charming dwelling built by extending both upwards and outwards from the original building.

During early 1980 the Plym Valley Railway, with a battlecry 'Resurgam' commenced a grandiose scheme to relay and reopen part of the branch from Marsh Mills to Bickleigh and thence possibly to Yelverton. At the time of writing, approximately a half mile of temporary track has been laid for storage purposes.

However, returning to this book, it was with some trepidation that I decided to embark upon 'The Tavistock & Launceston Branch' during December 1981.

My established patterns formulated over the last ten years, writing accounts of the Yealmpton, Ashburton, Princetown and Turnchapel branches, were now in need of modification. This was necessary to enable me to achieve the task of recording the history of a 36 mile line with over 100 years of history within the confines of a book, the parameters of which were more suited to branches less than half the length and with three quarters the history. In addition to this fact, the line had been the subject of two previous authors.

'Plymouth & Launceston' by the late T W E Roche, MA, first appeared in November 1962, just prior to closure. This first edition was published by Branch Line Handbooks; the second edition was a more professional attempt and followed in 1965 as a printed booklet by the same publishers.

"TWEE" Roche, as he was affectionately known to all railway buffs, was in fact, a personal friend of mine who encouraged me continuously during the early days of preservation and during my time as Chairman of the South West Group of the Great Western Society. He was dearly loved by all within every aspect of railway interest in which he partook. Professionally, he was until his retirement during the early 1970's, Chief Immigration Officer, Custom & Excise, for all principal airports in the British Isles. He projected his leadership, power of expression, and organising abilities into his love for railways. This affection, particularly of the Great Western, was both dedicated and absolute, and I am indebted to him for his book and articles in the various magazines.

'The Tavistock, Launceston & Princetown Railways' was published by the Oakwood Press during 1971. Its author, Mr G H Anthony MICT, on his retirement, had the distinction of being the last Station-master of

Plymouth, North Road. He too was a personal friend of mine and his help on 'The Princetown Branch' noticeably lessened the burden of research. Now, in his eighty fifth year and not quite as active as in the past he has kindly given permission to quote from and refer to his notes and other material, a gesture which I truly appreciate.

I am now faced with following into print, these two very able gentlemen. I count it an honour to have known them both and to have had them as my friends. My only hope is that this book may prove to be a worthy follower to their individual and informative efforts. Both professional and domestic pressures have protracted the writing of this book to a period of over three years. Such has been that protraction that two events, one major and one minor, have overtaken its completion. The major event was the control of the Oxford Publishing Co transferred to the Blandford Press, a member of Link House Publishing, during July 1982. Policy changes followed and consequently my established patterns of writing already referred to required further modifications. This I have been pleased to do, but it has had a delaying effect, compounding those already affecting the completion. The minor event was my relegation to being the fourth author to write about the Launceston Branch. 'The Branch' by Bernard Mills suddenly appeared during December 1983. Nil desperandum, non omnia possumus omnes!

Anthony R Kingdom
'Thalassa'
Newton Ferrers Devon   September 1984

View taken from a Plymouth-Exeter train on the SR main line just south of Lydford.
The WR Launceston-Plymouth branch train heads for Tavistock
past Lydford down fixed distant

L Crosier

Author's Note

Readers may well wonder why this book is published during 1989-90 and the introduction is dated 1984. I think an update to the events preceding and following that is called for. The agreement for 'The Launceston Branch' was signed with the original Oxford Publishing Co on 4 December 1981 and the book was completed 30 September 1984.

The fact has passed into history that the OPC has been taken over by several other publishing companies each in their turn. This painful process caused many of the old company's successful lines to be axed under the name of 'rationalisation', the 'Branch Line' series for one.

Attempts to interest many other, some well known, publishers each ended with the return of the manuscript. Reasons for refusal ranged from 'not our style' to 'too large' and 'the end product would not be of an economic size'.

The numerous publishers approached each were responsible for months of procrastination and in all, five years of delay until finally I decided to publish the book myself. Finding a printer who was interested was equally exasperating, especially within the confines of my meagre budget.

Finally Western Litho Printers of Plymouth under the direction of Peter Howell, gave me that vital chance to publish, and on 24 June 1989 the m.s. came to rest upon his desk.

Ad postremum!

Further Acknowledgements

My sincere and grateful thanks to Peter Howell for the chance to publish and to the 13 fellow enthusiasts who put up the necessary extra finance to produce this book. Their names are recorded within the general acknowledgements in order to protect their anonymity at their request.

To Bryan Gibson for producing the excellent map of the line; information on the omnibus services and the associated time tables; for final proof reading of the updated m.s. and the rechecking of the historical dates and operational data.

Anthony R. Kingdom
ARK Publications,
Newton Ferrers,
Devon

June 1989

An early exterior view of the original terminus, Plymouth Millbay.
c early 1900's   *Author's collection*

Plymouth, North Road station prior to the reconstruction of 1938. Launceston train has
arrived on platform 6?

Lens of Sutton

The 3.5 pm auto train from Tavistock passes the rear of the former Beechwood factory near the site of Lipson Vale Halt.

c late 1950's   *W.E. Stevens*

Mutley Station, closed during 1939, was the first stop from Plymouth, North Road.
c 1920's   *LGRP*

The former Lipson Vale Halt on the main line between Mutley and Laira Halt.
c 1922   *LGRP*

The former Laira Halt on the main line between Plymouth and Plympton.
c 1922   *LGRP*

THE ROUTE DESCRIBED
TAVISTOCK JUNCTION TO
TAVISTOCK SOUTH

The branch proper, left the main line at Tavistock Junction as it headed northwards towards the first station, Marsh Mills.

Tavistock Junction lay approximately half way between Laira M.P.D. and Plympton station on the main line from Plymouth to Paddington. Immediately the junction had been negotiated the train passed the 'down home' and under a two arch limestone bridge carrying the old A38 over the line. This bridge is at the southern end of Marsh Mills station and the train drew to a halt no more than 18 chains down the branch. Upon entering from the south, the line ran straight through the station on a rising gradient of 1 in 200 adjacent to the down platform. On its passage through, the train crosses trailing points on 0m 14c at the southern end, provided as a crossover to the up line. At the northern end another set of points, facing for up trains, provided access to the up platform. It was not a true 'passing loop' as such, for the up branch line continued south to join with the down main line independently of the down branch line. At 0m 26c a third set of points, again facing for up trains, gave access into the clay works which were situated in an easterly direction behind the up platform. This access consisted of one main siding which had 'loop connection' at the southern end at 0m 10c, before running further south parallel to the branch and ending at stop blocks just short of the junction itself. The northern end of the siding ran into the clay works whilst further to the east a second siding ran north and parallel on to stop blocks. Two chains further on at 0m 28c a set of facing points gave access into the M.O.D. depot at Coypool, the details of which are outside the scope of this book.

Turning attention to the station, its up and down platforms were of the normal construction for a branch line station in the area, namely earthfill behind brick facing. Both surfaces were of tarmac and gravel with brick end slopes, the edges of platforms were of the standard concrete slabs with rounded shoulders painted white in latter years. The down platform building was constructed of local stone with granite facings at its corners, windows and door linings. It had a slate roof set off by two chimney stacks, ornate by any standard, which provided means of heating the waiting room/ticket office. The up platform building was constructed of similar material, was smaller in size and was an 'open fronted' design type waiting shelter. These two buildings lay approximately at the centres of their respective platforms with a foot crossing for railway staff between them. On the up platform,

The 3.9 pm Plymouth to Launceston train leaves the main line at Tavistock Junction before entering Marsh Mills station.

c 1958   *W.E. Stevens*

An 0-6-0 PT number 6430 and train enter Marsh Mills on a winters day during the late 1950's   L. Crosier

Marsh Mills Station taken from the former A38 road bridge, looking north.
c 1950's   L. Crosier

adjacent to the shelter, stood the signal box which housed a 32 lever frame. It was built with a brick base, and timber top with white painted window frames along its platform side and ends. It controlled the double line section of the branch in conjunction with Tavistock Junction signal box, local movements to the respective sidings, together with any local shunting operations. One entrance only provided access to the platform even though there was no connecting footbridge for passengers. The down side was served by a path leading down from the road serving the M.O.D. depot, just in from the road bridge, whilst access to the up side was by means of a 'barrow' crossing at the south end. At the rear of the down platform was a fairly high earthwork bank topped by a deciduous hedgerow, at its base a low stone wall retained spoil from spilling onto the platform. The up platform by way of contrast, was lined along its entire length with the erection of a wood paling fence, behind which lay the clay works sidings. Platform lighting was by means of electric filament lamps hung from back curving brackets, fixed on modification from gas lighting. These fittings replaced the old 'Windsor' pattern gas lamps but left the original cast iron standards resplendent in their purple and buff stone colours.

Standing at the southern end of the up platform was a fine example of a G.W.R. wooden signal, the top arm was the 'up starter' and the lower arm was the 'inner distant' for Tavistock Junction signal box. Another such example stood at the top end of the down platform, this had a single arm, that of the 'down starter'. Further down the line adjacent to the siding pointwork stood two brackets facing in opposite directions. The down bracket consisted of the 'down main advanced starter' and the 'down main to Ordnance Depot advanced starter'. The up bracket signal carried the 'up main home' and the 'up main to up sidings home' signals. Note: There were no signals protecting the Lee Moor Tramway here but there was a ground frame on the LMT which prevented the LMT waggons fouling the entrance to the Ordnance Depot. The ground frame was situated 330 yds from Marsh Mills signal box.

The branch train, having completed its picking up and setting down of passengers at the station, heads out on a rising gradient of 1 in 60 for the next 4 miles towards Bickleigh. At the top end of the Laira, the river Plym becomes no longer navigable and adopts a meandering course running roughly parallel to the branch on its western side. This it does all the way to the next stop, Plym Bridge Platform, not so the Lee Moor Tramway which also accompanies the branch on its western flank. The Tramway runs parallel to the branch from Marsh Mills to a point 1m 9c along it northwards, whereupon they cross. On leaving Marsh Mills and passing the aforementioned signals the train heads in a north westerly direction passing the 'down advanced starter' and 'L.M. Crossing down distant signals', Shearwood Plantation to the east and then the skirting of the ruins of Cann Cottages to the west, follows next. Swinging to the north east the rear of 'Marsh Mills up distant' M.P.1 and the 'L.M. Crossing down home' are passed as the train approaches Woodford Wood situated on its eastern flank. At 1m 9c the site of the former L.M.T. level crossing is reached, where the 4'6" gauge clay line crossed the branch in a south west to north east direction. Here stands Lee Moor Crossing signal box on the west of the line with its two home signals protecting it. It was no more than a ground frame, but as it had to be manned during the years of heavy traffic on the L.M.T., a miniature signal box was provided to house the gateman. (The tramway closed during 1947 but the crossing remained in operation until 1955, after which the signals were taken out of use).

A view of the Lee Moor Tramway crossing at 1m 9c.
c 1933   *R.W. Kidner*

Heading north east again the train passes the rear of 'L.M.T. Crossing up home' and continues along the flank of Woodford Wood, the L.M.T. now pulling away to the east as it heads for Lee Moor through Cann Wood. It is here just prior to the two lines crossing the Plymbridge road by their independent bridges that the next stop, Plym Bridge Platform is reached at 1m 39c.

Plym Bridge Platform took its name from the old narrow granite bridge spanning the river immediately below the embankment upon which the train was now standing. The bridge also gave its name to the

The later concrete structure of Plym Bridge Platform during 1950's
Lens of Sutton

Two studies of Plym Bridge platform during the last year of operation
viewed from Plym Bridge itself.
A.R. Kingdom

surrounding woodland area, a favourite family picnic spot since the turn of the century on account of its outstanding sylvan beauty. The 'platform' as it was rebuilt in 1949, was a stark and ugly, non G.W.R. structure of huge concrete slabs laid upon pre-stressed concrete members spanning legs of the same construction. Concrete posts supported a wire fence at the rear of the platform, and every so often, longer posts provided for the mounting of oil lamps. Seating was more than adequate for the traffic during the 'fifties, several seats with wooden slats secured to concrete legs - cum - backrests proliferated the platform and for inclement weather, a corrugated asbestos, on a timber frame shelter, provided further seating under a small canopy. The original halt was 100 feet longer, was equipped with a Booking Office and was constructed entirely of timber. Heavy timber trestle legs, cross braced, carried long lengths of hardwood planking used for the walking area. The fencing too, was of timber supports threaded through with wire and providing at intervals mountings for several 'Windsor' type copper lanterns. (The oil wells to light them were provided by the guard of the last down train before dusk and retrieved by the first up train after daybreak the following day).

Leaving Plym Bridge Platform, the train, running on a high embankment, continues to run generally northwards to penetrate more deeply into the Plym Forest, on a ruling gradient of 1 in 60 in so doing, it immediately crosses the Plym Bridge road by means of a stone bridge parallel to the wooden trestle bridge carrying the Lee Moor Tramway to the east of it. Another crossing quickly follows over a disused Cann Quarry canal, the train now making its way past Towers and Boringdon Woods to the east, and Mainstone Wood to the west, passing the rear of 'up distant' for Lee Moor crossing adjacent to Towers Wood. The train now heads deeply into Cann Wood following the course of the river Plym on its west flank, passing M.P.2, and running in a north westerly direction until the site of the disused Cann Quarry is reached with its limestone accommodation bridge crossing above the line. At this point, with Rumple Quarry and Colwill Woods, together with the river Plym to the west, and Cann Quarry to the east, the line crosses the same river Plym by means of Cann Viaduct at 2m 15c. The viaduct, built in 1907 to replace an earlier structure of Brunel's timber design, was constructed of blue Staffordshire brick. It was 127 yards long, supporting six arches, the highest being 63 feet tall, a massive structure in comparison with the narrow river it spanned.

After crossing the viaduct and still heading north, the train retains its affinity for the Plym, this time located on its eastern side as it cascades over a weir and borders Great Shaugh Wood. This is followed by a stretch of line between Colwill and Great Shaugh Woods on which a series of small embankments and cuttings are negotiated, the line

An early view of Cann Viaduct in the Plym Valley
c 1920's   F. Frith & Co. Ltd.

passes under an accommodation bridge to an old quarry near Common Wood House. It then breaks out on to a longer embankment and crosses a tributary of the Plym by means of Riverford Viaduct at 2m 65c. This viaduct, again replacing an earlier structure during 1893, was 127 yards long and 97 feet high, its five arches were constructed of granite. Having crossed two viaducts, passed M.P.3, it continues the journey through Henroost Wood and Hatshill Wood, the line veers north westerly, negotiates a straight stretch of some 1000 yards before approaching a third viaduct. This is Bickleigh Viaduct at 3m 37$^1/_2$c, built of granite, 167 yards long and 123 feet high, sporting seven arches and spanning the valley between Hatshill and Cann Woods with its tributary to the Plym. By now the woodland is receding as the train enters on to a panoramic view of the lower slopes of Dartmoor having passed Bickleigh 'down fixed distant' on leaving the viaduct. Adjacent to Bickleigh Bridge Wood where the road from Bickleigh village to Elfordleigh crosses the line, the river Plym tires of the branches company and veers away south east and then quickly north west to run parallel to it at a greater distance to the east, preparing as it does to completely abandon company with the railway further to the north at Shaugh Bridge.

The line is taking a course almost due east of Bickleigh village and approximately one mile from it as it makes its final approach, emerging from a deep cutting past M.P.4 and the 'down home' signal, into Bickleigh station on a rising gradient of 1 in 60.

Bickleigh station was the epitome of a Devonian country station, situated as it was at the southern slopes of Dartmoor in the beautiful Vale of Bickleigh. It nestled below Bickleigh Down to its west and

Shaugh Prior to its north east. It was a passing place at 4m 9c, with its two platforms, served on the down side by the running line of 904 feet and on the up side by the loop line of 980 feet, the northern end of which continued on to form the Ham Green Siding. At the southern end of the down platform trailing points ran back to connect with a down goods siding at its centre point. Here too stood the 'Bickleigh up starter' signal, the rear of which is passed on our journey. The down platform was constructed of earthfill from cuttings, faced with stone, and a surface of blue Staffordshire bricks. The platform edging was the usual large concrete slabs painted white at their edges. Two buildings occupied this platform, the original Saxby and Farmer signal box, built of brick and now used as a goods shed, and the main station buildings. The main buildings were built of stone and covered with a cement rendering, the roof was slate, the apex running parallel to the platform. A tall brick chimney stack protruded from the centre, containing a solitary chimney pot. A single doorway and three windows lined the platform side over which was constructed a short stubby canopy giving cover to two bench type platform seats. A square, flat roofed extension faced the roadside with a doorway and a further three windows. This building housed the usual waiting rooms and ticket office and was built to South Devon Railway design.

The southern end was boardered with white painted wooden fencing, whilst the northern end was boardered with shrubbery and flower beds, the entire length was lit by Windsor pattern gas lamps on cast iron standards. At the northern end also stands a cylindrical type G.W.R. water crane and the 'down starter' signal with its 'shunt' arm below it. The latter gave access into the section for shunting purposes only.

The up platform was of similar construction, but with a surface of chippings, a 'barrow crossing' connected it to the down at its southern end, this being the only means of access for passengers. Two buildings stood upon it, the later brick built G.W.R. signal box, opened in 1913, was situated south of its centre whilst at the centre was situated the up waiting room building. This was a picturesque stone built open building with a slate roof, its doorway and window frames lined with granite. The window frames, one at either end and two along the platform side were small multi-paned frames with curved tops. Upon its entire length the platform was bordered by black spiked iron railings and was lit similarly to the afore mentioned down platform. The two platforms, in common with Marsh Mills and the other passing places, were very widely spaced apart, a relic of the former broad gauge days. This space was utilised at Bickleigh by the provision of the pointwork rodding, the signal wires however were slung through pulleys upon the platform facing.

A general view of the down platform and S.D.R. signal box at Bickleigh looking north.
Lens of Sutton

Two views of Bickleigh Station
    a. looking south and showing 0-6-0 PT No 6400 with a train for Plymouth
    b. looking north and showing an unidentified PT leaving for Shaugh Bridge.
L. Crosier / I. Hocking

Running parallel to the line and to the west of it was the road down from Bickleigh village to Shaugh Prior and Plympton. As it passed by the station, a short stub road branched from it forming the station entrance road and the entrance to the Station Master's house.

A few yards further on this same road turned sharp right over the line by means of an old timber sided bridge which could be clearly seen from both platforms. From this bridge the road ran down to a tee junction where its divergence allowed access northwards to Shaugh Prior via Shaugh Bridge, or southwards via Bickleigh Bridge and Elfordleigh to Plympton.

As the train gains the right of way out of Bickleigh station, it passes under a road bridge, through a cutting with the up refuge or Ham Green siding dropping away to the east. Here also the rear of the 'up home signal' is passed, standing as it does to control the crossing loop from the north. Following the cutting the line all too soon emerges out onto the fourth viaduct of the journey. This is Ham Green viaduct at 4m 27c, constructed with six arches, it measured 190 yards long and 91 feet high and spanned yet another tributary of the river Plym. This stream flows eastwards past the hamlets of Hele and Ham to join the main river opposite Thrill Wood, one of the many beautiful little woods that boardered the Plym on its eastern flank at this point in the journey. The view from the train between Ham Green viaduct and the Stygian gloom of Shaugh tunnel, a distance of just less than a mile, is one of the most breathtaking of the whole journey. The train still travelling north-wards, passes through a short cutting to emerge out onto a shelf cut into the hillside. A high bank reaches up westwards into the dense undergrowth of Heleball Wood and a deep embankment reaching down eastwards to Ham Green Plantation which itself, separates the line from the Bickleigh to Shaugh road running parallel to it in the valley.

The northern end of Heleball Wood is terminated by the progress of Hele Lane, a small backroad from Bickleigh village crossing both the line and platform of the next stop, Shaugh Bridge Platform, at 4m 79c. The stone bridge carrying Hele Lane dominates the southern end of the little halt it spans. This halt served the village of Shaugh Prior a mile away on the distant hill to its east, its location clearly etched on the skyline by the eminence of the tower of St Edwards parish church. Nearer to the halt, a mere quarter of a mile distant to the northeast, is the famous high rock mass named the Dewerstone, rising above the wooded confluence of the Meavy and Plym, to a peak of 745 feet a.s.l. Shaugh Bridge Platform was just a long, curving single platform faced with brick with a slab edging and a surface of chippings. To the western side of the line a colourful bank of Rhododendron bushes blossomed in early summertime. The only building to grace the scene was a typical

*Above and left
Two general views of Shaugh Bridge
platform looking south towards
Marsh Mills.
L. Crosier/
Lens of Sutton*

*An unusual photograph showing the
approach of 2-6-2T No. 5572 and
train to Shaugh tunnel entrance. View
taken from inside the tunnel by the
photographer who was a British Rail
employee.
L. Crosier*

corrugated iron sheeting 'Pagoda' shelter, which contained Booking Office and Waiting Room accommodation, equipped with wooden bench seats, although there were once tea rooms here also, their demise followed the outbreak of the Second World War. The rear of the platform was lined with more Rhododendrons, conifers and some deciduous trees. Passing through the sturdy growth was a concrete post and wire fencing interspersed with cast iron lamp posts carrying Windsor lamp standards into which fitted the oil lamps to be lit at the appropriate times. The exit led out by the shelter to join Hele Lane en route for Shaugh Bridge, $^1/_2$ mile away. It is at Shaugh Bridge that the river Plym finally parts company with the line to strike an easterly course back to its source between Great Gnats Head and the marshland of Carters Beam, high on the moor. It is now the turn of the river Meavy to accompany the train upon its next stage of the journey.

Leaving Shaugh Bridge Platform behind the train passes M.P.5 and heads along the latter half of the 'breathtaking mile' to Shaugh tunnel. Just before it plunges into the darkness of the 308 yards long tunnel at 5m 20c, it passes under the iron aquaduct standing high above the line on its slender stone legs. It carried the now disused Wheal Lopes leat over the railway on its journey to join the river Meavy at Hoo Meavy Bridge. Running out of the Vale of Bickleigh, the trains progress launches it upon another lovely stretch of line. Emerging from Shaugh tunnel into a deep cutting, the line continues along the valley of the Meavy on a low embankment, past the hamlet of Leighbeer and the plantation of the same name.

They lie to the west of the line whilst to the east lay the hamlets of Goodameavy, Lower Goodameavy and Willake. The river Meavy keeps close company with the line to the east whilst the disused leat meanders back and forth under it with a series of culverts.

The embankment develops a high shoulder to its western side as M.P.6 is passed but levels out again as the line arrives at Clearbrook Halt at 6m 25c. Clearbrook Halt was one of the more austere efforts of the G.W.R. The platform was constructed of, and edged with, old sleepers kept into place with sections of bridgerail. A loose chipping surface ran back to an unfenced rear, the boundary was formed by a grass bank and various shrubbery. A couple of concrete posts made provision for the usual Windsor pattern lamps, whilst the station nameboard was an over large wooden affair sporting large cast iron letters, and mounted upon old rails. At the northern end of the platform stood a 'bicycleshed' type of corrugated iron waiting room with a solitary bench standing adjacent to it. The exit from the halt ran past the waiting room and down the bank to the road below by means of steps. Clearbrook village encompassed the halt, the adjacent bridge over the road situated immediately after it and the entrance to it. This made the

Two views of the little halt at Clearbrook
   a. Looking south towards Shaugh Bridge.
   b. looking north towards Yelverton.

Lens of Sutton

latter difficult to locate from the road for a passing stranger or 'tripper'. A high embankment follows the bridge, which incidentally, carries the line over a little moorland road in from the main A386, Plymouth to Tavistock road, to serve the villages of Clearbrook and Meavy. Progressing still in a northerly direction, the line winds its way through a series of embankments and cuttings through Mabor and Chubbtor Woods and under the shoulder of Roborough Down. Between the disused Yeoland Console Mine and Elford Town Farm, almost opposite M.P.7 the river Meavy decides it is its turn to part company with the line and strike eastwards via Gratton Bridge and Meavy Village to the foot of the dam at Burrator Reservoir lake.

It was the damming of 116 acres of contiguous land to the river Meavy at Burrator that gave birth to the giant reservoir that serves Plymouth with its water. Commenced on the 9th August 1893 and opened on 21st September 1898, its 651 million gallons capacity was later increased to 1,026 million gallons between 1924 and 1928, by raising the height of the dam. From the northern end of the lake the river Meavy continues back to its source near Princetown, high on the moor. Following M.P.7 the train makes a dead straight approach, past the 'up distant' for the first major station on the branch, Yelverton. It was the junction for the Princetown branch at 7m 37c.

Entering Yelverton from the south, in the down direction, the track ran straight through the station adjacent to the main down platform and on into the tunnel beyond. On its journey through the station, it passed the rear of the 'up advanced starter', the 'down home' on its east side and the down refuge siding on its west side which was catered for by a set of trailing points allowing trains to reverse into it. To the east there was a passing loop which formed the up line. Facing points at the southern end of the station formed an exit for up trains protected by the 'up starter' situated at the end of that platform. Trailing points in the down line at the northern end formed the entrance to the up loop and was under control of the 'up home' situated adjacent to them. The down platform was the longer but was not completely opposite the up platform. The up platform was constructed in a 'V' formation (with the two arms pointing south) and the Princetown branch platform forming the left hand arm of the 'V'. These two platforms formed an island and passenger access to them, apart from the standard G.W.R iron overbridge, was by a footpath emerging from the angle of the 'V'. This footpath ran along the foot of the south side of the embankment of the Princetown branch, entering the Yelverton to Cornwood road just south of Gratton Cross. No less than three 'barrow crossings' connected the up and down platforms for the use of railway staff.

The down platform construction was of the usual earthfill behind brick facing. The surface was of blue Staffordshire bricks etched with

27

*General view of Yelverton Station looking north towards Yelverton tunnel
and Horrabridge.*

c 1934   *S. Taylor*

*The Tavistock train is stoked on the down branch whilst No. 4407 blows off as it awaits
departure in the "Princetown" platform.*

c November 1949   *R.C. Sambourne*

A deserted scene at Yelverton during the summer of 1957 following the closure of the Princetown branch. The station nameboard now just reads 'Yelverton.

Author's collection.

Yelverton signal box and down platform showing the gas lighting plant gantry to left of picture.

c 1910

W.R. Gay's Series
Courtesy of E.J. Thomas

a diamond pattern to provide better adhesion under foot. The platform edge was of the standard thick concrete slabs with rounded shoulders, painted white in latter years. The whole length of the platform was backed with iron round spiked railings, so separating it from the access road outside the station. Half way up the platform stood the building housing the Ticket Office and Waiting Rooms. This was of a vertical wood planking construction, braced with heavier timbers to strengthen it. A timber apex roof, dressed with slate and finished with blue Staffordshire ridge tiles completed the building. Although of a modest size, this did not prevent it having a canopy extending out half way over the platform. This was of 'wedge shape' construction formed of short lengths of wood planking mounted vertically with the conventional 'saw tooth' pattern.

To the south side of this building stood the ubiquitous corrugated iron 'Pagoda' shelter with double wooden doors and two quarter light windows. It was used in latter days as the parcels office. To the left of it, until 1956, there stood a large wooden nameboard with cast iron lettering declaring "Yelverton - change for Dousland and Princetown Branch". From 1956 to 1962 its replacement read just "Yelverton". At the northern end of the down platform stood a water crane accompanied by another cast iron notice which read "Passengers are requested to cross the line by the bridge". At the north end also stood the 'down starter' with its shunt signal below it. At the same distance from the signal box and adjacent to the up loop line stood the 'up to down starting' signal allowing access from the Princetown side out onto the running line via the loop. It too had a 'Shunt' arm mounted below it which allowed entry into the next section for shunting purposes only. At the southern end of the platform stood the 35 lever signal box. It was built of brick throughout with a high windowless back, a timber apex roof covered with slate and finished with ridge tiles similar to the main building. All around vision was accomplished by multi-panelled sliding windows which ran the whole length of the eastern side (front) and half of each end; the latter were completed to the apex with lateral wooden planking. It had a brick chimney at the back, a wooden door and steps at the southern end and sported the standard GW cast iron nameplate. The 'up' and Princetown branch platforms were of similar construction to that of the down, except the finished surfaces were of paving stones around the main building, giving way to tarred chippings at their extremities. An identical station name board to the down side stood on the island just under the footbridge whilst on the Princetown platform stood another which stated "Yelverton - change for Tavistock, Launceston & Plymouth". The Waiting Rooms/Ticket Office/Toilets were contained in a building of an unusual polygonal design. It was constructed and finished in identical manner and materials as the one on the down platform, except its design centred around a cemented chimney stack housing three chimney pots. Short wedge shape canopies protruded radially from all sides except the south which faced the turntable.

The track layout on the Princetown branch platform was reached from points leading off the up loop just north of the island platform. An 'up inner home' bracket signal stood adjacent, the left hand arm giving access to the Princetown face from the up loop and the right hand arm guarding progress further into the up loop. This constituted the 'main' or running line on the branch and consequently ran adjacent to the branch platform. Trailing points provided a small spur backwards on the eastern side whilst at the far end there was a turn out into a facing spur on the southern end. This siding was equipped with reversing facilities onto the turntable road and inspection pit. The former was provided to turn the snowploughs.

Standing on the platform at Yelverton, one could look down the steeply deepening rock cutting, into and through the straight bore of the tunnel beyond. The next stage of the journey down the branch had commenced with the negotiation of these two major engineering works. Yelverton tunnel, situated at 7m $49^1/_2$c was 641 yards long and was constructed deep under the village of Yelverton itself. Emergence from the tunnel at its northern end brought the train into sudden daylight shafting into another deep rock cutting as M.P.8 and the rear

An unidentified 0-6-0 PT leaves Yelverton tunnel, bunker first, with a train for Plymouth during Summer 1954

B. Gibson Collection

of Yelverton 'up distant' are passed. A veer to the north west over a long curving embankment carries the train over an underpass almost adjacent to which stands Horrabridge 'down distant'. The underpass serves to connect the hamlets of Hillsborough and Ashfield on opposite sides of the line. Gaining in tightness of curvature, the line negotiates a second underpass and an over bridge across a rock cutting. Both these allow for passage of backroads to and from Walkhampton and Horrabridge village to Harrowbeer, lying to the west. Swinging back northwards temporarily, the line then allows the train to break out onto a high embankment before returning to the north west crossing the steel bridge over the A386 road from Yelverton to Tavistock, and passing the 'down main home' for Horrabridge station. Here too commenced the down loop over which our train would pass using the facing points. The bridge over which the train just passed was of a slewed configuration with high curved sides and it was more of a

An unusual study of Horrabridge station showing the 'bowstring' girder bridge that spanned the A386 Plymouth to Tavistock road below. There is also a fine view of the 'up home' signal which is a typical early GWR wooden construction.

R. Goulding collection

landmark to the road travellers below it than to the rail traveller. Following the commencement of the down loop, the up and down lines cross over the road from Buckland Monachorum to Horrabridge village by means of a typical G.W.R. level crossing. This crossing is adjacent to the southern end of the main platforms and the train now enters the confines of Horrabridge station down an incline of 1 in 60, at 8m 77c.

Horrabridge station, one time terminus for Princetown, stood high over the village it served and about a quarter to half a mile from it. It served a large area surrounding the village which itself could be clearly seen by passengers from the train as it waited in the station. Through the village runs the river Walkham whose turn it will soon be to accompany the train but for a short distance to a viaduct named after it, and thereby passing below the line on its way to join the river Tavy, its means of reaching the sea.

The river Walkham approaches Horrabridge Village from a north easterly direction descending from the moor, around the rock basin to the west side of Great Mis Tor, and from its source further up to the north east of Lynch Tor some 1600 feet a.s.l. It is within the journey from Yelverton tunnel to Horrabridge station that another glorious vista is opened up unto the rail traveller, that of the Walkham valley to Great Mis Tor and to North Hessary Tor.

Turning to the track layout of Horrabridge station, the main running line ran through adjacent to the 'up' platform, the opposite from Yelverton. Facing and trailing pointwork at either end provided the access to a passing loop adjacent to the down platform. The points at the southern end were immediately after the bridge, whilst at the northern end the points were well past the ends of the platforms and were very near to the water tank tower and the weighbridge. The 'down' loop pointwork at the northern end continued on by means of another set of facing points into the 'down siding' which itself reversed back to 'stop blocks' at the platform end. Here alongside these buffer stops, stood the 'down main starter' and M.P.9. Trailing pointwork at the northern end of the 'up' platform provided access into a longer 'up siding', which ran parallel to both the running line and the 'down siding'. It also ran forward into a small goods dock slightly to the rear of the signal box. Between the 'up' main and 'up siding' stood the 'up main home' controlling entry into the station from the Tavistock direction.

Consideration of the buildings and platforms of the station were simple but rather depressing. Horrabridge station was ideally situated with a commanding view, but unfortunately was not pretty or well kept in later years. It consisted of two platforms, an 'up' and a 'down' built on a gentle curve. The 'down' was much the longer of the two and upon it stood a small stone building with a slate roof, similar to that at Bickleigh. This was the open fronted waiting room. The 'up' platform although shorter, was the principle one and upon this one stood the main building housing the usual waiting room and ticket office. It was of timber construction, namely of wide lateral planking, its short stubby canopy giving no more than essential cover to the platform outside it. Public entrance to the station was by road in from the main A386 or, using the level crossing at the southern end, from either Horrabridge village or Buckland Monachorum. Nearby the level crossing and, at the southern end of the 'up' platform stood the 'up starter' with its lower 'shunt' arm. Situated also on the 'up' side were a goods shed, loading bank, a $3^1/_2$ ton crane, a loading gauge etc all north of the signal box and contained behind a wooden fence equipped with a large pair of gates. The 'up' platform was fenced at its rear with white wooden paling fencing and was lit by gas lamps suspended from swan neck mountings upon 'Windsor' standards. The same was true of the 'down' platform with the exception that there was no fencing as the high grass bank interspersed with shrubbery, rising to above the height of the waiting room building, formed its boundary. At either end of the platforms were water cranes situated between the up and down lines, there was plenty of room thanks again to the passing of the broad gauge. The water cranes were supplied from the large tower standing at the northern approach to the station as previously mentioned. Both platforms were equipped with large wood and cast iron nameboards and the level crossing provided access to the down side. A warning notice informing passengers to "Stop, Look & Listen" stood close by and inside the entry gate in from the road. In addition a foot crossing for all station staff was positioned half way along the platforms length. The construction of the two platforms were of the usual rock and earth infill faced with stone and edged with slabs. The surfaces however have seen much repair and change over the years. The originals were of the diagonally etched blue Staffordshire bricks laid at right angles to the line, but by the 1950's chippings and paving stones added to the mixture. Further courses of brickwork were laid parallel to the line. The signal box, standing adjacent to the main station building on the up side, was the original Saxby & Farmer box of the South Devon railway. It consisted of a brick base with the usual windows at each end and along the platform side, but with the inclusion of small fanlight windows over each frame. This was the 'tell tale' sign that gave away its age and differentiated it from G.W.R. signal boxes. A small wooden porch and a set of steps gave entry at its north facing end, the whole box was equipped with slate roof capped with a brick chimney and metal ventilator.

The train is now ready to commence its journey to Tavistock and pulls out of the platform loop, past the 'down starter' in the off position, over the trailing points out onto the running line. It now heads north through Harwood Plantation and then north west past the 'up fixed distant' for Horrabridge. A long embankment, with a steep rock

Two views of Horrabridge station looking towards Yelverton during the late 1950's
  a) Shows the over road bridge in the centre background
  b) Shows both 'up' amd 'down' trains passing

Horrabridge Station looking towards Yelverton on a very sunny day
during the early 1950's

shoulder to its western side, then leads out onto Magpie Viaduct, which is situated at 9m 46c. This viaduct, opened during June 1902, replaced an earlier timber one. It was built of blue Staffordshire brick and stood 62 feet above the valley it crossed. From here, over its 216 yards length, one could see down to the ancient Bedford, or as it is locally known, Magpie Bridge. Standing adjacent to cottages of the same name, it spanned the river Walkham, carrying the A386 from Horrabridge to Tavistock. It must be said that it provides a serious hazard for modern traffic, for the road on either side approaches almost at right angles. The bridge itself is hump backed and of narrow width so exacerbating the situation. On a clear day, an added bonus may catch the travellers eye, that of the moors at Peek Hill and of the two coach

The picture of 1950 vintage, showing a four coach train for Launceston crossing Magpie Viaduct just north of Horrabridge.

Author's collection.

train to Princetown away in the distance beyond Walkhampton as it winds its way amongst the rocky moors to King's Tor on the horizon.

The train having crossed the viaduct, continues north westwards along a series of embankments, many having steep rocky shoulders on their south western sides, and runs parallel to both the A386 and the river Walkham along their northern flanks in the valley below. M.P.10 is followed by an accommodation bridge over the line as the road climbs out of the valley on the other side and disappears into dense deciduous growth. Soon afterwards and following a more northerly course, the train approaches Walkham Viaduct at 10m 14c, spanning the river Walkham on its new easterly course to join the river Tavy. The whole area is boardered by Sticklepath Wood to the west and Furzeland Down and Birchcleave Wood to the east.

The original timber structure of South Devon Railway days was known as one of the most mature of Brunel's designs. It had grace and beauty and blended in with the sylvan landscape around it. The description of the graceful Walkham Viaduct and its 1910 replacement is given in G H Anthony's book 'The Tavistock, Launceston & Princetown Railways' and with his permission I quote the following passage.

"This famous viaduct, 367 yards long and 132 feet high, described as 'the most matured design of Brunel's timber viaducts' was erected to span the valley of the river Walkham, between Horrabridge and Grenofen tunnel. Like all the famous engineer's timber viaducts in Devon and Cornwall, it had great beauty, and fitted gracefully into the local landscape.

The viaduct comprised 15 spans of 66 ft each and two end spans of approximately 59 ft 6 in each. The superstructure was carried on tall stone piers, with Gothic headed openings, with buttresses tapering from tip to base. Cast iron tips rested on top of the buttresses from which the timber beams sprang to support the longitudinal timbers. The timber, which came from the Baltic, was very strong, and had an average life of thirty years. It was kyanised as a precaution against fire.

The reconstructed viaduct was brought into use in September 1910. The same number of spans was adhered to and the piers were raised in brickwork to take the bedstones, each weighing six tons, which was lowered into position from a temporary gantry erected at floor level of the old viaduct. The main girders were placed into position on to the bedstones by two twelve-ton cranes, one at each end. This stage of the work was carried out on Sundays. The cross-girders and rail-bearers were fixed during weekdays, without disturbing the beams carrying the permanent way, the cross-girders being threaded in from the outside by three-ton cranes and the rail-bearers lowered on to cross girders from above by removing portions of the decking, which was eventually replaced by steel flooring for the permanent way.

The girders were conveyed, pair by pair, on 'Crocodile' type wagons from the makers works at Horsehay, Shropshire. The work was carried out by the railway's own bridge gangs, under the direction of the Plymouth Engineer, Mr H D Smith."

Leaving the viaduct behind, the train now runs over a number of smaller embankments between Grenofen House and Higher Grenofen. This is followed by a deep rock cutting from which the train plunges into the 374 yard long Grenofen tunnel at 10m 62c. The tunnel

Panoramic view of Walkham Viaduct. Note the maintenance engineer with ladder down to the super structure. Compare this photograph with the original on Page 96.

c early 1950's

Roy Nash

runs under a very high ridge of land directly under Grenofen village and it is interesting to note that some two miles to the west, under another such ridge, runs the former Southern Railway through Shillamill tunnel. That tunnel is situated on the other side of the river Walkham and carried the line between Bere Alston and Okehampton via Tavistock. At Grenofen's northern portal stands M.P.11 at the bottom of another deep rock cutting. Emerging from the tunnel and travelling roughly due north the train proceeds on its journey descending a 1 in 64 gradient over long stretches of embankments, to cross a high stone bridge over a road in from the A386 to Whitchurch. The line from here swings north west and crosses an underpass before entering Whitchurch Down Platform at 11m 65c. The train is now only just over a mile away from Tavistock station whereupon just less than half of its journey will be completed.

Whitchurch Down, a pretty little halt serving a suburb of Tavistock which in more recent times has become almost part of Tavistock itself. For its size and importance it was well constructed, far better in fact than Clearbrook Halt. It consisted of a long straight platform capable of serving long excursion trains. It was brick faced with slab edging and a tidy chipping surface. At its centre, adjacent to its large cast iron on wood nameboard, was its entrance leading in onto a paved section on which stood a square corrugated waiting shelter. No less than five lamp standards were spaced along its length two either side of the shelter were of cast iron and fitted with swan neck extensions carrying gas lamps. The others were similar fittings mounted upon wooden posts immediately in front of the timber and wire fence that bordered the rear. Onto the fence also bordered the back gardens of houses situated in Whitchurch Road and as a result it was adorned with many fine rambling roses. From this halt passengers can see the main A386 road away to the west running into Tavistock. Nearer to the train is the little Tiddy Brook crossing the nearby fields in its quest to join the river Tavy, which incidentally, will be the fourth river to take up station with the branch!

Upon leaving Whitchurch Down the train encounters the first real increase in population density since leaving Plymouth, as it heads firstly past Tavistock 'down fixed distant' at the rear of Fernhill Villas and then past Drake Gardens and Crelake Park to the east at a point where the line is quickly swinging north then north west on its final approach to Tavistock station. It was at a point just 28 chains out from Tavistock station that Crelake siding was situated during the early days of the line. It served the long defunct Crelake copper mine which closed in 1873. Since 1938, just a little further on from the site of Crelake siding there existed the Tavistock Gas Company's siding on the down side some 21 chains out from the station. Coal trains unloaded into a

Two views of Whitchurch Down Platform

a Looking north to Tavistock

b Looking south to Horrabridge
c 1950's   Lens of Sutton

hopper here, and it was delivered by chute down to lorries which, in turn, completed the delivery into the gas works itself. In later years the gas holder station has been connected to the national gas grid system and acts as a storage/booster depot. Finally as Pixon Lane passes under the line towards the cattle market, Tavistock station itself is reached at 12m 71c.

Tavistock 'South', as it was known after 1949, was the busiest and considered the main station on the whole branch. It also possessed the most complex and comprehensive of track layouts for a rural station of its size. Although a rebuild of the original Brunel design of the 1850's (the original burnt down in 1887), it was a superb example of an overall roof and one of the last to remain intact. Tavistock South was ideally situated very near to the centre of the town and slightly above it to its southern side. The river Tavy bisected that land upon which the town stood and that upon which the station was situated. A first class subject for any modeller, its total trackwork exceeded $1^1/_2$ miles in length, and was so arranged as to contain all the various impedimenta of a busy G.W.R. station of a rural moorland market town.

Approaching from the south the train would first encounter the 'down home' signal just before it crossed the 25 foot span of the limestone bridge over Pixon Lane. When actually crossing the bridge, facing points connected the separate up and down lines through the whole length of the station, to join again at the northern end just prior to the bridge over Abbey Road. In addition a middle siding also ran the entire length of the station, joining the up line by further pointwork inside those previously mentioned. Catch points in the middle siding prevented accidental entry onto the running line against the signals. Additional pointwork allowed the southern end of the middle siding access over the down line into a selection of sidings on the stations north side. Here two main sidings ran towards Lydford direction, through the ample goods shed to stop blocks at the far end. A third siding branched out from these opposite the signal box to run in a gentle curve behind the goods shed. This third siding also ran back in a southerly direction to the timber stores, coal stores and weighbridge. Finally a turntable road ran south from the down line and a small siding ran north into cattle pens at the rear of the signal box from the up line. All the sidings were equipped with catch points to protect the running lines from accidental entry.

The platforms were well built, brick faced with slab edging and blue Staffordshire brick surfaces through their entire lengths. The up platform was the largest at 480 feet in length and it was the direct access to the main station buildings and the approach road outside. The narrower down platform was 320 feet in length and was connected at the northern end by an ornate steel covered footbridge for passengers. A large notice over its stairway requested the passengers to use it and not cross the lines.

The main station building was constructed of cut limestone with red brick surrounds on each window and doorway. This was enhanced by a fine cut Welsh slate roof interspersed with several fine red brick chimney stacks of a square chunky design. The stacks were capped by one or a pair of plain buff chimney pots. It is true to say, that this was one of the most photographed stations in the Westcountry but alas, there seems to be little or no record of the sturdy, well built frontage of Tavistock South! The only pictures I have been able to include were taken at its demise and after its demolition was commenced. However entry into the station buildings was by private road in from the old Plymouth Road as it rose out of Tavistock under the line at Abbey Bridge en route for Whitchurch Down. This rising roadway formed a steep bank along the frontage of the station buildings and dwarfing them in summertime with copious arrays of flowering rhododendrons.

The many entrance doorways and windows along the road side were completely protected by a long square canopy, whilst those on the lineside were under cover from the overall roof. This made the lineside windows very dark on all but the brightest of days, but cover was certain for passengers waiting in the winds and rain that often blasted off the surrounding moorland. Large additional fanlight roof panels were once provided (but now denuded of glass) along the entire centre section of the roof apex but this tended to lighten the middle siding rather than the unfortunate platforms. The main trusses of the roof were supported on the up side by wall supports and on the down side by no less than 14 timber uprights rising from the platform foundation level. The whole station roof was braced with longitudinal and traversing iron tie bars, onto which many more vertical drop rods secured the spans with deft certainty against force nine gales. Long lateral timber planking framed the wall between the roof supports on the down side, every third section was fitted with a window but in earlier days every section had a window fitted.

At the southern end of the platform stood a typical G.W.R. signal box, brick based with large timber window frames at each end and along the platform side. It had a 37 lever frame and entry to it was by a small wooden staircase. It was one of many signal boxes to be built at Tavistock. The first box was situated in the centre of the station. The Board of Trade refused to pass it fit for use because the points were over the maximum permitted distance for operation from the box. This original box was replaced by two boxes, one at each end of the station. This was before the advent of LSWR trains on the branch, afterwards however, when they were using their own route to Plymouth, the

0-6-0 pannier tank No. 6410 blows off as it waits to depart with the 6.35 pm auto train to Plymouth during the summer of 1959
R.S. Carpenter

A sad view of the outside approach to Tavistock South during the last months of service before closure.

Lens of Sutton

Tavistock south during 8 August 1961. No 5572 waits to work the 4.30 pm to Plymouth whilst No 5569 takes on water before setting off with the Plymouth to Launceston train.

Hugh Ballantyne

A general view of the northern end of Tavistock South showing clearly the Tavistock-Whitchurch Road and the station road departing from it.

L. Crosier

a

b

c

d

e

Arrivals and departures at Tavistock South during September 1962 taken by the author.

a 0-6-0 PT No. 6430 and auto train after arrival on the down platform as the 2.10 pm from Plymouth.

b The same train shunts out of the station in order to form the 4.30 pm Tavistock to Plymouth on the up platform line.

c The author's wife and son pose by the 4.30 pm from Tavistock, he after experiencing his very first train ride on it earlier as the 2.10 pm from Plymouth

d The 5.25 pm from Plymouth enters Tavistock from the South at 6.11 pm

e The 5.40 pm Launceston to Plymouth train arrives at Tavistock at 6.30 pm whilst the 5.25 pm waits on the down line to form the 7.10 pm Tavistock to Plymouth

length of the crossing station was reduced. A new box was built and the former boxes closed, the one at the northern end of the station was demolished, whilst the one at the southern end of the station on the down side very near to the large square water tower and turntable remained. This box was now used as a signal telegraph maintenance hut, a worthy new use for the fine brick base, supporting the large lateral planking which formed the top section. The design was S.D.R. and the toplights over the main window frames were very much in evidence. At this end of the platform, adjacent to the present signal box stands a water crane with its fire devil tucked under its arm. The 'up starter' too stands near here at the end of the platform slope. Between here and the final pointwork to the running line stand the 'up interme-diate starter' and the 'up advanced starter', the latter equipped with a lower shunt arm. Similarly the 'down starter' has its usual place at the end of the down platform by another water crane, this time supple-mented by a 'down advanced starter' over the bridge spanning Abbey Road.

By here, but nearer the bridge is the 'up home' for Tavistock. Over the years the ancillary buildings have altered quite a bit and few have little of their original structure left but perhaps the framework. One such a building was the goods shed, this building had been modified, repaired and extended. By the 1950's the original framework, together with much of the vertical planking, suitably pitched for protection, remained. Corrugated sheeting however covered the side walls and provided an extension at the station end whilst its other end was extended in later years by a modern brick building with a concrete roof. Of the remaining buildings within the station complex, some, such as the old workshops, remained as original but by the time of our journey many ugly prefabricated buildings had sprung up. These were often in a poorer state of repair than many of the older counterparts.

Leaving Tavistock on a journey to stations en route for Launceston was always a wrench for any traveller who knew the line well for here was what for a short time, was the terminus of the branch and it still retained that air of importance. The scenery from here on could not compete in variety with that already passed except for the section between Mary Tavy and Coryton, and there was 19 miles yet to go.

Two charming studies taken at Tavistock South, featuring auto-trains awaiting departure for Plymouth. The first is 1408 & W157W forming the 12.33pm train on 19 December 1955; the second is 6400 & W230W forming the 12.35pm train on 8 August 1961.
Hugh Ballantyne

TAVISTOCK SOUTH TO LAUNCESTON NORTH

'The down starter' drops and the train is on the move again. Over the long steel spans of a single track bridge with its white painted railings on either side, crossing the old Plymouth Road. From here on a long embankment takes over high above the old cemetery, past M.P.13 and leaving Tavistock in a north easterly direction. Further bridges carry the train over Mount Tavy Road and the river Tavy in quick succession as it gathers speed past the 'up fixed distant' and Mount House School to the east and Kelly College, a boys' public school to the west. It is by this part of the line that the river Wallabrook flows down through Wilminstone Quarry from its source on the Beacon, a hill 966 feet a.s.l to the north west, and joins the river Tavy near M.P.14. The branch, the road and now the Southern main line move ever closer, all to vie with one another to share the narrow river valley for the land rises steeply on either side. The A386 road adjoining, having left Tavistock heads for Okehampton via Mary Tavy. The Southern main line however, cuts into the hillside, only 200 - 300 yards away, also heads for Okehampton but via Brentor and Lydford. The river Tavy at this point parts company with the line and heads north east and out upon the open moor and to its source. In compensation it leaves its tributary, the river

The 3.10 pm Plymouth to Launceston train hauled by 0-6-2T No 5541 near Mary Tavy on 10 May 1961

S.C. Nash

A view from the leading coach of the 2.22pm Launceston to Plymouth train between Mary Tavy and Tavistock on 20 August 1954. The SR main line from Okehampton to Tavistock North is to the right of the picture.

H.C. Casserley

Burn in company with the line at the end of Rowden Wood. At this same point, at 14m 17c is the site of Pitts Cleave Quarry sidings which opened during 1922 for the loading of roadstone. An entry road into the quarry crosses the line by means of an occupational level crossing here. As the branch swings to the north the A386 crosses it using a small stone bridge, and climbs steeply upwards towards Mary Tavy village. A few yards past this bridge M.P.15 is passed. The Southern main line, on a large embankment draws even closer to the branch whilst the river Burn meanders gaily to the western side until Wringworthy is reached. Here two events happen at the same time, the main line crosses the branch and the river crosses under both from east to west. All three head due north running at the base of gentle sloping land, passing M.P.16 between Grendon and Burnford; away to the east lies the larger village of Peter Tavy. This run over the last three miles of the lower pastoral slopes of Dartmoor to the north of Tavistock is typical of this part of Devon. Eventually the train reaches Mary Tavy and Blackdown Halt at 16m 23c.

The halt was formerly an early passing place and station and was sited just north of a small bridge carrying the station road down from the two villages to the east and onto Burnford hamlet to the west. This station was semi derelict for many years before its eventual closure and

A solitary passenger alights from the train at Mary Tavy and Blackdown on 20 August 1954. The station was then an unstaffed halt.
H.C. Casserley

Mary Tavy & Blackdown station as an unmanned halt during the last days of service.
Lens of Sutton

during the 1950's a passenger would find an old stone faced platform on the up side of a single line. (On the other side the overgrown remains of the down platform and building, closed during 1892 could just be detected). On the up platform stood a neat but small station building built of stone with its doorways, windows and corners lined with buff bricks. The doorways and windows were boarded up since it became an unstaffed halt. The platform surface was of chippings and blue Staffordshire brick, interlaced with ample sproutings of grass and weeds behind the slab edging which was tinged with former coatings of whitewash paint. In addition there was an original signal box, long disused, built of brick throughout and standing on the northern side of the station building. A solitary concrete lamp standard supporting a Windsor style oil lamp was the sole means of illuminating the platform although there was evidence of a wall version fixed to the wall of the signal box earlier. The station nameboard was necessarily large and pretentious for such a halt by virtue of its long name. The platform rear was bordered by a wooden fence and much undergrowth, whilst the former station master's house with its double gabled front stood at the southern end and to the rear.

Upon leaving the halt the branch and accompanying main line and river Burn run almost parallel to one another and swing north west through Smallacombe Bottom to the east and Heathfield Plantation to the west. At M.P.17 the river dives under both lines as they run on their long shallow embankments, but it returns to the western side again as the lines turn northwards and head for Brentor. Both lines are spanned by Wortha Mill bridge as it carries a byroad in from South Brentor to Wortha Mill, near Blackmoor Park. High above Wortha Mill stands Brent Tor itself at 1095 feet a.s.l. Upon the Tor stands the little church of St Michael de Rupe whose origin dates back to 1130 A.D. It was later reconsecrated in 1319 A.D. by Bishop Stapledon of Exeter. Nowadays occasional services are held here by candlelight, the most enchanting of which is the Christmas service, for there are no public main services on such a remote spot and candles together with oil lamps, are the only means of heating and lighting here.

North west of Brentor is North Brentor village and to the front of the hill on its eastern side is situated Brentor station on the Southern Railway main line. It is interesting to note that approximately two miles to the north east of this point is situated Liddaton Halt. However returning to our journey, M.P.18 is passed and as the G.W.R chose to ignore Brentor, the line continues north easterly parallel to the river Burn and that same S.R main line. Two over bridges are quickly negotiated the first bringing Station Road and the second bringing Burn Lane, in from North Brentor village to the west of Blackdown. High upon the eastern side of the valley at this point stands Gibbet Hill at 1158 feet a.s.l, the highest point on Blackdown. This hill overlooks the next stop for the train, namely the double G.W.R/S.R station of Lydford. By this spot the river is following an agitated course meandering from one side of the line to the other, finally deciding upon the west side at the second of the overbridges. It eventually parts company with the line by crossing under Lydford station to surface to the east of Lyd Cottage and the Southern main line as it heads in direction for its source high upon Blackdown. Meanwhile the train is passing M.P.19 and the 'down fixed distant' for Lydford as it steers a north west route on a rising gradient of 1 in 77 for Lydford station itself at 19m 43c.

Lydford station was the highest point on the Launceston branch at 650 feet a.s.l. It was an anachronistic yet unique station, it commenced as broad gauge 'Lidford' in 1865; later in 1876 it was joined by the standard gauge and thereby became a junction equipped with mixed gauge. A little after 1890 it ceased to be a junction but instead became a 'dual company' station; the main L.S.W.R. and the G.W.R. branch co-habiting the same site, but each independent of the other. By the first world war, the L.S.W.R. was supervising and staffing both sides and before the end of the war each company's separate signal box was closed upon the construction and opening of a new joint box. The two companies lines were not reconnected again until the period of the second world war, during 1943. This pre-nationalisation directive remained until closure of the branch to freight during 1966, when Lydford became the main line station only, of the Southern, then Western Region of British Railways. This situation remained until complete closure and demolition during 1968. A full description of the main line station is outside the scope of this book and only obtuse references will be made to it where illustration of particulars regarding the branch station need enhancing.

If Lydford history was somewhat of an anachronism, its geography was most certainly not. It was situated in an area of outstanding natural beauty below the high slopes of west Dartmoor, to its eastern flank and the deep glacial valley of the river Lyd to its northern flank. Here the tempestuous Lyd, rising on the slopes of Great Links Tor, which peaked at 1908 feet a.s.l, descended south of the village of Lydford, some two miles from the station. It then flowed through the lovely Lydford Gorge, a beauty spot now owned by the National Trust. The Southern main line heads north east, crossing the river at Lydford Viaduct south east of the village. The acute change of direction to almost due west by the branch at Lydford, was to make the Lyd the sixth river to accompany the branch along part of its route since Marsh Mills. Approaching Lydford station from its southern end, the rear of the 'up advanced starter' is passed approximately one third of a mile out. As the final approaches are made, the facing pointwork turning

Lydford GWR Station showing the down platform and associated buildings.
Lens of Sutton

A general view of Lydford GWR Station looking South and showing a joint signal box and island up platform with the SR main line.

Lens of Sutton

An up train from Launceston running bunker first enters the northern end of Lydford station. In the distance can be seen the SR goods shed., sidings and main line.

L. Crosier

2-6-2 Tank, No. 5544 with the up goods at Lydford on 9th June 1962.

R.A. Lumber

out towards the S.R. up and down main lines, are encountered 300 yards from the signal box. Although the actual points were controlled by the G.W.R. frame, the connections to the main lines were under the control of the S.R.frame. Here at the departure from the branch, a bracket signal carries the 'up home' and the 'branch to S.R.main' arms. The running line ran straight through the down side of the station with provision for a 567 foot up loop, and reverse pointwork just south of the platform, ran back into down sidings. At the other end of the up loop further pointwork allowed for the extension of the loop northward, parallel to the running line for over 200 yards as the up relief siding. Provision was also made for a turnout into a siding northwards to the goods shed and southwards to a dock terminating at stop blocks at the end of the signal box. The principal platform on the branch was the down side and upon it stood the main station building housing the waiting room/ticket office etc. It was a small long building built in three sections with a square, short canopy spanning the length of its centre section. Differing from other stations on the line, this building was constructed of brick and finished with a cement rendering. Windows were of a twelve panel sash type which made them look very tall in comparison with the height of the building. There were eight sets in all along the platform side, some constructed with ornate plaster surrounds, whilst some remained plain in finish. The slate roof was stepped to a reduced height for the end sections, whilst two double chimneys, built of red brick, were situated at the ends of the main section. The platform was brick faced, slab edged, which kept in check the chipping surface. The goods dock at the southern end was fenced with concrete post and wire fencing, but the station buildings were fenced off in white painted palings. At the north end of the fence, a wooden gate, sporting a "Tickets must be shewn here" sign in blue and white enamel, opened in from the access road outside. Also at this end of the platform stood the 'up starter' and a stopboard for mineral trains. On the other side of an adjacent barrow crossing, used for passenger access to the up platform, stood a cylindrical G.W.R. water tower. The up platform with which the crossing connected, was a compromise between the G.W.R. and the S.R. It consisted of two distinct sides, the G.W.R.up branch side and the S.R. up main side. Common to each of course, was a signal box, which itself had two sides, or rather two frames. This box had timber window frames mounted upon a low brick wall plinth giving all round vision. A G.W.R. nameplate appeared one side and a S.R. one on the other! The building on this platform was of L.S.W.R. design and was more ornate than the main on the down side, and it served both sides of this common platform. It was that shorter, built of brick and cement rendered with much decoration, particularly on its flat roofed end, housing the toilets. The main sloping roof was constructed of slate and two brick double chimneys were situated at opposite ends of its apex. The main difference in appearance from the G.W.R. brick building, was that the walls of these were painted white with contrasting black paint picking out the woodwork, forming an impressive sight on this bleak moorland spot. The double sided platform was stone faced and brick edged on the S.R. side, and brick faced and slab edged on the G.W.R. side. The joint surfaces ranged from blue Staffordshire brick to chippings, the former in the centre, near the buildings and the latter at the platform ends. The only marring feature was the erection of the tall square concrete lamp standards with their lower quadrant and bar suspension for the small green and white lampshades for the electric lights. They also served to suspend the cables feeding these lights. (Unfortunately one found these on the G.W.R. platforms too in later years, together with the 'ring and bar' type station nameplates for lamp standards.) A pre-cast concrete open footbridge connected the up and the down S.R. platforms, an obvious replacement, its ugliness did little credit to its usefulness. Along the centre of the common platform stood a tall telegraph route, the poles supporting their mixture of 2-way and 4-way arms carrying the Southern main line signalling wires. Finally station nameboards for Lydford were very large, the usual wooden ones with large cast iron letters for the G.W.R. branch and fine white on green enamel ones for the S.R. main lines. The common platform had one of each at either end. The remaining signals were the 'up starter' at the south end of the platform and the 'up home' at the approaches to its northern end.

As the 'up starter' drops, our imaginary journey of the 1950's is on its way again. The train briefly heads north east before a spectacular change in direction to the west, commencing as it does on a descending gradient of 1 in 77. The swing to the west from north east veers away from the village of Lydford and accompanies the river Lyd on the next stage of the journey. Running out from Lydford station, past the rear of the 'up fixed distant', the train passes close to the Manor Hotel to the west, Lyd Cottage to the east and under the bridge that carries the road between them. It then passes the disused Westford Mill at M.P.20 and on into the wooded Lyd valley which culminates in the spectacular and beautiful waterfall cascading 100 feet over its rocky drop. The line then skirts Westford Wood to the north, running through a series of rock cuttings and embankments as it continues past Broadridge Wood and Coles Wood to its north side. To the southern side however, firstly the smaller Wastor Wood at M.P.21 and later, Langstone, Ashelter and Davies Woods are negotiated with M.P.22 situated between the latter two. The much longer Lydford Forest, Waddlestone and Longham Downs lay further to the north on the other side of the river Lyd, which itself is running parallel to the line and only 300 - 400 yards from it, also

Two views of Liddaton Halt during the 1920's showing
above: Up train arriving to pick up lady passenger
below: General view looking east from the overbridge.
Chapman & Son

to the north. For some three miles one travels through the breath-takingly beautiful Lyd valley with the Dartmoor Tors soaring high above it before the next stop is reached. This is Liddaton Halt serving the farming communities of East and West Liddaton, Liddaton Green, and Bowdenhill which are all situated south of the halt. As previously mentioned, the distance between here and the Southern Railway's Brentor station is approximately two miles, Brentor station being adjacent to the branch at that point. Contained within the geographical envelope encompassed by just four miles of track, are many square miles of moorland known as Brentor, the entire section bisected by the Tavistock to Okehampton road via Milton Abbot and Lydford, running along its crown. This road runs at the foot of Brent Tor, the church of St Michael, perched tantalizingly upon its peak surveys all without obstruction.

Liddaton Halt is reached at 22m 35c as the train passes under the Coryton to Lydford Green girder road bridge, all situated in a rather more pastoral setting. The halt was constructed entirely of timber with the platform's planking supported upon bulky timber legs, cross braced for strength. The halt was built alongside the byroad from Broadpark on the west side of the halt to Higher Woodpark to the east. This road was fenced off from the railway by wooden post and wire fencing. A small white painted gateway gave access over a small walkway to the platform and the small timber planked shelter. Two oil lamps housed in copper 'Windsor' pattern lanterns, lit the platform. A further one lit the entrance, and a fourth 'wall version' was affixed to the eastern end of the waiting shelter. More wooden fencing posts and steel wire lined the rear of the platform and one large timber name-board with its cast iron letters proclaimed our arrival here.

After a brief stay the train commences the one and a half short miles to the next station on the branch, Coryton. The direction of departure from Liddaton Halt is just south of due west, the line descending on a 1 in 55 gradient passing East Liddaton, Liddaton Green and West Liddaton to the south. An underpass is crossed at M.P.23 carrying a road into West Liddaton, just as the train is negotiating a shallow embankment. An accommodation overbridge is passed as the line veers north west, the embankments gaining height as yet another but deeper underpass is reached. Nearing the Chillaton to Lewtrenchard road, near Coryton station, the river Lyd closes quickly with the line and passes under it 300 yards away. Now flowing to the south of the line, the river Lyd passes within 100 yards of the station. In so doing its course carries it under the road employing a bridge of local stone. The line too passes under the road on its immediate approach to Coryton station, but however employing a steel girder bridge. The station at Coryton is reached at 23m 76c on a 1 in 55 gradient falling towards

Lifton.

Coryton was an original station, constructed using local stone but, with its window and door frames, its corners including the large chimney stack at its eastern end, were all lined with limestone. Slate sills graced the three windows on the platform side and each were equipped with decorative yet functional pairs of wooden shutters. The station building had a delightful rural atmosphere about it and when caught in the rays of the early morning sunlight, its relief was clear and decisive. A small building occupying the centre of the platform on the up side, had a slate roof with an ample stone chimney stack to the western end and it housed the normal provision of a waiting room/ ticket office. A square extension at the western end housed the toilets and provided space for numerous posters to be appended in earlier days. Again with reference to earlier days the stone faced, slab edged, and paving stone with chippings surfaced platform was fenced with a neat wooden slatted fence at the rear. A bold nameboard stood above it raised to the height by means of two lengths of old bull head rail.

The railway land opposite the station was once a fine allotment garden but the sight to greet the traveller in the early 'fifties was less orderly and more mundane. The fencing had been changed for the more economically maintained concrete post and wire fence, whilst the garden had given way to wild unattended grassland. All but one of the Windsor pattern oil lamps in their standards had also disappeared and their replacements were rather ugly metal poles with hooks at their tops from which could be hung hurricane lamps. A telephone kiosk of the former Post Office Telephones design stood near the platform entrance. It's presence was advertised by, what itself is fast becoming a relic, namely a 'You may telephone from here' sign in bright blue and white enamel. Presumably it alluded to the telephone within the station in days gone by before Coryton became an unstaffed halt, Telegraph poles, often with a distinct list, and arms askew, added to the rustic charm and carried the telegraph wires in both directions. In addition they also carried the public telephone into the former station master's house, standing within the grounds behind the station. This double gabled house with diamond latticed windows could be reached from either station entrance, that is from the Chillaton road via steps down to the station forecourt or in from the Coryton village to Sydenham road running at right angles to it via the station forecourt and yard. Trackwork was a single line through the station with up and down cross overs to a siding running parallel, westwards to the cattle pens and weighbridge, and eastwards to a dock at the rear of the west end of the platform. A small hut housing a ground frame, stands clear of the platform on the down side, and further to the west but slightly behind, there stands the square, brick outline of a P.Way hut. Further

Overall picture of Coryton during April 1957 taken from the overbridge and looking east.
P.M. Pollinger

A general view of Coryton station looking east towards Lydford.
c 1959   *Lens of Sutton*

towards Lifton in a westerly direction M.P.24 is passed as another road bridge spans the line. This bridge carries the road from Marystowe to meet with the Coryton village to Sydenham road and was just prior to the spot where the confluence of the rivers Lew and Lyd is situated. The river Lew rises beyond Bridestowe, and Sourton villages to the south, on the lower slopes of the common shared by both parishes. From its source it flowed south past Lewtrenchard village down to join the Lyd between Coryton station and Sydenham Wood. (Lewtrenchard church is noted for the fact that the Rev S Baring Gould wrote the hymn `Onward Christian Soldiers' there).

Leaving Coryton station, the train gathers speed again as it negotiated the aforementioned cross over and passes under a steel road bridge, past the point where the river Lew flows under the line, and westwards towards Lifton. A long stretch of line is traversed south of Lee Quarry as the river Lyd deviates away from the company of the line for a short distance taking up in the process a position further south but parallel to it. Both river and line veer north westerly at this point where the road from Marystowe to Lee Wood crosses, firstly the river at Marystowe Bridge and then the line at Bow Cottage. Continuing north west, around the edge of Sydenham Wood, the line passes M.P.25 as the river commences to move nearer to the line again. It passes the Elizabethan mansion near Sydenham, to the south. The road from Marystowe and Chillaton crosses the river at Sydenham Bridge and the line immediately afterwards. The two almost embrace as they

No 4591 heads for Coryton near Sydenham House, west of the station during the summer of 1962.

R.M. Pollinger

pass between Blackdown Wood to the south and Warren Wood to the north. At the western end of Warren Wood however, the river Lyd suddenly swings northward, passes under the line in order to take up residence on the northern side again. The line in the meantime traverses along the northern edge of Twelvepenny and Hartley Woods and adjusts to a more westerly course. M.P.26 is passed at the junction of these two woods as the line runs in the flat bottomed river valley. The river itself, drops over a weir north of Hartley Wood and commences to meander somewhat as it accompanies Mill Leat and Spry Farm to its north. At this point, where the Lifton 'down fixed distant' is passed, the A30 trunk road from Okehampton to Launceston closes quickly with the line and the river Lyd and becomes adjacent to them at Tinhay just east of Lifton. Prior to this the river straightened its former course and closes with the line near Sprymill Cottages as the rear of Lifton 'up advanced starter' is passed. M.P.27 follows next with the river now passing under the line just before the 'down home' for Lifton station. The station was named after the larger village over half a mile to the west, but was in fact, situated on a falling gradient of 1 in 40 towards Launceston, at 27m 14c within the village of Tinhay.

Lifton station during the 'twenties and 'thirties was a modeller's delight with its enchanting layout. It sported its small platforms, the passing loop, the level crossing at its west end whilst at its east end were situated the collection of sidings into the 'Ambrosia' factory where "Dried milk for infants" was made on the station's northern flank. The main A30 road ran close by, also to the north flank and the cluster of vintage country buildings grouped around the little village of Tinhay enhanced the rural scene accordingly.

To the south of the station lay an extensive area of verdant pasture whilst in the area to the north, between the factory and the level crossing, was a well kept allotment garden, abundant in its produce. Alas! as the train of our journey during the 'fifties arrives at Lifton, the scene is far less rural and far more industrialised. The A30 has been widened and carries much too heavy traffic both in weight and capacity, the factory has expanded considerably with predicted encroachment onto the former pastures south of the station. This was but a prelude to the time of writing, whereupon the entire station site has been overwhelmed and replaced by a far larger factory. Ambrosia today is a supermarket byword for tinned rice and other milk products, sadly all shipped out by road transport to the many and varied destinations.

However returning to the station, it consisted of a down through line with an up passing loop. Its platforms were of hardfill construction with stone facing, chipping surfaces and slab edging. Some paving did exist on the sloping ends and within the area immediately in front of

Panoramic view of Lifton taken from the bridge over the line during the 1920's showing from left to right a deserted A30 trunk road, a comparatively small Ambrosia dairy produce factory, and an up freight departing.

Chapman & Son

A 45XX class runs bunker first with an 'up' passenger train to Plymouth during the 1960's. The defunct overbridge the far side of the level crossing is a relic of the former Tinhay Quarry line.

L.W. Crosier

the main buildings. The main buildings were on the up side with their entrances in from the A30 at Tinhay. The station building was constructed mainly of limestone but also of Cornish stone and using dressed granite framing windows, doorways and cornering to walls. Its roof was of slate formed into long overhanging eaves at the front and along the platform side. A double and a single chimney were situated at each end of the roof catering for the waiting room and ticket office etc. The second building to the west of it, was the goods shed, built of Cornish stone, it had a slate roof with large overhanging eaves on all sides. A large wooden door hung on a steel rail offered entry from the platform and a similar construction was erected at the roadside with a high platform for off-loading onto horse drawn and later motor transport. A typical G.W.R. corrugated iron shed stood adjacent to the goods shed on its western side. This was the lamp hut where paraffin and lamp maintenance equipment were kept. Alongside it stood the station nameboard, large, ornate and of wood, its cast iron letters spelt out Lifton. The whole lengths of both up and down platforms were bounded by a concrete post and wire fence, replacing earlier wooden slat fencing, but there was little evidence at this time of any lighting. Originally there were no less than five 'Windsor' pattern standard lamps with their oil lamp inserts, two of these lit the barrow crossing joining the western end of the platforms which gave passengers access to the down side.

Nothing but a small waiting shelter stood upon the down platform. It was constructed of limestone with a dressed granite damp course plinth, the roof was of slate and the difference from the main building was the window surrounds and cornering was of blue Staffordshire brick. At the western end of the station was situated the level crossing with its accompanying hut built of lateral timber planking. The crossing gates protected the road in from Tinhay to Tavistock via Chillaton and Milton Abbot on the A384 Tavistock to Launceston road. Two long G.W.R. pattern gates crossed the single line with the accompanying wicket gates for pedestrians to pass over the line when the level crossing was closed to trains. These, of course, were locked mechanically when the main gates were opened to trains. Wooden paling fencing and two oil lamps completed the installation but for the $27^1/_4$ MP and its adjacent gradient post on the up side. Just west of here stood the 'up home' signal and behind it the high edifice of the defunct overbridge of the former narrow gauge Tinhay Quarry line, a favourite vantage point over the years for photographing the station site. Finally at the far eastern end of the station stood the small signal box with the 'up starter' adjacent to the platforms end. It was constructed of lateral planking in true G.W. style and because of its size and location, was reminiscent of a summer house in a country garden! This signal box controlled the passing loop, the level crossing and sidings into the factory behind it. It differed from other signal boxes on the branch in so much as it did not possess token instruments. These were kept within the ticket office for sound economic reasons of staffing. The signalman could therefore undertake many other tasks or duties on the station as a result. The level crossing was also controlled by the signal box, as stated, this was achieved by means of a lever dedicated to the unlocking mechanically of the mechanism to permit the hand operation of the gates.

With an impatient whistle, the train is ready to depart on the last stage of the journey to Launceston. The 'down starter' is off and the crossing closed to road traffic as the train pulls out of Lifton, over the crossing itself, and under the defunct bridge and swings south west. In so doing it crosses the river yet again at its confluence with the river Thrushel flowing down from the north. The line now swings south with the river Lyd on its western side as the two converge after passing the hamlet of Leat. At Leat there was a siding at 27m 51c connected by trailing points from the up direction and served Leat corn mills.

Also at Leat was the site of the 'up fixed distant' for Lifton. Little evidence of the siding was visible to travellers on our journey as its demise and subsequent lifting was during November 1943. Two and a half miles further on was the site of yet another siding, that of the very much older Cawdron Siding at 29m 12c. It served Arundell's Quarry from 1865 to 1894.

From Leat both river and rail continue south past Leat Wood to the east and the longer Lifton Wood to the west, within the latter was the site of the country house and pheasantry of Lifton Park. Veering quickly westwards at Moon House Plantation, M.P.28 is passed as the train crosses the river Lyd yet again. The Lyd suddenly swings away westwards then southwards to Gatherly Wood and to change sides with the railway as it makes for the river Tamar just south of M.P.29, and so becomes its tributary. The line changes its direction to north west with the river Tamar as its new and seventh travelling companion. This river is significant by its presence as it forms the county boundary between Cornwall and Devon. The branch train continues to head west, south of Lifton Quarry and the site of the aforementioned Cawdron siding, with the river Tamar and Gordonhill Plantation lying to its south.

The river Tamar is crossed by a small railway viaduct just south of Polson. (Polson Bridge to the north at this point, carries the main A30 road over the river as it leave Polson Wood). The river crossed, the train now enters Cornwall for its final run into Launceston, M.P.30 having just been passed. This final run commences as the train continues its travel just south of the confluence of the Tamar with another of its tributaries, the river Kensey. The river Kensey is the eighth and final river to accompany the line since its long journey from Marsh Mills. (It is interesting to note that, to the north of this point two other tributaries of the river Tamar join it, namely the river Carey and the river Ottery - not to be confused with the river Otter near Exeter).

The main A30 road crosses the line here from north to south by means of a steel girder bridge just east of St Leonards and heads past Lower and Middle Bamham. In the distance can be seen the town of Launceston, the former county town of Cornwall dominated by its ancient castle. Launceston Castle is situated at the town's centre and towers high above it. West of St Leonards the line runs close to the river Kensey to its north and the old Mill Leat to its south as M.P.31 is passed. As the Launceston 'down distant' is sighted the line swings north west and passes under the former London & South Western Railway, later Southern Railway line from Ashwater and Tower Hill. This was the North Cornwall Line en route from Exeter Central via Okehampton and Halwill Junction to Launceston (S.R.) and thence on via Wade-bridge to Padstow, its terminus.

(At a distance of 31m $33^1/_2$c along the Launceston branch, the G.W.R. formed a wartime connection with the S.R. North Cornwall Line and this remained until its closure). Continuing the journey north westwards, with the Southern line to the south, the branch and its new companions pass under Ridgegrove Hill by means of separate bridges, whilst the river Kensey emulates the railway by means of Ridgegrove Bridge a little to the north. Finally at 31m $64^1/_2$c from March Mills or 35m 38c from Plymouth, North Road (Prior to 1941, 36m 18c from Plymouth Millbay), on a rising gradient of 1 : 126, Launceston station is reached.

The G.W.R. station at Launceston was the terminus for the branch. Entry into the station, following a plethora of signals guarding the 1943 vintage connection to the S.R's North Cornwall Line, is less than complicated. The train passes the rear of the 'advanced up starter', a signal guarding entry into the southernmost siding, turntable and loco shed roads, a signal guarding the northernmost dock road and sidings, also the loop, and finally the rear of the 'up starter'. The multiple pointwork can be seen on the 1943 signal box diagram for Launceston elsewhere in this book.

The platform layout at this time was of a square 'U' shape configuration with the northern arm constituting the main up/down platform into which the branch or running line ran to stop blocks at its western end. The centre line formed the running around loop, this too ran into stops at the western end. Finally the southernmost arm, slightly shorter, backed onto the S.R. station at its northern side and since 1915 a joint signal box stood common to both railways. Like Lydford it had separate G.W.R/S.R frames but was under the control of the S.R. The siding in from the turntable and loco shed roads ran into this point and terminated at a third pair of stop blocks alongside the other two.

The platforms were constructed of Cornish stone facing, with a hardcore backfill, the surfaces were of chippings except for the station building area which was of paving stones.

Large rounded slabs and a single brick course formed the platform edging. The main station building was the original Launceston and South Devon Railway construction, built of Cornish stone with granite blockwork forming cornering, giving added strength and appearance. The northern side was equipped with 8 windows and 3 doorways. The main doorway and its 4 attendant windows were sheltered by a short, square canopy for they formed the centre section of the building and as such were set back from the roadway more than the east and west ends as an architectural feature. The southern or platform side was equipped with 6 doorways and 7 windows along its length. All the windows and doorways were ornamentally framed with scroll plasterwork and a dummy keystone. This side of the building was cement rendered. All doors were solid panelled hardwood in their construction and all the windows were 8 paned with an additional 2 quadrant fanlights at the apex. One doorway and 2 windows were situated at the west end and 2 doorways were at the east end. The whole platform was covered with a long square canopy upon its entire length. This was supported with anchoring girders along the upstand of the south wall. The latter stood proud of the apex roof and consequently the roof formed a short side down to it. Additional supports for the main canopy were formed by 12 inch square timber piers standing upon cast iron supports at the platforms centre. A main girder ran along their top line, onto which the supporting timber framework was erected. The skirt was formed by short wooden slats cut into the usual saw tooth pattern. The apex roof was constructed with Delebole slate and sported 3 ornate cement rendered chimneys. This station had the usual accommodation for a branch line terminus. It contained a booking office; ladies and general waiting rooms; gents toilets and in addition, it housed goods and other offices. The station lighting was even to its eventual demise, by gas and the familiar 'Windsor' pattern lamps were suspended upon shaped hangers fastened to cast iron lamp posts along the entire run of the platform. Outside the station entrance however, the lamp was suspended from a wall bracket over the main doorway. The goods shed was on the northern side of the station building and set back from its eastern end. It was constructed of Cornish stone with a slate roof

General view of Launceston GW/SR stations with respective trains arriving during the 1930s. Note the joint signal box.

Lens of Sutton

An up train awaits departure from Launceston north during 1949 whilst wagons of sawn timber occupy the dock line.

C. Barrett

Loco No 5532 at rest outside Launceston engine shed during 1959.
R.S. Carpenter

An unusual view of Launceston WR/SR goods yard showing an SR class N loco
on a west bound freight and the WR branch in the foreground.
A.R. Kingdom

matching the main building itself. The main goods siding ran through it at its southern side, large curving arches being let into the timber ends for this purpose. Three matching windows adorned this side whilst the northern or road side was equipped with the familiar loading bay with platform and sliding doors. The engine shed was erected in 1899 and was also built of Cornish stone, as were the small offices adjacent to the south wall. The shed was 100 feet long by 22 feet wide, the offices were 35 feet by 15 feet in size. To the west end of the engine shed stood a large square G.W.R. water tank standing on a girder framework and supported upon 6 tubular legs. The main water supply pipe to it was boxed in against inclement weather and the gravity fed crane was accompanied by its 'fire devil' for a similar reason. Alongside the water tower and immediately outside the engine shed was the ash pit. From 1952 onwards a large storage shed for agricultural feeding stuffs etc was erected adjacent to it and to the east opposite an existing crane. This building was constructed of wide corrugated asbestos sheeting used for both its walls and roof. It was over 150 feet long and stood upon brick legs to enable its floor to be positioned level to that of the attendant trucks. Ironically, at the time of writing, it is the only surviving evidence of Launceston's branch line terminus, still functional but definitely very 'un G.W.R' in appearance. To add to the irony, 103 years of railway history is epitaphed by a small cement plaque which reads 'British Railways 1952' snugly adorning its southern side!

Launceston's two railway stations were situated deep in the valley below the ancient market town. This area is known as Kensey Vale, after the little river flowing through it. The original layout was complex, with firstly the 1865 branch terminus to the north of the common site, and then the 1886 L.S.W.R through station of the North Cornwall line to the south of the site. It can be seen in its original layout (approx 1907) on page 100 viewed from Dockacre Road high above on the hill to its south. Higher still, indeed upon the highest point for miles around stands the oldest inhabitant of the area, that of Launceston Castle after which the Great Western named its No 5000 Locomotive. The first mention of this castle was in the Domesday survey of 1086. Robert of Mortain, a Norman Earl with William the Conqueror was rewarded with a large earldom, the administration centre was sited at Dunheved (Launceston). It was initially constructed as a simple earthworks castle and remained so until 1216. No evidence survives regarding the construction of the later stonework castle but the first reference to it was made by a survey officer of the Black Prince in 1337. At the time of the Civil War, town and castle held out for the King until the army of Fairfax took it in 1646. With the end of the Civil War, the castle's life was at a virtual end and as such, later became the property of the Duchy of Cornwall. It was subsequently leased to the Corporation of Launceston and was laid out as a public park. In 1951 the guardianship passed onto the Ministry of Works. It is now maintained by the Department of the Environment. It has observed many eras as they came and went, not least the towns two railways, for many visitors to Launceston have alighted from the train to include this ancient monument within their tour of the town.

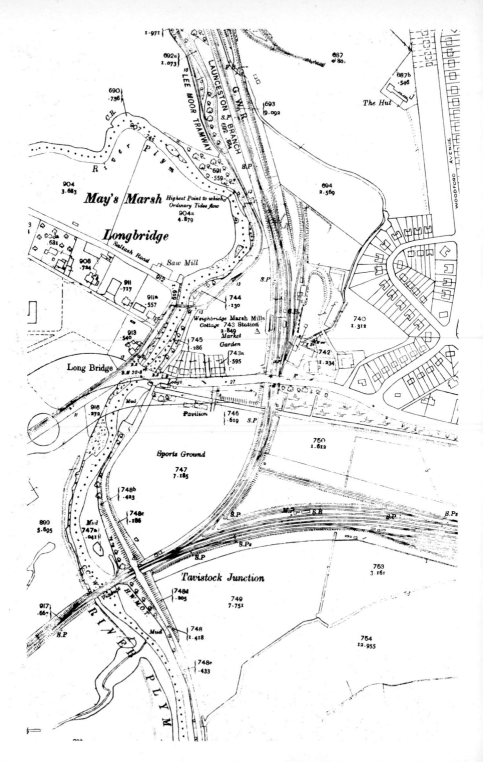

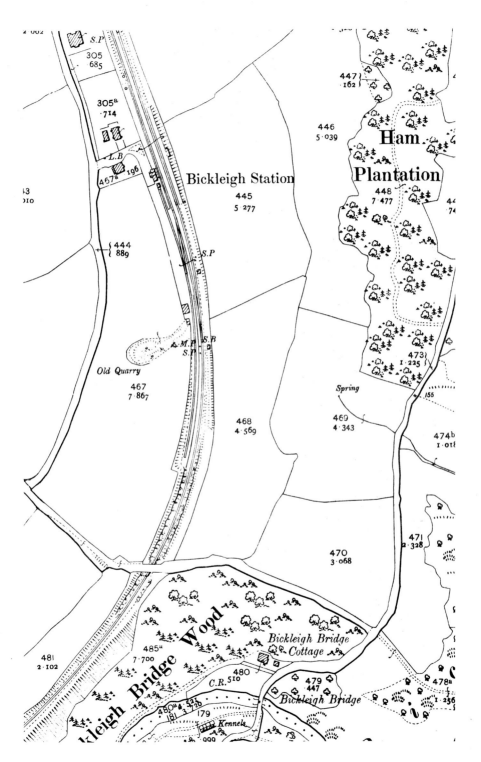

Bickleigh Station

Ham Plantation

Old Quarry

Bickleigh Bridge Wood

Bickleigh Bridge Cottage

Bickleigh Bridge

Kennels

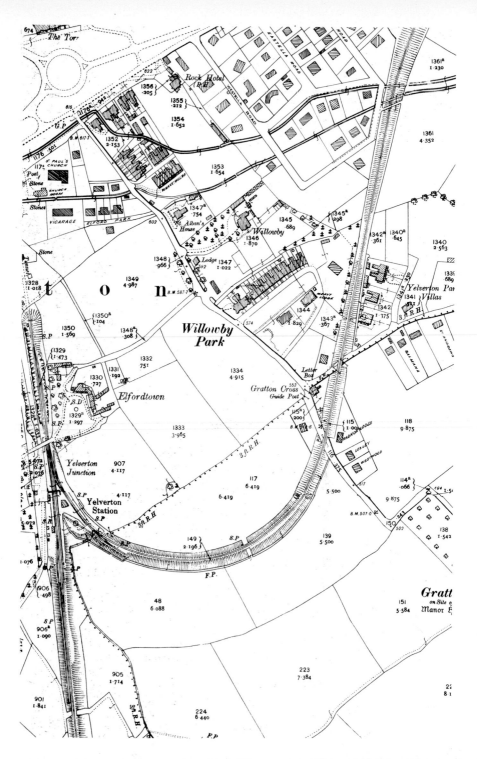

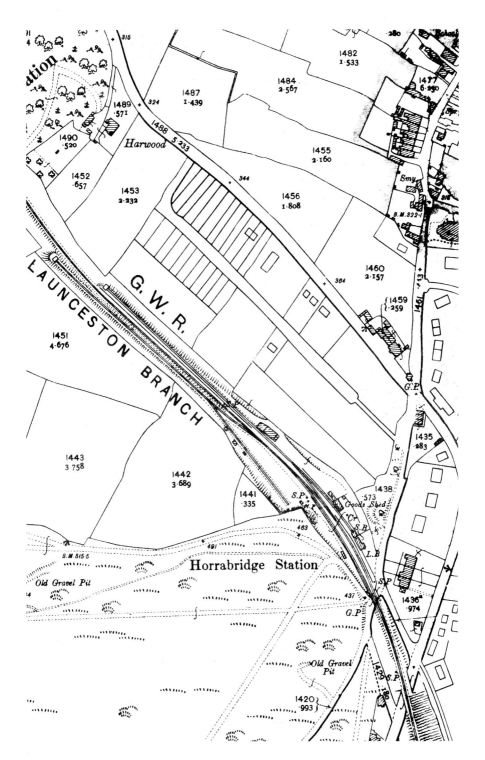

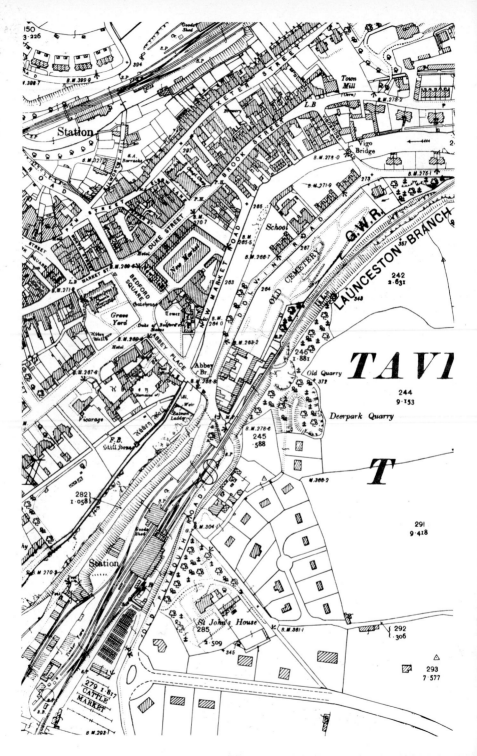

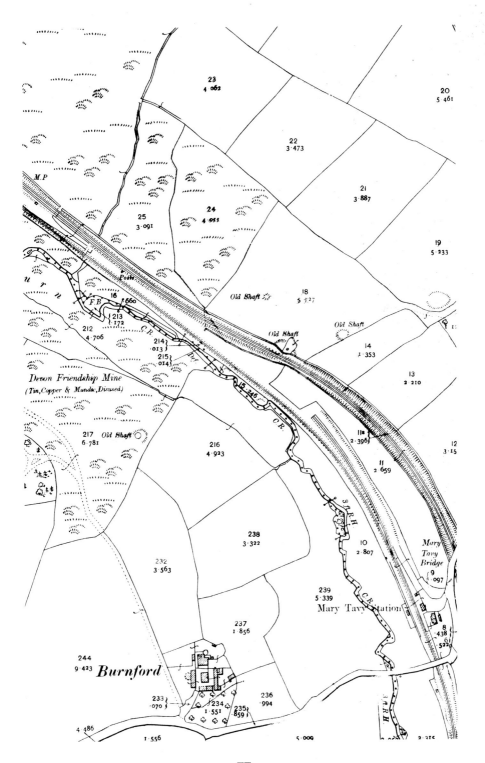

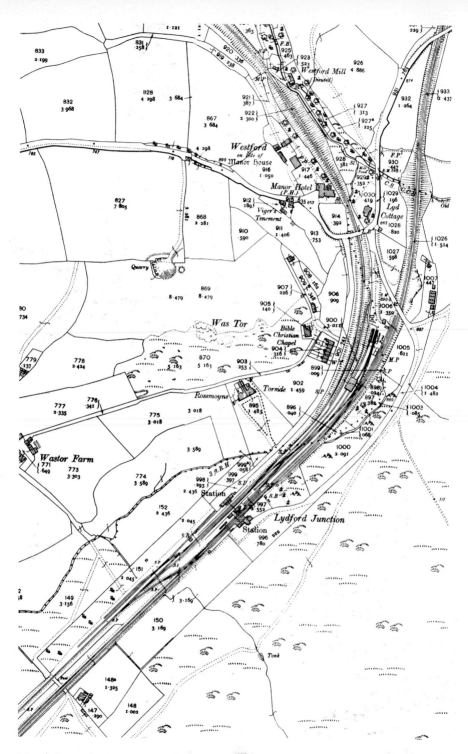

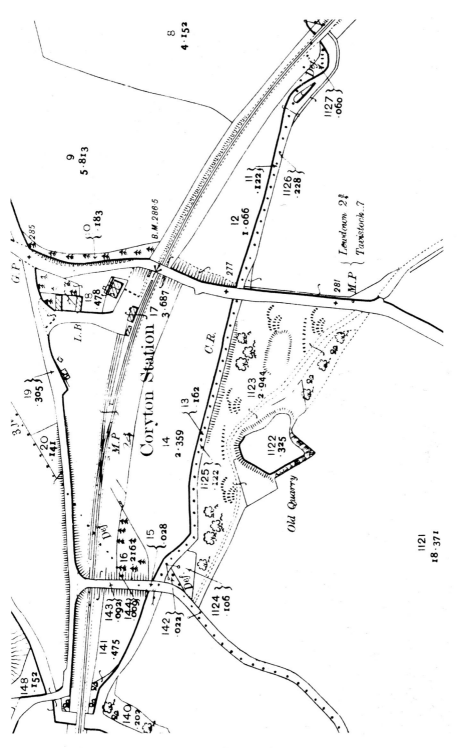

Coryton Station

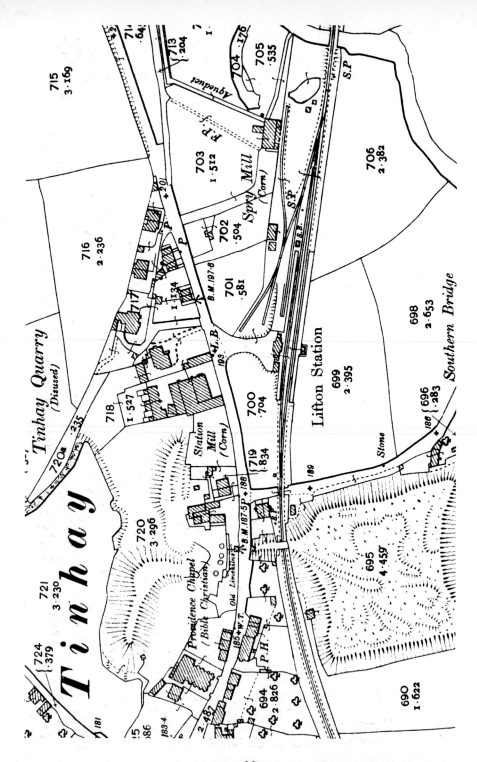

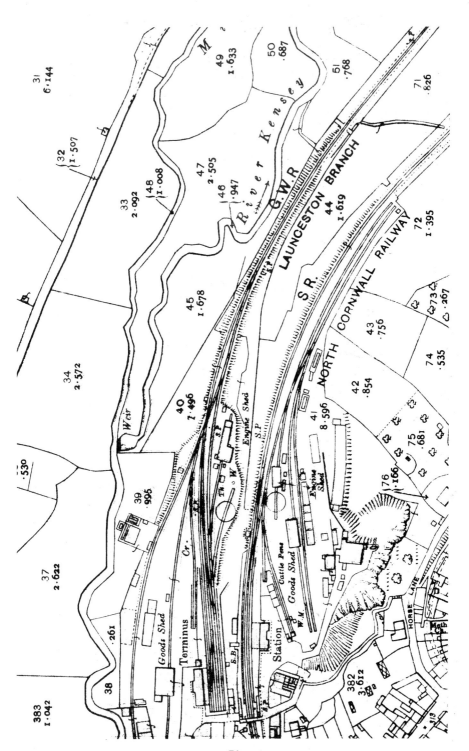

The Tavistock Launceston Branch
History

Phase 1 The Broad and Mixed Gauge Era, 1859 - 1892

The history of the Plymouth to Launceston branch is both long and complex. It dates back in association to the arrival of the South Devon Railway in Plymouth, Millbay during 1849. In fact, the railway to Tavistock was the first important extension to the South Devon Railway to be made. This Company had, in 1845 proposed its own branch to Tavistock to counteract the ever pressing designs of the so called 'narrow gauge' companies to invade south and central Devon. Conversely the broad gauge companies had connived with and supported the Great Western Dock Co in 1848 in reply to the LSWR scheme to link Sutton Harbour with Tavistock via a Plymouth branch.

Prior to 1849, the 1830's and '40's saw the generation of many proposals for Devonshire and the Westcountry. The 1830's produced the following:

a   The incorporation of the GWR on 31 August 1835.

b   Issue of prospectus of the Bristol & Exeter Railway during September 1835, which became law by the 19th of that month.

c   Survey of a line from Plymouth to Exeter via the South Hams by Brunel during 1836 and its failure due to lack of funds.

d   Francis Giles, original engineer of the London Southampton Railway proposed a line north of Dartmoor via Crediton, Okehampton to Tavistock.

e   Rendle commenced a seven year study and investigation into railway communications between Plymouth and Exeter with an attendant branch to Tavistock.

f   The failure of the Launceston & Victoria Railway during 1836, coupled with the Tremoutha Haven, St Gennys Harbour scheme.

The 1840's produced the following in their turn:

a   Depositing of plans for a railway from Plymouth, Devonport & Stonehouse over Dartmoor with a branch to Tavistock. The brainchild of James Meadows Rendle and surveyed by a Mr H Beardmore. Three routes were offered as alternatives each of them costly and needing many and complicated engineering works.

b   A Mr McNeil's survey in 1841 following doubts of the viability of the 1840 proposals.

c   Captain W S Moorsom's survey of a Cornwall and Devon Railway from Falmouth to Exeter via Launceston, at Tavistock a branch would diverge to Plymouth.

d   With the formation of the Plymouth, Devonport & Exeter Railway completed in 1843, a prospectus was issued for a railway from Plymouth to Exeter via the South Hams as surveyed by Brunel in 1836.

e   Also during 1843 the final decision was taken to construct the line of, and change the name of the company to, The South Devon Railway Company. A Bill for these plans was deposited on 30 November of that year. It came before the 'Commons Committee' 26 April 1844.

f   1844 also saw a prospectus for the South Devon & Tavistock Railway issued following the re-engagement of James Rendle to survey the project. Provisional directors for the SDR agreed with Lord Morley not to erect a station on his land without prior agreement, so dashing hopes of a junction station at the junction of the main line and the branch.

g   The same year saw the adoption of the 'Atmospheric System' for the whole of the SDR. This led to the rejection of the Bill for a line to Tavistock. On 28 August the South Devon & Tavistock Co engaged Brunel to survey the proposed branch to Tavistock.

h   Plans were deposited on 30 November 1844 for a railway from the SDR main line to Tavistock at Crabtree Marsh (Later Marsh Mills).

j   The SDR lent support for Launceston in its bid for an atmospheric system to join that of the main line to Tavistock. This line would follow the later route of 1862 bypassing Milton Abbot but with a detour via Lidford to join with the North Devon line from Okehampton to Launceston. The Bill for the above scheme failed in Parliament and the Launceston company was dissolved. The failure of the atmospheric railway of the SDR was also evident at this time.

k   On 8 July 1845 the Tavistock section of the Plymouth to Launceston railway scheme was brought before Parliament's Commons Committee and was read unopposed as part of an 'Omnibus Bill'.

And so the proposals, counter proposals, schemes and plans were conceived and died throughout these years before the final opening of the line to Tavistock. However, the main battle for the Plymouth to Tavistock railway was fought during 1852-53 by two rival but gallant armies of Devonian men. The two 'sides' were the 'Plymouth and Tavistock' faction led by Thomas Gill, ex Chairman of the SDR. (He had just resigned over the abysmal failure of the atmospheric railway), and the South Devon & Tavistock' faction led by Lord Morley who had impressed the SDR directors.

The former faction sought sustenance from further north in Devon and the resultant company had the omnipotent title of the 'Plymouth, Tavistock, Okehampton, North Devon & Exeter Railway'. This plan was defeated in 1853 by the Commons Committee at the first reading. The South Devon & Tavistock faction did however succeed in getting its plans passed by the Commons only to fail in the House of Lords. The Plymouth & Tavistock faction again rallied under a third company name, that of the 'Tavistock & Devon Central Railway' but failed to impress Parliament. The time for manoeuvres was over and it was in 1854, the very same year that the 'South Devon & Tavistock' faction under the leadership of Lord Morley achieved an easy victory resulting in the 'first sod' being cut at Mrs Davey's farm on Roborough Down for the company on 25 August 1856.

The company's engineer, Mr A H Bampton, did not begin works until 24 September 1856. He lived for only a few months after the commencement and his untimely death the following Spring saw the appointment of I K Brunel as his successor. The half yearly meeting of 29 August 1857 proposed another branch from Yelverton to Princetown. In the meantime, progress on the line, which contained en route, many heavy earthworks and engineering works, was swiftly achieved and on 8 February 1858 Brunel gave his first reassuring report as engineer. During June the following year, Brunel was travelling over the completed line engaged upon a personal inspection.

Illustrated London News

Opening of the South Devon & Tavistock Railway,
Scene at Tavistock station, 21 June 1859.

The line was formally opened on 21 June 1859 between Plymouth and Tavistock. The first train from Millbay had for its human cargo all those, including the Tavistock Brass Band, the 96th Warwickshire Militia, and the Tavistock Fife and Drum Band, who could not be accommodated on the special train. The special train was due out of Millbay at 2.00 pm, and was to carry the Directors, Company officials, dignitaries and up to 300 guests within the confines of its ten coaches. The reception at Tavistock for the special train was quite spectacular. It was presided over by the Portreeve of the Court Leet and the Court Baron of Tavistock. The climax to the celebrations was a comprehensive and detailed procession through the town, formed of floats depicting all the trades and occupations of the district. Two nonagenarians were guests of honour of the Portreeve's carriage, a John Eddy and a Mary Doidge. The whole procession took a considerable time to pass through the many narrow streets of the town, but it finally came to a halt in Bedford Square where the official party and guests totalling 120 were entertained to dinner at the Bedford Hotel.

The following day the branch opened for normal passenger traffic with stations such as Bickleigh, Horrabridge and Tavistock opening as well. It was not until 1 February 1860 that these stations opened for goods traffic.

Marsh Mills, on the other hand, was opened for goods with Bickleigh and Horrabridge but its passenger traffic did not materialise until as late as 15 March 1861.

The year 1861 saw the beginning of the extension of the branch from Tavistock to Launceston. A Bill proposing a line from Launceston to Coleford Junction, joining the Exeter to Barnstaple branch failed that year.

Throughout the months between August and November, much activity was experienced in obtaining proposals to connect Launceston to the railway network. A 42 mile long line from Exeter via Crediton, Okehampton and Tavistock to Launceston was considered at a meeting in Plymouth. Other meetings were organised to hear proposals for Launceston from the SDR Co and to decide between the SDR schemes and the alternative Mid Cornwall scheme, which actually lost. A more detailed consideration was given at yet another meeting to debate the Tavistock to Launceston line proposed by the SDR and finally on 30 November 1861 plans were deposited for the same, a line 19 miles long via Lifton, Lidford and Mary Tavy.

On 13/14 March 1862 the Bill came before the House of Commons and became an Act of incorporation on 30 June the same year for the Launceston & South Devon Railway Company.

Meanwhile over 2000 citizens of Launceston and its surrounding districts signed a petition on 23 April 1862 for a railway for their town and presented it to Westminster on the following 15 May, such was its concern at being left off the railway map. During this year also, the recently opened Tavistock railway from Plymouth had its history marred by a minor accident. It was on 18 April 1862 the locomotive of the 9.20 am passenger train from Tavistock broke its pistons just after passing Magpie Viaduct. Returning to the Tavistock to Launceston project, a further Act of Parliament for a deviation between Lifton and Coryton was passed on 29 June 1863.

The 1 June 1865 witnessed the formal opening of the Launceston & South Devon Railway from Tavistock to Launceston. A special train of 14 coaches (hauled by two SDR 'Hawk' class locomotives, 'Giraffe' and 'Dart', departed Millbay at 10.45 am and later gained an additional coach at Tavistock. Enthusiastic celebrations were expounded at Launceston to greet the trains arrival in torrential rain.

Through the remainder of June Col Yolland, Inspector of the Board of Trade, and Mr P J Margary, the Company's Engineer, held various inspections of the finished line to supervise minor rearrangements and improvements made in the interests of public safety. Finally on 1 July 1865 the branch was publicly opened to passenger traffic, Mary Tavy, Lidford, Coryton, Lifton and Launceston opened simultaneously. The same date saw the amalgamation of the South Devon & Tavistock Railway with the South Devon Railway by an Act of Parliament. On the following 21 August 1865 Launceston opened for goods traffic. Ten days later, on 31 August 1865 the last meeting of the South Devon & Tavistock Railway occurred. Track extension in the form of Cawdron

The first train at Launceston, 1st July 1865

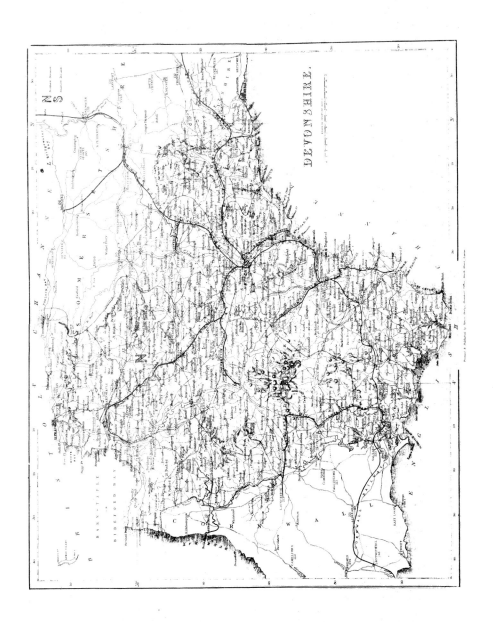

Map of Devon's railway companies. Circa 1865.

siding at 29m 12c near Launceston was completed and put into use at the instigation of the Board of Trade. It was to serve Mr Arundell's quarry until 1894. Another siding at 18m 17c was constructed at Brentor between Mary Tavy and Lidford, during 1866 for the use of farmers and tradesmen in the area.

The absorption of the Launceston and South Devon Railway by the South Devon Railway resulted on 24 June 1869 but its amalgamation did not follow until 31 December 1873. At Shaugh Bridge, the works siding opened for the building of Shaugh tunnel, re-opened during 1870 for the loading of low grade iron ore for smelting in South Wales. It was being mined on the east side of the River Plym. Lifton however, was equipped with a new goods station during 1870 and the company was planning a canopy for Launceston station platform.

1874 was a particular year of note in the history of the branch for on 12 October the arrival of the opposing 4' 8$\frac{1}{2}$" gauge of the London & South Western Railway made considerable impact at Lidford. Construction of the line from Okehampton commenced in 1865 following powers derived from an Act two years earlier. This Act was also responsible for changing the name of the former Okehampton Railway to the Devon & Cornwall Railway. During the two years that followed, the LSWR became dissatisfied with its passengers having to change trains because of differing gauges at Lidford. It therefore set out to secure a mixed gauge from there to Marsh Mills. This was finally achieved and opened on 17 May 1876 so completing the LSWR route from London via Lidford and Marsh Mills section of the branch to its new terminus at Devonport, latterly Kings Road. This was made possible by implementing newly acquired running rights over South Devon and Cornwall Railways metals. Lidford thus became the busiest station on the branch. During 1876 also, the narrower gauge East Cornwall Mineral Railway obtained an Act to extend its line from Calstock to Tavistock joining the South Devon & Tavistock Railway there. It was to convert its 3' 6" gauge to 4' 8$\frac{1}{2}$" in so doing. This project failed to materialise however and it was much later that a branch emerged from 'Beer' (from 1897 Bere) Alston to Callington. It was on 22 July 1878 that the GWR took over the former Launceston & South Devon Railway, only four years before another Bill came before Parliament. This time it was for an independent line from Lidford to Plymouth for the LSWR. It was authorised by the House of Commons but was later abandoned. The Company was gaining nothing but dissatisfaction from the arrangement with the GWR to run over its metals from Lidford to Devonport Junction via Plymouth.

The following year, 1883 was an important year historically for the branch for two main reasons. The first was the commencement on 11 August of a passenger train service to Princetown from Horrabridge.

The opening of the Princetown Railway from a junction at Yelverton had reached fruition. The second reason was the formation of the Plymouth, Devonport & South Western Junction Railway following an Act of Parliament dated 25 August 1883 for an independent line from Lidford to Devonport via Tavistock and Bere Alston, and thence to a new central station at Plymouth Friary. This occurrence was not a moment too soon for the hapless LSWR as the climax to their discontent arrived during the following year. The 11 am train from Waterloo to Devonport hauled by an Adams 0-6-0 tender locomotive, No 442, was derailed at MP $6^1/_2$ near Clearbrook. It was apparently due to a broken coupling but the rigid wheelbase of the loco was considered to be a contributory cause of the accident and it terminated the employment of that class upon the branch. It is sad to record that the toppling over the embankment of the loco after the derailment caused the death of the driver.

LSWR '395 class' loco No 442 off the road at Clearbrook on 18 November 1887. The accident happened between Good-a-Meavy Bridge and just below Clearbrook Halt.
Courtesy of R.T. Coxon and E. Thomas

Earlier during the year, on 1 May 1885 Yelverton station was opened to passenger traffic at 7m 37c, but goods traffic was still originating from Horrabridge. Just over a year later another station celebrated its opening. On 21 July 1886 Launceston LSWR station handled its first passenger traffic.

During the Summer of 1887 the branch suffered another setback, this time for the GWR, when the original all wooden building built by

Brunel at Tavistock, burnt down. The replacement which followed during 1888 and served until closure was constructed of both stone and timber, but still sported an all over roof.

1888 was the peak year for flour traffic at Marsh Mills for about that time a large flour mill occupied the site adjacent to the station.

An historically momentous year for the branch was 1890 for on 2 June that year the LSWR trains enjoyed their own main line route to Plymouth from Lidford. (This was followed by the opening of the new station at Plymouth Friary on 1 July 1891). This, in fact, resulted in the junction at Lidford and the 'third rail' from Lidford to Tavistock Junction being taken out of use on and from the early 1890's. The third rail was returned to use again with the eventful passing of the broad gauge on the weekend of 21/22 May 1892. However the adjacent broad gauge rail became redundant in its turn and resulted in the mixed gauge from Lidford to Plymouth becoming the standard 4'8$^1/_2$" gauge. So with the end of the broad gauge era Phase 1 of the branch history concludes. (Not before the recovery of the passing loop at Mary Tavy during the previous year is recorded).

View showing the original timber construction of Plym Bridge Halt, together with the approach of a steam rail motor.

c early 1900's   LGRP

Shaugh Bridge Platform circa 1907. The newly denuded surroundings were the result of its recent construction.
Courtesy of King Street Curios, Tavistock

Yelverton Station during the summer of 1905. Note the longitudinal track and the double turn out to Princetown branch at the end of the 'up' platform. A Princetown coach can be seen to the right of the picture.
Photomatic Ltd

Launceston to Plymouth train entering Yelverton from the north hauled by 4-4-0 "Duke".
c 1910   *Author's Collection*

A turn of the century study of Yelverton during 1912. A steam railmotor arrives with an
excursion from Plymouth.
Lens of Sutton
Courtesy of King Street Curios, Tavistock

The Princetown line is just visible in the background as a Launceston to Plymouth train heads south out of Yelverton Station behind a class '517' tank during the late 1890's
F. Frith & Co Ltd

View of Horrabridge village from the station during 1920's period. Trucks in the sidings include examples from the Great North of Scotland and Furness Railways.
Chapman & Son

A six coach train for Plymouth heads for Yelverton after its departure from Horrabridge.
Note its 4 and 6 wheeled stock.

c 1913

S Taylor

Horrabridge Station looking towards Tavistock. GWR "3521 class" 4-4-0 No 3531
arriving with a "up train" for Plymouth. From a postcard dated 1916.
W.R. Gay's Series
Courtesy R.T. Coxon

Rare picture of Horrabridge "Bowstring" bridge taken from the roadway below looking towards Tavistock.

c 1914   *S. Taylor*

A scene of the former level crossing at the southern end of Horrabridge Station.
c early 1920's   *S. Taylor*

Two differing views of Brunel's original Walkham (or Grenofen) Viaduct showing the massive timber superstructure replaced with steel by 1910.

F. Frith & Co Ltd   Launceston Railway Circle
c 1905   Courtesy of R.T. Coxon   Courtesy of C. Barrett

A five coach train heading for Tavistock crosses Walkham Viaduct during the summer of 1903

S. Taylor

GWR 0-6-2T No 4409 leaves Tavistock with two railmotor coaches. The loco was proper to the Princetown branch and it is interesting to note its use beyond Yelverton.
c 1930   Courtesy of King Street Curios, Tavistock

Mary Tavy and Blackdown Station during the halcyon days of 1914.
It shows the original SDR signal box then, still in use.

S. Taylor

A 1920 study of the picturesque country station of Coryton complete with orderly
allotments.

Chapman & Son

A copy from an original photograph showing the two companies' station at Lydford around the 1900 period. View taken from Was Tor looking eastwards towards Black Down.

F. Frith & Co. Ltd.

An earlier scene to the one shown previously in this book of Lifton station looking east. The factory sign here shows 'Ambrosia Ltd, Dried Milk Works'.
c 1910's   Lens of Sutton

The two Launceston Stations at the turn of the century. Viewed from Dockacre Road area and looking north. It shows the extensive layouts of both companies including their individual signal boxes, current at the time.

Launceston Railway Circle

A very early view of the two stations at Launceston looking from the other direction to that of the previous picture and at a greater distance from them.

Lens of Sutton

Phase 2 - GWR Standard Gauge Branch - Nationalisation 1892-1947

The first year of the new era saw the replacement of Riverford and Bickleigh Viaducts. They were rebuilt in granite and brought into service on the same day 12 March 1893. Two years later, during late 1895, the defunct GWR to LSWR junction was taken out at Lidford. This was followed with a change of spelling of the name of the station to 'Lydford' on and from 3 June 1897.

The last year of the 19th century was 'celebrated' by the reconstruction of Ham Green Viaduct. It was brought into use on 19 November 1899, so just making it! It was reconstructed in stone with a brick top above the level of the trackwork. Following closely in 1902, it was Magpie Viaduct's turn for replacement, and it was reconstructed wholly in blue Staffordshire brick and duly opened on 8 June that year.

Cann Viaduct's replacement commenced on 2 February 1905 but it was not until 10 March 1907 that its blue Staffordshire brick construction was opened to traffic. Meanwhile during 1906, Plym Bridge Platform opened on 1 May and Whitchurch Down Platform opened on 1 September. On 19 August 1907 the third platform opened on the branch to cater for the increasing 'day tripper' traffic, this time it was at Shaugh Bridge, on the site of the old mine siding.

It was also during 1907 that the words "& Blackdown" were added to Mary Tavy station. On and around these years work had commenced on replacing the giant timber superstructure of the graceful Walkham Viaduct. The same limestone piers which previously carried the huge timbers carried the new brickwork with their Gothic headed openings emulating those existing within the original stonework bases. The new viaduct was completed by placing steel superstructures and flooring over its fifteen spans using two twelve ton cranes. It was opened for traffic, proper during September 1910 but interruptions to trains during engineering works were minimal, generally Sundays and only whilst the positioning of the main girders was achieved. (See account in the geographical chapter).

The years running up to the first World War saw the construction of a new signal box at Bickleigh which opened on 4 December 1913, and the supervision of the GW branch station at Lydford transferring over to the LSWR staff on 1 March 1914. The GWR signalman was withdrawn but one porter remained there until as late as 1917.

The increase of all types of traffic on the branch and the LSWR main line during the war was responsible for an agreement between the two companies for the GWR to restore the Lydford Junction line on 28 days notice for wartime emergency working.

Further co-operation between the companies was established during 1917 when on 8 June that year both the GWR and the LSWR signal boxes were closed and a new joint box was opened on the centre platform, manned by LSWR signalmen.

Raw materials were in ever increasing demand for the war effort and so on 15 February 1918 a siding was opened at 1m 20c near Plym Bridge to serve the Canadian Forestry Commission engaged upon loading timber here for pit props. The siding was controlled by a ground frame locked by a key on the ET system. It finally closed down during 1920 following the cessation of hostilities in November 1918.

The first signs of the branch's insecurity was apparent the following year. It was during 1919 the Devon Motor Transport was inaugurated at Okehampton and bus services started within the area between there and Tavistock. By 1925 the services had expanded to include Princetown and the area local to it. Seeing the competition, the Great Western commenced its own bus services in the area soon afterwards. By 1922 the Devon Motor Transport had established services covering Plymouth, Tavistock, Princetown, Lydford, Okehampton and many other places throughout the area. By 1924 the GWR had opened a depot at Bovey (Tracey) on the Moretonhampstead branch. Its buses ran to Haytor, Lustleigh and Manaton all the year around and to Moretonhampstead, Postbridge, Princetown and Tavistock during the summer only.

Apart from the aforementioned, the early 1920's observed a multitude of minor events taking place on the branch. Firstly, on 7 June 1921 the private sidings for the Dartmoor China Clay Co (Later ECLP Ltd), opened at Marsh Mills. Settling tanks were also installed at Woodford.

At the commencement of the severe winter of 1921, lineside loading of firewood was specially authorised. This was at 2m 0c, near Cann Cottages and authorisation was on and from 18 December 1921. (The Canadian Forestry Commission's siding near Plym Bridge was reopened for a time on 13 July 1922 but its reclosure date is unknown). Earlier in 1922, on 30 March, the first of the Pitts Cleave Quarry sidings was brought into use. Three more followed by the month of June that year and they were all situated between MP's 14 and $14^1/_2$.

Between 1923 and 1928, the raising of the height of the dam at Burrator on the Princetown branch, increased both the passenger and freight traffic over the Marsh Mills to Yelverton section of the branch. This took the form of workmen, stores and equipment mainly, added to which were sightseers and trippers, especially during the summer, augmenting the existing traffic.

1923 was the year of the amalgamation of the country's railways into the 'Big Four'. This did not directly affect the branch save for the new adjacent company at Lydford and Launceston was now the Southern

Railway. The winter of 1927-28 was another very severe one, and the railway to Princetown via Yelverton was the only link for many weeks after being cleared of snowdrifts. The increase of the day tripper traffic encouraged the GWR to open Clearbrook Halt for passengers on 29 october 1928, too late for the summer traffic that year. By November 1928 the station house at Lifton was completed and occupied.

The 1930's commenced with the run down of the quarries on Dartmoor so affecting the freight over the Princetown branch and the Marsh Mills to Yelverton section of the branch. This poor start to a new decade was however, partly balanced by the opening of a new Tarmac Works belonging to Messrs Hoare Bros of Tavistock. From 14 March 1932 new roadstone traffic in private hopper waggons provided heavy traffic from Pitts Cleave Quarry near Tavistock to the new Marsh Mills works.

The bay platform for Princetown trains at Yelverton was shortened by 22 May 1933, the connection from the down loop to branch was removed and consequently the curve improved. On 28 February 1933 the motor trolley P Way maintenance system was introduced between Marsh Mills and Horrabridge. On 6 June it was extended from Horrabridge to Launceston. The loop at Bickleigh station was extended and brought into use on 13 March 1935.

The decade ended with the halt at Liddaton opening on 4 April 1938 and the Tavistock Gas Co's siding opening on the down side $21^1/_2$c from Tavistock on 20 July the same year.

At the commencement of 1939 the second War War was well in view and by 3 September hostilities had broken out. Resulting from this, new sidings were installed at Marsh Mills for a large government complex at Coypool. (Later MOD Depot, Coypool). It was situated adjacent to the western side of the branch and just to the north of the station and was opened on 3 November 1939. This new depot was to result in much wartime and post war freight traffic. (The sidings were closed and taken out of use during the early 1980's).

The war accelerated during 1940 into a sinister setback for the Allied powers. France, together with the rest of Europe had fallen which resulted in the famous Battle of Britain being fought and won during the August and September months. Nazi Germany had now turned its attention onto our cities and their subsequent destruction by aerial bombing.

1941 saw the bombing intensify and all principal cities were attacked in their turn. It was the turn of Plymouth on the nights of 20 and 21 March, followed by three more attacks on the nights of 22, 23 and 24 April 1941. Five full scale blitz raids laid the city in ruin and qualified it as the most heavily bombed city outside London in terms of bombs per square mile, and this included Coventry! The result was that the city's weary citizens flocked in their droves to the surrounding countryside to escape further onslaughts. Many extra trains were run to Tavistock and Yelverton and other places on the branch to cater for these unfortunate souls. It is interesting to note at this juncture that during the massive clear up that followed by men and women from the Services and from the city itself during 1941-2, much of the rubble from the streets was brought to Yelverton station. It was unloaded from trucks and dumped at the southern end of the station forming a high embankment adjacent to the up refuge siding. Broken crockery and other railway items were also dumped there, a little known fact, one may add.

Of lesser consequence but worthy nevertheless of mentioning was the ground frame provided on the down side of the Lee Moor Tramway at a point 330 yards from Marsh Mills signal box. It provided for the LMT crossing the new Government Depot line and it opened on 12 February 1941. On 11 August that year Mary Tavy and Blackdown became an unstaffed halt.

The progress of the war into 1943 brought the preparations for the invasion of Europe which culminated in the D Day landings of 1944. By now the 'Big Four' railways were working together closely and by their very act of co-operation, were effectively 'Nationalised'. 1943 marked the opening of a junction at Launceston between the GWR branch and the SR main line at $31m\ 33^1/_2c$ along the branch. The junction had a new east ground frame on the up side as an engineering department siding. It was SR property and was brought into use for emergency war traffic on 22 September of that year.

Lydford followed the example on 15 November that year with its own junction between the two companies. (This was the second time such had existed here).

On 21 November 1943 the ground frame and siding at Leat between Lifton and Launceston at 27m 51c was removed on the other hand. It had existed on the site since 1876. Finally 1943 witnessed the large scale alteration and extension of Marsh Mills signal box. War traffic reached its peak during 1944 following the D Day landings on 6 June. Much wartime freight was passing over the branch from many depots set up in country places served by the line. This continued until the cessation of hostilities in Europe on 8 May 1945.

By 1947 the reverse was beginning to happen, motor traffic was on the increase with the availability of petrol. That year the LMT closed and the Dartmoor Clay Co was taken over by English China Clays Ltd and its sidings at Marsh Mills were extended.

November 1947 saw the wartime junction at Lydford taken out of use. The end of the year brought the most momentous change since the passing of the broad gauge. Not so noticeable at first the impact was nevertheless as effective, for 31 December was the last day of GWR ownership. The following day all Britain's railways were nationalised and that sounded the death knell for the first time for the branch. The onslaught of the motor car and government policy during the following years were to eventually destroy the branch. With that sad note the second phase of the history of the line concludes.

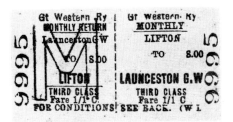

Lineside view of the former Launceston passenger station during 1959, showing its use as a goods depot and office.

Lens of Sutton

Launceston former GWR station used as goods offices during 1959. Loco No 5532 waits with a train in the SR station to the right of the picture.

R.S. Carpenter

Launceston SR station during the mid 1950's
The arrival of No 4591 on the WR branch train from Plymouth on a sunny day during August 1953. Another member of its class shunts goods in the former GWR station.

Real Photos Co Ltd

Shows No 5567 taking on water following its arrival with the mid morning train from Plymouth. Another 45XX class couples to the other end as it prepares to return the stock on the next service to Plymouth.

c 20 December 1955   *Hugh Ballantyne*

Lineside view of the former Launceston passenger station during 1959, showing its use as a goods depot and office.

Lens of Sutton

Phase 3 - Nationalisation & Demise to Closure & Lifting, 1948-1968

The first year of nationalisation opened with a minor demolition, a bad omen for what was to follow. The siding, ground frame and disc were removed from Mary Tavy and Blackdown on 14 December 1948. The balance was redressed however, the following year when Plym Bridge Platform was reconstructed in pre-cast concrete and shortened by 100 feet. This structure, built during May 1949, remained until closure and is described in the previous chapter.

On 26 September 1949 the suffix 'South' was added to Tavistock station nameboards. This was followed two years later with the suffix 'North' being added to the GW Launceston station nameboards, on 18 June 1951 to be exact.

This latter act was both ironic and a total waste of time, as Launceston North closed to passengers on 30 June 1952. From this date all WR passenger trains were diverted over the wartime connection into Launceston SR station. Further closures on the branch during 1952 were the level crossing at Horrabridge on 5 March and Hoare Bros Tarmac Works at Marsh Mills during the autumn.

In the first month of 1955 the Lee Moor Tramway crossing was closed, the signals were taken out of use and the catchpoints were locked in the 'open' position. The gateman was withdrawn also.

On 5 March 1956 the Princetown branch closed to all traffic. This was a heavy blow to the branch in terms of its own passengers and freight below Yelverton. Changes in the signalling at the lower end of the branch were also in evidence during 1956. Marsh Mills to Bickleigh electric staff was replaced by the electric token on 2 May followed by the same action being taken over the Bickleigh to Yelverton section on 4 May.

With the closure of the Princetown Branch, the rundown of Yelverton station was inevitable and on 28 April the connection from the 'up main to Princetown branch' was put out of use.

In January 1957 the *Western Morning News* bore a report of a runaway truck. "Runaway truck diverted to avoid collision with train. Shortly before a passenger train was due along the same line, a steel-built 'BBC' truck for recovered rails from the Princetown branch ran away at Yelverton Station and trundled back towards the oncoming train.

The truck - three times the length of ordinary rail trucks - rapidly picked up speed on the steep gradient, and within seconds was hurtling towards Plymouth at over 40 miles an hour.

Shunting staff at Yelverton warned the traffic control and the oncoming train from Plymouth was stopped at Marsh Mills.

Seven men working on the line at Shaugh Tunnel heard a rumbling and looked up to see the truck speeding towards them. They quickly scattered and the truck raced past them and vanished into the tunnel.

At Bickleigh Station catchpoints had been set to divert the truck to a "throw off", where it would run off the line and be checked on soft ground. Station-master Mr S Taylor stood on the platform waiting for the truck to appear. "I heard a rattle like thunder and it came at me like a shot out of a gun" he said. "As it went over the catchpoint the rear end of the truck rode up on the platform. Showers of sparks made it seem like a ball of fire. I immediately dived under cover.

The truck careered on over the soft ground for nearly 200 yards before finally coming to rest. It damaged signalling gear and part of the platform. The truck was later removed by a breakdown wagon."

Three years later on 4 May 1959 the signal box was closed, the signals disconnected, the down line converted to single line, the up line secured and closed. The new electric token section Horrabridge to Bickleigh was brought into use as a direct result. Later on 14 September 1959, Coryton was reduced to an unstaffed halt with public siding status. The decay was now beginning to accelerate and by 1960 rumours of pending closure were beginning to circulate. The only fact worth recording for the following year was the withdrawal of the ex LSWR locomotive No 442, involved in the 1885 accident at Clearbrook, as BR (SR) No 30582 during May 1961.

The arrival of 1962 brought the dawn of the "Beeching Era" and the criminal repercussions of his savage policies. Closure rumours were proven correct and the end of the branch was decided in January that year. The posting of the foreboding notices declaring the pending closure were abundantly displayed at all main and branch line stations. Later the same year further notices declaring 31 December 1962 as the date from which all services should cease, 14 years to the day from the date of nationalisation. The closure saga itself is now a landmark in Westcountry railway history and its details are prolifically recorded. As is now well known, the closure of the branch was unique for the last scheduled trains failed to run, the immediately preceding ones were stranded in stations at the height of the blizzard. This commenced on 29 December and was the foretaste of the worst winter conditions since 1891 and 1947. (The following diagrammatic representation records the last trains movements or lack of them, on the branch for the last days running).

BRITISH TRANSPORT COMMISSION

WESTERN BRITISH RAILWAYS REGION

NOTICE TO THE PUBLIC

In view of the British Transport Commission's financial position and its statutory obligation to pay its way, it can no longer continue to provide services which are not economic. As a consequence all facilities whose ability "to pay their way" is in doubt have been or will be examined. The passenger train service between Plymouth, Tavistock South and Launceston falls within this category and it has been established that the Commission would benefit financially to a substantial degree if this service was withdrawn. The introduction of new diesel units would not effect an improvement to an extent whereby the service could be made remunerative, and it would be unreasonable to expect the Commission to incur a capital expenditure in the provision of these units when there would be no hope of any return.

The Commission have no alternative but to submit to the South Western Area Transport Users' Consultative Committee for their consideration, a proposal to withdraw the passenger train service between Plymouth, Tavistock South and Launceston; withdraw the parcels facilities from Marsh Mills, Tavistock South and Lifton; withdraw freight facilities from Coryton Siding and close the line for all purposes between Marsh Mills (exclusive) and Tavistock South (exclusive) and Lifton (exclusive) and Launceston (exclusive).

The Western National Omnibus Co. Ltd. operate between Plymouth and Tavistock and Launceston and the Southern National Omnibus Co. Ltd., Plymouth Joint Services, and, to a limited degree, Mr. E. P. Down and Mr. N. C. Born also operate services in the area. In addition, Tavistock, Lydford and Launceston would continue to be served from Plymouth and Exeter via the Southern Region and it is considered these rail services, together with the road services would provide a reasonable alternative.

Omnibus services by virtue of their flexibility in route, etc., are more adequate to cater for areas of this nature and this to a large extent has brought about the drift from rail to road transport.

Public Notices are on exhibition at all the stations affected indicating the Commission's proposals and a copy of the memorandum submitted to the Transport Users' Consultative Committee has been forwarded to the Members of Parliament, Local Authorities and other interested parties concerned.

When considered from a logical viewpoint, it is obvious that the traffic potential available in the area concerned is insufficient to support both rail and road passenger services and the elimination of the rail service, which is by far the more costly means of conveying a limited number of passengers, would result in a minimum of inconvenience.

The Section of line between Tavistock South (inclusive) and Lifton (inclusive) would be retained for freight and milk traffic. Freight facilities at Marsh Mills and Launceston would also be maintained. The withdrawal of freight facilities from other points on the branch would not, therefore, result in any undue hardship.

The circumstances which have led to the Commission's decision, to seek the agreement of the Consultative Committee to their proposals, are regretted. The change, however, which has taken place over the years in the method of travel preferred by the general public, so far as short distance journeys are concerned, is a facet over which the Commission have no control and can only accept, revising their services accordingly.

January 1962   S. E. RAYMOND
Paddington Station   *General Manager.*

R1198   Printed by   Trend & Co. Ltd., Plymouth.

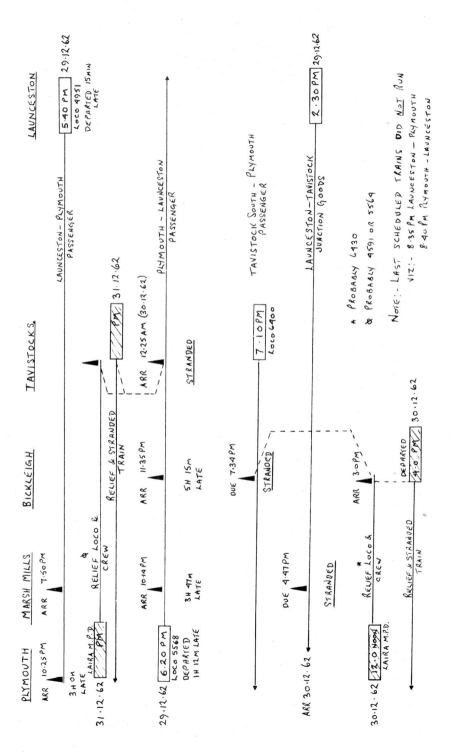

However, the official closure was on and from 29 December 1962 whereupon all stations closed to passengers from Marsh Mills to Launceston. Marsh Mills (exclusive) to Tavistock South (exclusive) and Lifton (exclusive) to Launceston (exclusive) were closed to all traffic. Launceston goods depot was reduced to siding status under supervision of SR staff. Launceston engine shed was closed and its turn-table recovered. After 103 years of service for the Marsh Mills to Tavistock section and 97 years of service for the Tavistock to Launceston section, the line had finally ceased to carry passengers and only the few miles between Tavistock South and Lifton remained open for freight traffic. The last train to be rescued was the one stranded at Tavistock and it was not until late afternoon on Monday 31 December that it was reached. Therefore it can be technically considered the actual closure was on and from Tuesday 1 January 1963!

1964 produced a miscellany of incidents still further degrading the remaining portion of the branch. 29 April marked the completion of the recovery of the centre road and miscellaneous sidings at Launceston station. 15 May produced the unusual sight of a BR Ivatt tank locomotive and an engineering train running over the closed Launceston to Lifton section of the remaining track. The section Lifton to Lydford was still open for 'Ambrosia' freight traffic and BR was then considering re-opening the section back to Launceston. This was to facilitate a Plymouth-Launceston freight service via the PDSWJ line to Lydford and then over the former GW track to Launceston. June marked the closing of Marsh Mills station to goods traffic, the closure of Tavistock signal box and its conversion to a ground frame (15.6.64). The Tavistock to Lydford electric token system was replaced by a wooden staff and a 'one engine in steam' working. By 29 July all signals at Tavistock were removed excepting the 'up fixed distant'; all points were worked by ground frame. The arrival of September marked the electric tokens at Lydford, Lifton and Launceston being removed and 'one engine in steam' operation being introduced. Lifton signal box was reduced to a ground frame and all signals at the station were removed except for the 'up and down fixed distants'. 7 September in particular was marked by the re-opening of the Lifton-Launceston section for freight following the 'special' in May and the results of its investigations. It was to be short lived however for the closure of Ambrosia sidings at Lifton was 'on the cards' and reclosure came less than eighteen months later.

During April 1964 the lifting of track commenced just south of Tavistock, by May the recovery had advanced as far as Horrabridge. During the summer work progressed on the removal of Walkham Viaduct and the over bridge across the A386 at Horrabridge station. By the end of 1964 the complete recovery of the whole railway from Tavistock South to Marsh Mills was achieved. Through 1965 the

The inevitable closure notice as it appeared at Bickleigh Station during January 1962
R.E. Taylor

0-6-0 PT No 6400 complete with wreath. Veteran of the branch, it leaves Plym Bridge Halt with one of the final day's trains during the Winter of December 1962.
L. Crosier

*Waiting for the last day's train which never arrived. Local
people from the district at Coryton Station.*
P.M. Pollinger

*Drifted snow blocking Bickleigh Station at the northern end.
Looking north*
c 30 December 1962
R.E. Taylor

Drifted snow blocking Bickleigh Station at the northern end.
Looking south

c 30 December 1962   R.E. Taylor

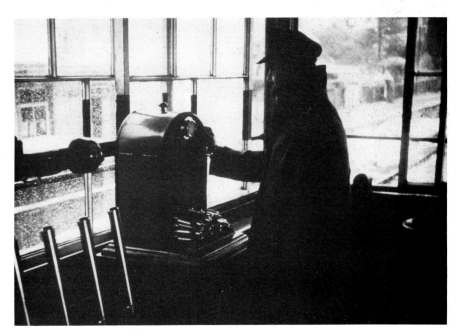

Signalman Morris at Bickleigh signal box rings 'train out of section' to Horrabridge
Signalman on 31 December 1962, the last time this act was executed.
R.E. Taylor

inexorable and terminal cancer of destruction carried on. At Coryton the ground frame and sidings were taken out of use on 31 March. On 4 April, Marsh Mills signal box closed, the signals were removed and points converted to hand working. In addition the branch connection to the main line was removed and replaced by a connection from number 4 road at Tavistock Junction goods sidings.

The end of the 'reprieve' for the last remaining section occurred on 28 February 1966. The closure of the 'Ambrosia' sidings at Lifton meant the end of the milk product traffic outwards and the tin traffic inwards. The latter were the ready made tins used to pack the rice pudding and other milk products).The same day Launceston GW and the Launceston to Lydford section closed to goods traffic and the only traffic the branch was to receive afterwards was the storage of some 200 or so condemned waggons on the Tavistock to Mary Tavy section, but this was not for long.

On 3 October 1966 the Southern Railway main line at Launceston closed to all traffic and the town was 'off the railway map' for the first time in 107 years. The final blow fell during December 1967 when the remaining track between Tavistock and Launceston was lifted, completion followed during early 1968.

During the two decades since the demise of the line, the intrusion of nature over much of the open countryside, minor stations and halts has been virile and complete. Demolition of Tavistock station site commenced during the Summer of 1968 and continued late into the Spring of 1969. The prime factor governing the early start on demolition was the need for the removal of the bridge over Abbey Road and the subsequent realignment of the roadway below. The severe bend caused by the bridge was straightened out by the removal of many tons of earthworks leading to the bridge from its southern end. This completed, the arc like section of the remaining roadway was later converted into a car park. The site remained undeveloped until early in the 1980's although it was sold to the Devon County Council soon after track lifting was completed in 1968.

Development of the former station site during 1981 to 1984 included the building of a Health Centre; Fire Station; an Ambulance Station; a small factory for Fairy Winches; and a building housing the Social Services Training Department.

The layout of the sole remaining stub of the branch at Marsh Mills station site was revised considerably during 1973, completion was by 25 October that year. The revised layout is of a single curving track running in from Tavistock Junction for approximatley $^1/_4$ mile to stop blocks. A further siding ran into the clayworks to the east and a second siding running into MOD Coypool to the west. The latter however was

116

Condemned stock stored on the branch during 1966 between Tavistock South and Mary Tavy

A. R. Kingdom

Marsh Mills Station during April 1967 looking north. Lines still in situ for MOD and clay traffic.

C.G. Lennox-Jones

Viewed over roadway wall looking towards Plymouth and showing close up of station buildings and foot bridge.

View of goods shed showing details and more recent additons to it.

Looking north towards Lydford showing also the turntable pit, water tower, goods shed and signal box.

Three studies of Tavistock South Station during June 1967
C.G. Lennox-Jones

General view westwards showing engine shed in foreground, station, goods shed and later goods shed in distance.

Station buildings looking west with goods dock trackbed in foreground.

Trackbed area looking east towards Lifton. The engine shed can be seen in the distance.

Three studies of Launceston GW Station during June 1967
C.G. Lennox-Jones

redundant at the time of writing, and is now recovered. On 5 May 1975 a new public level crossing was put into use across the siding at a point 0m 20c from Tavistock Junction. (During the late 1980's a second level crossing was constructed south of the overbridge of the old A38.) Coryton the other hand is the only remaining station building to survive all the demolition activities. Early during 1974, the station site and its buildings were sold to a private builder and by March of that year had undergone extensive building rearrangements. Planning permission had been obtained to convert the station building into a private dwelling, and in so doing the new owner had a second story added and an increase to the overall floor area of the original building. It is now a very desirable country dwelling standing in its own grounds and almost defies the existence of a railway having passed there. Coincident with the rebuilding, the Devon County Council removed the adjacent overbridge and filled the cutting beneath it.

It was the turn of the GWR/SR station sites at Launceston to be demolished during the early 1970's. Rubble from the site was dumped at the Lanstephen housing site on the Bude road north of the town from the station. The present day estate contains flats for OAPs and it is interesting to surmise that the stonework forming the foundations of their flats may well have served many of the inhabitants in earlier days on their rail trips to Tavistock and Plymouth etc!

Development of what is now known as Launceston's Newport Industrial Estate during the period of the mid 1970's to the mid 1980's has been determined but steady and mostly given over to the service of the great god 'Car'. No less than six car suppliers and motor engineers have residence on the site. Other firms include fuel merchants for coal, coke, oil and calor gas. Builders merchants, Electrical and TV engineers, Wholesale food suppliers are also in residence and of course all are served by road transport. The only opposition to the worship of this modern day god is the little narrow gauge Launceston Steam Railway situated on the former SR trackbed just west of the former station site.

What of the fate of the other stations along the branch? All have had their buildings demolished and Plym Bridge, Bickleigh, Shaugh Bridge, Clearbrook, Yelverton, Whitchurch Down, Mary Tavy, Lydford and Liddaton Halt have all returned to nature. Only the contour 'ghosts' of railway works remain beneath the undergrowth. Bickleigh station site has returned to Maristow Estates; Yelverton station site has returned to Col Spencer of Elfordtown. Clearbrook has been purchased by a local resident and turned into a garden.

Horrabridge too was sold to a firm of agricultural engineers who, during 1979 demolished the buildings and replaced them with a small factory in the early 1980's.

Lifton followed the same fate and was purchased by Ambrosia Ltd, now greatly enlarged and covering not only the former station site but land on the far side of it.

Events have returned the line full circle, much of the countryside out of which it was hewn has returned to nature. Only where urban life intrudes into the quiet shadows does it spill over and engulf the memories, but then this same urban growth would have invaded earlier if the line was never there!

Author's Footnote

During the early 1980's an organisation was formed dedicated to the relaying and reopening of the Marsh Mills to Yelverton section of the branch. The first stage embarked upon was the Marsh Mills to Plym Bridge section commencing from its home base north of the level crossing at Marsh Mills. (Coincident with this formation, the author's participation was sought by the committee primarily to advise them from his preservation experience). The conception of such an idea, although daunting, was nevertheless not an impossibility and could prove to be one of the most exciting feats within the preservation field. The Plym Valley Railway as it is now known is armed with boundless enthusiasm and much local support. In my opinion it does however lack a sense of planning employing an up to date approach, it also lacks the professionalism often identified with other preserved lines. One feels too much effort has been channelled into acquiring locomotives, often foreign to the line (one foreign to the country), in need of much expensive restoration rather than to the acquisition of good quality track and its associated facilities. Had the latter been achieved at an early date, owners of preserved and restored locomotives and stock would have come forward prepared to operate from a new base. Much needed revenue would have, by now been earned for consolidation and extension. In short one cannot employ 1960 methods of preservation to the 1980's, withdrawn BR locos can no longer be purchased in working order and those remaining for sale have deteriorated often beyond economic repair. Whilst I am no longer a member, I remain loyal to its aims, at variance with its approach, but nevertheless look forward to its success, with steam again running alongside the River Plym. To their battlecry 'Resurgam' one can only reply 'Quando et Quomodo?'

Author's Footnote Update 1990

When one is prepared to criticize, albeit constructively, an organisation which operates at variance with ones personal views, one ought to be prepared to congratulate it also when the occasion arises.

Recently, during the latter part of 1989, newspaper reports and my own frequent visits to site provide the grounds for such congratulation.

The PVR has completed the purchase from BR of the land and track at Marsh Mills and is preparing for possible Easter 1990 operation.

I have seen a large amount of good track laid and the demolition of Billacombe station (former Yealmpton Branch) is well under way for re-erection at Marsh Mills, a gift from English China Clays Ltd. Also waiting for erection is the old LSWR footbridge from Tavistock (north) and the refreshment bar from Millbay Docks.

Good work PVR - keep up these efforts and forget expensive loco restoration for the forseeable future!

Marsh Mills Station in the Spring of 1981 looking south. A single track forming a siding from Tavistock Junction is all that remains to serve clay traffic.
C.G. Lennox-Jones

Demolition of Tavistock South during Summer 1968-Spring 1969
Outside of station building and approach road from bank.
The late F.J.T. Elliott

Demolition of Tavistock South during Summer 1968-Spring 1969
Signal box and cattle dock looking south from wreckage of station buildings.
The late F.J.T. Elliott

Lydford SR Station during its last month of passenger service.
Looking east with the Exeter-Plymouth local service arriving.The destruction of the GWR
branch , running away to far left of picture is in evidence.

c 7 April 1963   *R.A. Lumber*

Lydford SR Station during its last month of passenger service.
Looking west with the Exeter-Plymouth local service leaving. The destruction of the GWR
branch towards Tavistock and the former World War II connections to the SR
can clearly be seen .

c 7 April 1963   *R.A. Lumber*

The only station to survive to date, Coryton.
Trackless during July 1967, looking east.
C.G. Lennox-Jones

The only station to survive to date, Coryton.
Reconstruction during March 1974 as a private dwelling
R.M. Pollinger

Broad gauge 4-4-0 ST of the South Devon Railway No 593 "Castor" at Launceston Station during the late 1860's. Jameson Davies, nearest the camera is its driver.
The late J.B.N. Ashford

TIME TABLES AND BRANCH WORKING
SOUTH DEVON TAVISTOCK AND LAUNCESTON SOUTH DEVON RAILWAYS

Motive Power employed.

Early days -   GWR 'Leo' class 2-4-0, these were not suitable and were withdrawn   before the branch's completion to Tavistock.

Late 1850's -   SDR 4-4-OST's 'Corsair' and 'Brigand' used on passenger traffic.

1865   -   4-4-OST No 2112 'Giraffe' transferred to Launceston from Tavistock where it was stationed since it first arrived in 1859/60. Drivers included Joe Booth, its regular one, the Fireman was usually Joe Rowland. Passenger traffic locomotive.

4-4-OST No 2121 'Castor' also stationed at Launceston for passenger traffic working, Driver Jameson Davies.

1860's   -   Goods traffic handled by 0-6-OST's of the SDR, 'Dido' and 'Ajax' (Diagram 1 refers).

1872   -   Goods motive power supplemented by ex GWR, 0-6-0 ST 'Bulkeley'.
Driver Dan Ware and Fireman, George West.

1876   -   Third rail laid for LSWR trains between Lidford and Plymouth.
This company's 318 'Metro' class 4-4-0 tanks were employed on the branch below Lidford. They were found to be not suitable and were replaced by 'Beattie' 2-4-0 tanks.

1878   -   Following takeover by GWR, 'Hawthorn' class 2-4-0's 'Melling' and 'Ostrich'.

1880's   -   GWR 3541 class 0-4-2ST, designed by Dean - several stationed at Millbay. (Diagram 2 refers).
Other LSWR classes in use were 'Adams' '415' class, 4-4-2 tanks and '395' class 0-6-0 tender engines.

1892   -   GWR locomotives for passenger working included 'Dean' 35XX tanks.

* (Diagram 3 refers).

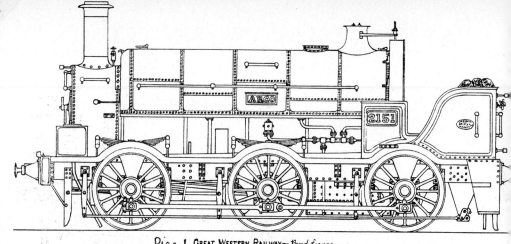

Diag 1. Great. Western. Railway.~ Broad Gauge.

Nº 2151. "Argo"

This was a South Devon Railway Cos Engine. { 17"×24" } Shewn above with G.W.R. chimney, sandbox,
built by Slaughter Gunning & Cos (Nº 523) Bristol 1863. 57" } cab, buffers, Nº, & brake gear & smoke box door.
This type engine runs from Exeter to Penzance & over all B.G. Branches in SDR & CR districts

Engines of this type below.

{ 2145 Rora : 2146 Ada }   2144 Hero.   2150 Brutus.   2153 Juno.   { For further details }
{ & 2147 ... were }   2148 Hebe   2151 Argo   2154 Remus   { refer to page 87. }
{ SlO. gaug.. type engines }   2149 Saturn   2152 Atlas.   2155 Romulus.   { of this Book. }
   2149 Saturn   2143 Dido.

Wheel base L to D. 7·10. D to T. 7·8"

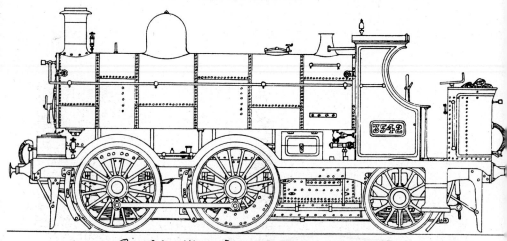

Diag 2. Great. Western. Railway.~ Broad Gauge.

Nº 3542.

Designed by Mr. W. Dean, & built by   Nº 3542. Fitted with trailing radial axle boxes.
G.W.R. Cos Swindon Works.   1888.   { 18"×26" }   Saunders & Bolitho vacuum & Steam brakes.
N.G. engine in B.G. frames. (Nº 3541 ... side tanks)   60".   Boiler pressure 160 lbs. Wheel centers 3ft 9.3"
This class run between Exeter & Penzance, also on the Branch lines. Several stationed at Millbay.

Numbers of this type below.

3541. 3542. 3543. 3544. 3545. 3546. 3547. 3548. 3549. 3550. 3551.
3552. 3553. 3554. 3555. 3556. 3557. 3558. 3559. (3560 never had Saddle. Tk.
All the above Engines, also 3560 were re-built with a trailing Bogie; & short side
tanks being substituted for the Saddle Tanks.

Diagrams of early Loco's working the Branch
by the late J.B.N. Ashford

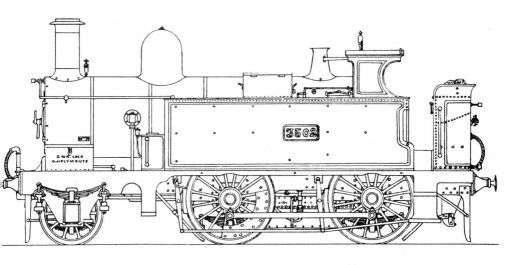

Diag 3. GREAT. WESTERN. RAILWAY. ~ Broad Gauge.

Designed by Mr W Dean. No in Bk of 3502.   Built by G W R Co. Swindon
Steam Brake to Engine & Vacuum (18" x 26") These two engines were stationed at (Millbay)
for train (Saunders & Boltho.)   60"   Plymouth from 1885 to 189 . They ran regularly
from Taunton to Penzance, also over the Launceston & Torquay Branches. Wheelcentres 7.3. 2½.9.
                    Numbers of this type
Weight Leading 7.C.2.   3501. 3502. 3503. 3504. 3505. 3506. 3507. 3508. 3509. 3510.
         10.14.0
       Driving 16.12.0
       Trailing 16.12.0
       Total. 43.18.0

GWR 0-6-0 Broad gauge loco No 2157 "Bulkeley" sold to SDR in June 1872.
Photographed at Millbay MPD.   *The late J.B.N. Ashford*

129

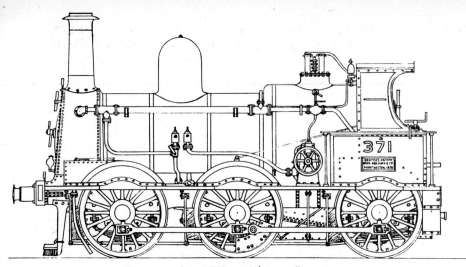

A. LONDON. & SOUTH. WESTERN. RAILWAY.

Designed by Mr. W. Beattie   No 371.   Nos of this type were
Built by Beyer Peacock & Co.   (17"x22")   151 Morthoe, 152 Marmion,
Manchester, 1878.   60"   160 Thames, 62 Severn, 229.
L&SWR 371 is B.P&Co 1784.   230, 368, 369, 370, 371, 372, 373.
This type were called "Beatties double brake goods" - they were the last he desig. d for L&SWR.
Fitted with Beatties paten t apparatus & firebox; 371 at Exeter 1878-1895 running Devonport,
Friary, Holsworthy, Torrington, Yeovil & Salisbury goods & passenger trains.

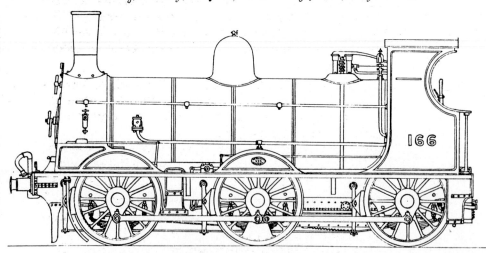

B. LONDON. & SOUTH. WESTERN. RAILWAY.

Designed by Mr. W. Adams, built by   No 166.   Fitted with Steam Brake to engine & tender & Gresham's
Neilson & Co, Glasgow, 1883. "Jumbo" type. (17½"x26")   Automatic Vacuum for train. - No 166 runs goods &
Weight (full loaders). 13. 8. 0   Total weight   61."   passenger trains between Salisbury, Exeter, Devonport, North
{underneath} drivers 14. 0. 0. {38-16. 0   Total engine & tender   Devon line, and also over the Friary Holsworthy &
{1500 gallons   trailer 11. 8. 0. {30-2. 0   68. 18. 0.   Launceston Branches. (166 stationed at Exeter.) -
{of water.
Numbers of above type.- 153. 159. 161. 164. 165. 166. 167. 395. 396. 397. 398. 399. 400. 401. 402. 403. 404. 405. 406. 433.
434. 435. 436. 437. 438. 439. 440. 441. 442. 443. 464. 158.
No 395-406, built 1882 when new they had no vacuum brake, nor motion plate to step.

| 1899-1902 | - | GWR 3521 class as rebuilt 4-4-0 tender engines, appeared on the branch and remained until 1914. Those stationed at Launceston included No's 3528/3535/3550/3554 & 3556. Goods traffic was mainly in the hands of 0-6-0 ST No 1897. |

* The locomotive to have the distinction of hauling the last broad gauge train on the branch was 4-4-0 ST No 2134, 'Heron'. It worked the 9.44 pm Tavistock ex Plymouth on 20 May 1892, returning with empty stock for Swindon, later.

Early 1900's Introduction of steam rail motors, Plymouth to Tavistock.
Replaced with auto fitted 0-4-2T's of '517' class; 2-4-0T's of 'Metro' class and 0-6-0ST's of '2021' and '1076' classes.
(1903 Churchwards '31XX' class tried but not retained).
Examples of these classes recorded as working on the branch were:
'2021' class, No's 2120 & 2140.
'1076' class, No's 738; 1167; 1284; 1570 & 1600.
'Duke' class with small tenders were permitted to run the branch and it is recorded that '3251 class No 3527 'King Arthur' was stationed at Launceston during 1912-13 and banker between Tavistock and Lidford was No 3284, Isles of Jersey. Steam railcars were also in evidence around 1912.

1920's - Branch mainly run by 2-6-2T's of '45XX' class; '44XX' class also but mostly reserved for the Yelverton to Princetown section, however 4409 was recorded at Tavistock during this time.
Note:- Engines of the larger classes were allowed as far as Yelverton on specials etc, they included 'Star', 'Dukedog', 'Bulldog', 'Castle', 'Hall' & 'Grange' classes.

In 1931 No 5031 'Abergavenny Castle' was recorded at Yelverton, No 3289 'St Austell' at Lydford and No 1570 double framed 0-6-0PT recorded at Tavistock.
Examples of 45XX class recorded were:No's 4511; 4520; 4522; 4547; 4548; 4551; 4557 & 4560 as first arrivals.

1930's - Further members of '45XX' class were introduced, examples recorded were:-
No's 4526; 4531; 4542; 4544; 4561; 4581; 4591 & 4598.

Post 1945 (World War II) Additions were as follows:-
No's 4524; 4533; 4555; 4568; 4570; 4574 & 4583.

Also during this period the following other classes were introduced:-
0-4-2T's of '1400' (4800) class.
0-6-OPT's of the '57XX' and '64XX' class.

1950's - 1960's - '55XX' class 2-6-2T's appeared.

During 1954-55 some examples of the '87XX'; '36XX' '37XX' were employed on the branch.

Examples of the '55XX' class recorded were:-
No's 5511; 5531; 5532; 5541; 5544; 5548; 5557; 5560; 5564; 5567; 5568; 5569 & 5572.

Examples of the '64XX' class recorded were:
No's 6400; 6410; 6420; 6430 6438.

Examples of other classes were:-
No's 1408; 1421; 1434; 3686; 4658; 9770.

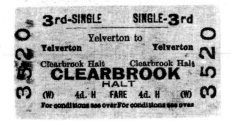

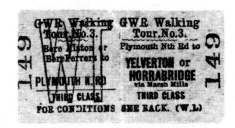

A rare sight of a 63XX class diesel upon the branch. This occasion was its unscheduled arrival with a breakdown train for shunting at Bickleigh on 1 October 1961.
R.E. Taylor

An Ivatt class tank No 43081 with an engineering train on the closed branch. It is seen passing the former Leat Corn Mills and Lifton up distant en route for Launceston.
c 15 May 1964. *Western Evening Herald*
Courtesy Devon Library Services

*The author's young son
and daughter pose for
the camera on the platform
at Coryton on
11 December 1965.
The occasion was the
last passenger train
direct from Plymouth
to Launceston run by
the GW Society (SW Group).
A.R. Kingdom*

*DMU W51062 with the '
Devon Rambler'
at Bickleigh
on 11 April 1959.
This excursion was
organised by the
Railway Enthusiast Club
of Farnborough covering
one of many West
country branch lines.
R.E. Taylor*

*Midland class II tank
No 41283
halts for photographs
at Liddaton Halt
5 September 1965.
It was hauling the
Launceston Branch
Centenary Special
run by the GW Society
(SW Group).
The late T.W.E. Roche
can be seen just above
the cab strolling
along the platform.
R.A. Lumber*

Special traffic

11 April 1959 - Railway Enthusiasts Club of Farnborough
Diesel Multiple Unit W 51062 'Devon Rambler'

1 October 1961 - Unauthorised diesel of D 63XX class and breakdown
train
Shunting operations to Bickleigh.

29 December 1962 - Last official passenger trains.
Locos 5568; 5564; 6430 4591

March 1963 - Loco 4555 on a 'fittings recovery' train.

April 1964 - Contractors train for track recovery: south of Tavistock
back to just north of Marsh Mills. Private 0-4-0 diesel
shunter.

15 May 1964 - BR Ivatt Tank No 41308 on an engineering inspection
train, Lydford to Launceston via Lifton and return.

5 September 1965 - Launceston Branch Centenary between Lydford
and Launceston run by the Great Western Society.
BR Midland class 2 loco No 41238.

11 December 1965 - Last train Plymouth to Launceston direct, run by
the GWS.
SR line Plymouth to Lydford, GW line Lydford to
Launceston and reverse. (First 3 car dmu to run on
branch).

26 February 1966 - Final freight from Launceston GWR station hauled
by North British diesel No D6311. (Launceston Railway
Circle aboard).

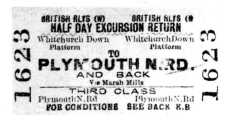

N.B.—London Time is kept at all the Stations on the Railway.

	WEEK DAYS.									SUNDAY TRAINS.				
STATIONS.	Ex. Train 1 & 2 class		Ex. Mil. Train to Brixham 1, 2, 3 1 & 2 class class		Ex. 1 & 2 class		Mil. to Reading and Paddington		Mil. 1, 2, 3 class class		1, 2, 3 class	Mil. 1 & 2 class		Mil. 1 & 2 class	1, 2, 3 class
PENZANCE, per W.C.R.		6 10		11			2 40					a.m.		p.m.	a.m.
FALMOUTH, per C. Ra.		7 25	12 15 12 41			1 17	6					6 4		4	8 54
TAVISTOCK	7 30		9 35	12 45		A	6 13 8 2		1, 2, 3	1, 2, 3		9 32		6 15	1, 2, 3
HORRABRIDGE	7 42		9 41	12 53			6 38 8 33					9 33		6 13	6
BICKLEIGH	7 55		9 56	1 13			6 43 8 43					9 46		6	
PLYMOUTH	8 2		10 2	1 35			7 5 9 3					11 1			6 55
Plymouth Dep.	6 45 8 30	9 2 1 45 12 46 1, 2, 3			4 30				6 45 12 42	2 30		6 45 12 42	2 30		
PLYMPTON Arrive	6 57	9 32	12 4 1 57			5 22 7 32			6 57 12 52	2 37		7 24			
CORNWOOD ROAD	7 12		1 2			5 37			7 12						
IVYBRIDGE	7 19	9 52	1 12 1 10 3 43			5 3 7 52			7 15 1 12 3 21			7 52			
KINGSBRIDGE ROAD	7 27	10 c	1 30 2 27			6 0			7 27 1 30 3 7						
BRENT	7 35	10 8	2 35			6 10 8 2			7 35 3 15						
TOTNESS	7 55	10 25 11 30 1 48 2 55 4 30				6 28 8 20			7 55 1 48 3 35			8 20			
NEWTON Arrive	8 20 9 34 10 48 11 51 2 10 3 20 4 31					6 53 8 43			8 20 2 10 4 0			8 43			
KINGSKERSWELL	8 35	10 56	2 30			7 4			8 35						
TORRE	8 44	11 8	2 34			7 49			8 44 4 17						
TORQUAY	8 49	11 8	2 39 3 46 5 21			7 55			8 49 4 22						
PAIGNTON	9 4	11 15	2 51 4 5 5 28			8 5			8 56 4 29						
BRIXHAM Rd. Arr.	9 6	11 23	3 0 4 13 5 37			8 16			9 6 4 37						
KINGSWEAR	9 20	11 35	3 13 4 25 5 48			8 38			9 20 4 50 class						
DARTMOUTH		11 45	3 25 4 35 6 0			8 56						1, 2, 3			
DARTMOUTH	7 15 8 45		3 30			5 45 7 35									
KINGSWEAR	7 25 8 54 9 53	1 18	3 44			5 57 7 25			7 15 7 10 c						
BRIXHAM Rd. Dep.	7 4 9 6 10 5	1 3	3 55			6 15 8 c			7 4 3 2 7 5						
PAIGNTON	7 47 9 15 10 12 11 3	1 37	4 6			6 22 8 8			7 47 3 7 7 33						
TORQUAY	7 54 9 33 10 5 11 4	1 44	4 12			6 39 8 15			7 54 3 34 7 42						
TORRE	7 57	10 24	1 40			6 35 8 25			7 59 3 47 7 45						
KINGSKERSWELL		12 31	1 50			6 43			8 6 7 53						
NEWTON Depart	8 25 9 40 10 53 12 c 2 15 3 35 4 37					6 58 8 5c			8 25 2 15 4 55 8 5c						
TEIGNMOUTH Arriv.	8 37 9 51 11 11 12 7 2 27 3 47 4 50					7 10 9 2			8 42 2 27 4 38 8 32 9 2						
DAWLISH	8 33 10 0 11 15 12 16 2 37 3 56 5 0					7 30 9 12			8 53 3 37 4 36 8 50 9 12						
STARCROSS	9 3	11 25 12 26 2 47 4 0				7 39 9 22			9 3 4 47 4 42 8 59 9 22						
EXMINSTER	9 13	11 35 4 10				7 50 9 32			9 13 4 50 9 32						
St. Thomas (Exeter)	9 23	11 45 4 1				7 56 9 37			9 23 3 c 9 0 9 37						
Exeter	9 30 10 20 11 55 12 45 3 10 4 30 5 c					8 0 9 45			9 30 3 10 5 0 9 10 9 45						
Bristol fm. B. & E.R.	1 0 12 12 4 5 5 45 6 15 8 38 7 35					11 25 12 25			1 30 6 15						
PADDINGTON, by Gr. Western Railway	4 45 3 0 9 c 6 1c		11 5			4 35 4 35			6 55 11 15				12 35	

** Third Class Return Tickets issued from Brent and lower stations to Plymouth, on Saturdays, will be available to return by this Train on the day of issue, or by the regular 3rd class Trains on the following Sunday or Monday.

A 3rd class from C.R. below Menheniot to Totnes & higher S. D. Stations, and to R. & E Stations, will be booked to Newton. · Passengers from the Torquay and Dartmouth Branch will not be booked by this Train to any Station below Newton.

	WEEK DAYS.									SUNDAYS.				
STATIONS.	Mil. 1 & 2 class	1, 2, 3 class.	Mil. 1 & 2 class.	1 & 2 class	Ex. 1 & 2 class.	1, 2, 3 class.	Ex. 1 & 2 class			Mil. 1 & 2 class	Mil. 1 & 2 class.	1, 2, 3 class.	
PADDINGTON, per Gr. Western Railway	p.m. 8 10	a.m.	a.m.	a.m.	a.m. 9 15	a.m. 6 0 11 45	a.m.			a.m. 10 c	p.m. 4 30	p.m. 8 10		
Bristol, per B. & E.R.		12 40	6 45	9 50	12 33 11 20					10 c	6 45		3 45
Exeter per S. D. R.		3 30	7 25	9 45	1 10 2 35 4 43 4 25					6 25 10 10	3 30 7 15 9 45 3 30		
St. Thomas (Exeter) Ar.			7 28 9 48	1 13	4 43					6 28	7 18 9 48 3 33		7 3
EXMINSTER			7 38	1 23	4 57					6 40	7 28	3 45	7 15
STARCROSS		3 35	7 48 10 c	1 32 3 51 5 7						6 50	7 38 10 c 3 55		7 25
DAWLISH		3 44	7 58 10 15	1 43 3 17						7 c 10 11	7 48 10 15 3 5		7 35
TEIGNMOUTH		3 53	8 10 15	1 52 3 1c 5 27 4 50						7 10 10 40	8 5 10 25 3 45		7 45
NEWTON Arrive		4 5	8 20 10 37	2 5 3 23 5 40 5 0						7 25 10 50	8 15 10 37 3 30		
KINGSKERSWELL			8 33 10 56	2 10	5 56					7 41	8 36	8 10	
TORRE			8 41 11 4	2 34	6 c					7 49	8 47 4 17	8 16	
TORQUAY			8 50 11 8	2 39 3 46 6 6 5 15						7 55	8 55 4 22	8 25	
PAIGNTON			8 56 11 15	2 51 4 5 6 22 5 28						8 5 11 15	9 2 4 29	8 45	
BRIXHAM Rd. Arr.			9 6 11 23	3 0 4 13 6 30 5 36						8 16 11 23	9 11 4 37	8 45	
KINGSWEAR			9 20 11 35	3 13 4 25 6 42 5 48						8 38 11 40	9 32 4 50		
DARTMOUTH			9 30 11 45	3 25 4 35 6 55 6 0						8 40			
DARTMOUTH				3 30									
KINGSWEAR			7 35 9 40	3 35						6 33			
BRIXHAM Rd. Dep.			7 40 10 c	1 30 3 36						6 55	7 40	7 35	
PAIGNTON			7 47 10 12	1 37	4 20					7 c	7 47	7 33	
TORQUAY			7 54 10 19	1 44	4 20					7 8	7 54	7 42	
TORRE			7 57 10 24	1 49						7 10	7 57	7 45	
KINGSKERSWELL			8 4 10 31	2 c						7 20	8 5	7 53	
NEWTON Depart		4 8 8 25 10 41	2 10 3 28 5 45 5 c				8 25 10 52		4 8 8 17 10 43		8 5	
TOTNESS Arrive		4 33 8 37 11 c	2 25 3 48 6 10				8 37		4 33 8 25 11 8		8 25	
BRENT			8 48 11 10	2 40	6 32					8 48		8 43	
KINGSBRIDGE ROAD			8 52 11 16	2 52	6 43					8 57		8 52	
IVY BRIDGE		4 58	9 0 11 25	3 c	6 32 class					4 58 9 0 11 25		9 3	
CORNWOOD ROAD	class		9 36	3 21	a.m. 1, 2, 3					9 5		9 10	
PLYMPTON	1, 2, 3		9 52 11 8	3 31	6 52 8 30					5 20 9 44 11 8		9 30	
Plymouth Arrive	a.m.	5 35 10 c 11 25	3 55 4 35 7 15 6 10				9 45 9 15 11 25		5 35 10 c 11 25		9 50	
Plymouth		7 5	10 35 1 15	1 & 2 3, 1, 2, 3 5 c 7 35 8 3o 1, 2, 3 p.m.						1, 2, 3	1, 2, 3		
BICKLEIGH		7 15	10 39 1 19	5 7 8 7						8 15	4 5o		
HORRABRIDGE		7 41	10 52 1 37	5 22 8 22						8 43	5 18		
TAVISTOCK Arrive		7 55	11 7 1 52	5 35 8 37						8 55	5 30		
FALMOUTH, per C. Ra.			8 41 1 17	6 50						4 55	5 51		
PENZANCE, per W.C.R.			9 31 1 42 6 58	8 20						9 40	11 51		

+ 1 & 2 Class, also 3rd Class from G.W. and R. & E. R. to S. D. & C. R. and 3rd Class from S. D. to C. R. below Menheniot.

N.B.—Passengers may be booked at St. Thomas' Station to Stations on the Bristol and Exeter and Great Western Railways.

Passengers cannot be booked from Exeter (St David's Station) to St. Thomas, or vice versa ; nor from Torre to the Torquay Station, or vice versa.

The Tavistock Branch Trains marked " 1, 2, 3," are Third Class Trains on this Branch only.

Third Class Return Tickets (available for the return journey until the following Monday) are issued on Saturdays from Ivybridge and Plympton to Plymouth by the train which leaves Exeter at 4.00 p.m.

Return Tickets taken at Ivybridge and Plympton by the Train leaving Exeter at 4.00 p.m., and at the Tavistock Branch Stations by the Train leaving Tavistock at 6.15 p.m., will be available for the return journey on the day of issue, or by the trains advertised to leave Plymouth at 6.45 a.m., 8.30 a.m., and at 9.20 a.m., on the following morning.

From G.W.R. Time Table for 1865

Plymouth, Princetown, Tavistock, and Launceston.

DOWN TRAINS.

	WEEK DAYS.				SUNDAYS.

PLYMOUTH { Millbay .....dep.
{ North Rd. "
{ Mutley "
Marsh Mills
Bickleigh
Yelverton
Dousland
PRINCETOWN arr.
Horrabridge
Tavistock
Marytavy
Lydford
Coryton
Lifton
LAUNCESTON arr.

UP TRAINS.

	WEEK DAYS.			SUNDAYS.

LAUNCESTON .....dep.
Lifton
Coryton
Lydford
Marytavy
Tavistock
Horrabridge
PRINCETOWN .....dep.
Dousland
Yelverton
Yelverton
Bickleigh
Marsh Mills
PLYMOUTH { Mutley arr.
{ North Rd. "
{ Millbay "

Jan. – Apl. 1896.

Plymouth, Princetown, Tavistock and Launceston.

	WEEK DAYS.				SUNDAYS.

PLYM'TH { Millbay dep.
{ Mutley "
Marsh Mills
Bickleigh
Yelverton
Yelverton
Dousland
PRINCETOWN arr.
Horrabridge
Tavistock
Marytavy
Lydford
Coryton
Lifton
LAUNCESTON arr.

Jan. – Apl. 1905.

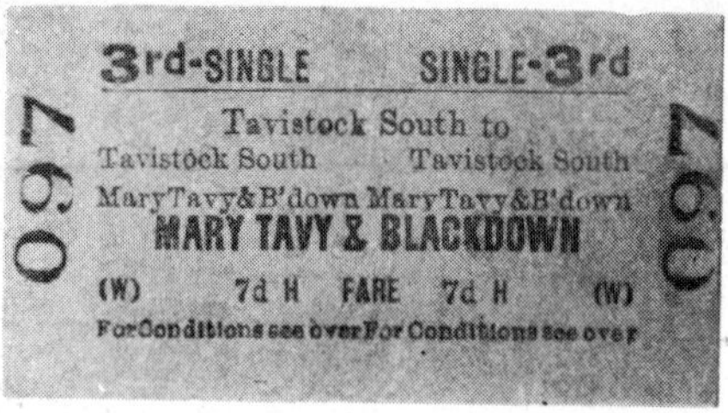

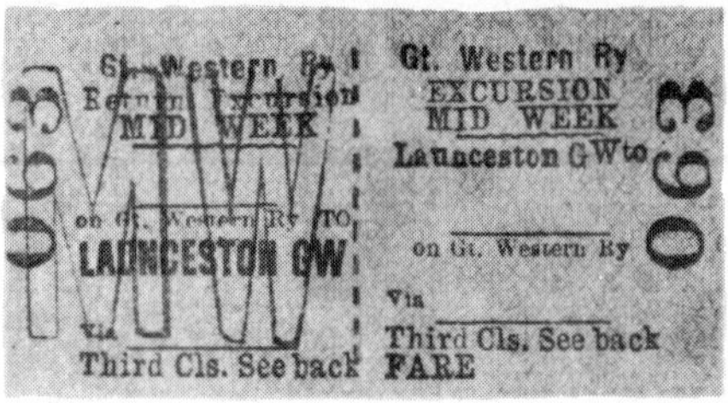

PLYMOUTH, PRINCETOWN, TAVISTOCK AND LAUNCESTON.

Week Days.

Mls.	Station		M		M	M				M					M		M
			a.m.	a.m.	a.m.	a.m.	p.m.	p.m.	Saturdays only.	p.m.	p.m.	p.m. Commences June 6th, 1932.	p.m.	p.m.	p.m.	p.m.	p.m.
	Plymouth Millbay	dep.	6 17	7 33	8 25	10 40	12 8	*12 46*		2 5	3 0	*4 30*	5 25	6 8	7 12	9 5	10 55
¾	**Plymouth** North Rd.	,,	6 25	7†48	8 30	10 44	12 14	*12 49*		2 10	3 6	*4 34*	5 30	6 16	7 17	9 10	10 59
1¼	**Plymouth** Mutley	,,	6 27	7 50	8 32	10 46	12 16	*12 51*		2 13	3 8	*4 36*	5 32	6 18	7 19	9 12	11 1
4	**Marsh Mills**	,,	6 33	7 57	8 40	10 52	12 22	*12 57*		2 19	3 15	*4 42*	5 38	6 24	7 25	9 18	11 7
5	**Plym Bridge Platform**	,,				10 55	12 25	*1 0*		2 23	3 19	*4 45*	5 41		7 28	9 21	
7¾	**Bickleigh**	,,	6 43	8 7	8 50	11 3	12 34	*1 12*		2 32	3 30	*4 57*	5 49	6 35	7 40	9 29	11 17
8¾	**Shaugh Bridge Platform**	,,		8 10	8 53	11 6	12 37	*1 15*		2 36	3 33	*5 0*	5 52	6 38	7 43	9 32	11 20
10	**Clearbrook Halt**	,,		8 16	8 59	11 12	12 43	*1 21*		2 42	3 39	*5 6*	5 58	6 44	7 49	9 38	11 26
11	**Yelverton**	,,	6 54	8 22	9 3	11 18	12 48	*1 27*		2 47	3 44	*5 9*	6 2	6 50	7 53	9 42	11 30
—	Yelverton	dep.		8 36		11 23				2 50	4 51			6 55		9S47	
1½	Dousland	,,		8 41		11 29				2 56	4 57			7 1		9S53	
3	Burrator Halt QQ	,,		8 54		11 35				3 6	5 3			7 7			
9	King Tor Halt	,,		9 20		11 56				3 32	5 24			7 28		10S14	
10½	**Princetown**	arr.		9 29		12 3				3 41	5 30			7 34		10S20	
12¼	**Horrabridge**	dep.	6 58	8 27	9 7	11 22	12 56	*1 31*		2 51	3 48		6 6	6 55	7 57	9 46	11 34
15½	**Whitchurch Down P'form**	,,	7 5	8 34	9 14	11 29	1 3	*1 38*		2 58	3 55		6 13	7 2	8 4	9 53	11 41
16½	**Tavistock ¶**	,,	7 8	8 45	9 17	11 32	1 8	*1 41*		3 1	4 0		6 16	7 9	8 7	9 56	11 44
20	**Marytavy and Blackdown**	,,		8 54			1 19				4 8			7 17			
23¾	**Lydford**	,,		9 4			1 28				4 17			7 26			
27¼	**Coryton**	,,		9 14			1 37				4 26			7 35			
30¾	**Lifton**	,,		9 25			1 45				4 34			7 43			
35¼	**Launceston**	arr		9 35			1 54				4 43			7 52			

Station																
		a.m.	a.m.	a.m.	a.m.	p.m.	p.m.	Saturdays only.	p.m.	p.m.	p.m. Commences June 6th, 1932.	p.m.	p.m.	p.m.	p.m.	p.m.
Launceston	dep.		7 13		10 5				2 10				6 25			
Lifton	,,		7 23		10 16				2 22				6 34			
Coryton	,,		7 31		10 24				2 29				6 41			
Lydford	,,		7 45		10 38				2 43				6 54			
Marytavy and Blackdown	,,	M	7 53	M	10 46	M			2 51	M			7 2	M		M
Tavistock ¶	,,	7 17	8 2	9 40	10 59	12 45	*2 4*		3 2	4 30		6 28	7 11	8 30	10 10	11 50
Whitchurch Down Platform	,,	7 20	8 5	9 43	11 2	12 48	*2 7*		3 5	4 33		6 31	7 14	8 33	10 13	11 53
Horrabridge	,,	7 28	8 13	9 51	11 10	12 56	*2 15*		3 13	4 41		6 39	7 22	8 41	10 21	12 1
Princetown	dep.		7 30		10 30	*12T14*				4 0		6 0		8S0		
King Tor Halt	,,		7 36		10 36	*12T21*				4 6		6 6		8S6		
Burrator Halt QQ	,,		7 57		10 57	*12T43*				4 27		6 26		8S27		
Dousland	,,		8 3		11 3	*12T50*				4 33		6 32		8S33		
Yelverton	arr.		8 8		11 8	*12T54*				4 38		6 37		8S38		
Yelverton	dep.	7 33	8 20	9 57	11 17	1 1	*2 21*		3 18	4 47	*6 25*	6 48	7 28	8 46	10 26	12 6
Clearbrook Halt	,,	7 36	8 23	10 0	11 20	1 4	*2 24*		3 21	4 50	*6 28*	6 51	7 31	8 49	10 29	
Shaugh Bridge Platform	,,	7 40	8 27	10 4	11 24	1 8	*2 28*		3 25	4 54	*6 32*	6 55	7 35	8 53	10 33	
Bickleigh	,,	7 43	8 30	10 8	11 27	1 12	*2 33*		3 28	4 58	*6 37*	6 58	7 39	8 56	10 36	12 14
Plym Bridge Platform	,,	7 49	8 36	10 14		1 18	*2 39*			5 4	*6 43*	7 4		9 2		
Marsh Mills	,,	7 52	8 39	10 17	11 36	1 21	*2 43*		3 36	5 7	*6 46*	7 7	7 47	9 5	10 44	
Plymouth Mutley	arr.	7 57	8 44	10 22	11 41	1 28	*2 47*		3 42	5 13	*6 52*	7 18	7 52	9 10	10 50	
Plymouth North Road	,,	7 59	8 46	10 24	11 43	1 30	*2 49*		3 44	5 17	*6 54*	7 20	7 54	9 12	10 52	12 28
Plymouth Millbay	,,	8 4	8 52	10 30	11 50	1 35	*2 54*		3 55	5 22	*7 0*	7 26	8 0	9 18	10 58	12 33

Sundays.

Station		Z		Z		Z	Z
		a.m.	a.m. Commences May 15th, 1932.	p.m.	p.m. Commences May 15th, 1932.	p.m.	p.m.
Plymouth Millbay	dep.	10 35	*11 25*	2 5	*2 25*	4 30	8 25
Plymouth North Road	,,	10 40	*11 30*	2 10	*2 30*	4 35	8 31
Plymouth Mutley	,,	10 42	*11 32*	2 12	*2 32*	4 38	8 33
Marsh Mills	,,	10 48	*11 38*	2 18	*2 38*	4 45	8 39
Plym Bridge Platform	,,						
Bickleigh	,,	10 58	*11 48*	2 28	*2 48*	4 55	8 50
Shaugh Bridge Platform	,,	11 2	*11 52*	2 32	*2 52*	4 58	8 53
Clearbrook Halt	,,	11 8	*11 58*	2 38	*2 58*	5 4	8 59
Yelverton	,,	11 13	*12 1*	2 43	*3 1*	5 7	9 3
Yelverton	dep.						
Dousland	,,						
Burrator Halt	,,						
King Tor Halt	,,						
Princetown	arr.						
Horrabridge	dep.	11 17		2 47			9 7
Whitchurch Down Platform	,,	11 24		2 54			9 14
Tavistock ¶	,,	11 27		2 57			9 17
Marytavy and Blackdown	,,						
Lydford	,,						
Coryton	,,						
Lifton	,,						
Launceston	arr.						

Sundays.

Station		Z		Z	Z		Z
		a.m.	p.m. Commences May 15th, 1932.	p.m.	p.m.	p.m. Commences May 15th, 1932.	p.m.
Launceston	dep.						
Lifton	,,						
Coryton	,,						
Lydford	,,						
Marytavy and Blackdown	,,						
Tavistock ¶	,,	11 50		3 20			9 25
Whitchurch Down Platform	,,	11 53		3 23			9 28
Horrabridge	,,	12 1		3 31			9 36
Princetown	dep.						
King Tor Halt	,,						
Burrator Halt	,,						
Dousland	,,						
Yelverton	arr.						
Yelverton	dep.	12 8	*1 10*	3 36	6 35	*8 0*	9 41
Clearbrook Halt	,,	12 11	*1 13*	3 39	6 38	*8 3*	9 44
Shaugh Bridge Platform	,,	12 15	*1 17*	3 43	6 42	*8 7*	9 48
Bickleigh	,,	12 18	*1 20*	3 46	6 45	*8 10*	9 51
Plym Bridge Platform	,,						
Marsh Mills	,,	12 26	*1 28*	3 54	6 53	*8 18*	9 59
Plymouth Mutley	arr.	12 31	*1 33*	3 59	6 58	*8 23*	10 4
Plymouth North Road	,,	12 33	*1 35*	4 1	7 0	*8 25*	10 6
Plymouth Millbay	,,	12 38	*1 40*	4 6	7 10	*8 32*	10 11

M—Rail Motor Car, one class only. QQ—Trains call at Burrator Halt during the hours of daylight only.
S—Saturdays only. T—Tuesdays, Thursdays and Saturdays only. Z—Rail Motor Car (one class only) until May 8th, 1932. Train (1st and 3rd) commencing May 15th, 1932. †—Arrive North Road 7.36 a.m. ¶—One mile to Southern Railway Station.

G.W.R. Passenger Time Table for September 14th 1931 & U.F.N.

Week Days only.

		a.m.	a.m.	a.m.	a.m.	a.m.		a.m.	p.m.	p.m.		p.m.	p.m.	p.m.	p.m.		p.m.	p.m.		p.m.		p.m.
Plymouth (North Road)	dep.	5 50	7 10	7 45		10 45		12 5	12 50	2 10		3 9		5 25		6 23			7 40		9 30
Marsh Mills	„	5 57	7 18	7 52		10 52		12 14	12 58	2 18		3 17		5 32		6 30			7 47		9 37
Plym Bridge Platform	„					10 56		12 19	1 6	2 23		3 21		5 36							
Bickleigh	„	6 7	7 29	8 2		11 3		12 28	1 15	2 30		3 31		5 43		6 40			7 57		9 47
Shaugh Bridge Platform	„		7 33	8 6		11 7		12 34	1 17	2 35		3 35		5 48		6 45			8 2		9 52
Clearbrook Halt	„			8 11		11 12		12 40	1 22	2 40		3 40		5 53		6 50			8 7		9 57
Yelverton	arr.	6 16	7 40	8 15		11 16		12 47	1 26	2 44		3 44		5 58		6 54			8 12		10 2
Yelverton	dep.				8 36		11 20			2 50		4 51				7 0					
Dousland	„				8 42		11 26			2 56		4 56				7 6					
Burrator Halt	„				8 54		11 32			3 2		5 3				7 12					
Ingra Tor Halt	„				9 9		11 44			3 14		5 15				7 24					
King Tor Halt	„				9 22		11 55			3 25		5 26				7 35					
Princetown	arr.				9 31		12 1			3 32		5 32				7 41					
Yelverton	dep.	6 17	7 41	8 16		11 19		12 50	1 27	2 45		3 45		5 59		6 56			8 13		10 5
Horrabridge	„	6 21	7 44	8 20		11 23		12 55	1 31	2 49		3 49		6 2		7 0			8 17		10 7
Whitchurch Down Platform	„	6 26	7 50	8 25		11 28		1 1	1 36	2 54		3 54		6 8		7 5			8 22		10 12
Tavistock	„	6 29	7 54	8 30		11 31		1 8	1 39	2 58		4 0		6 11		7 12			8 25		10 20
Mary Tavy and Blackdown	„			8 39				1 15				4 7				7 21					10 27
Lydford §	„			8 47				1 24				4 14				7 29					10 35
Liddaton Halt	„			8 55				1 31				4 21				7 36					10 41
Coryton	„			8 59				1 36				4 25				7 40					10 45
Lifton	„			9 7				1 44				4 31				7 47					10 51
Launceston	arr.			9 16				1 52				4 39				7 55					11 0

		a.m.	a.m.	a.m.	a.m.	a.m.	p.m.	p.m.		p.m.		p.m.	p.m.	p.m.	p.m.	p.m.		p.m.	p.m.		p.m.
Launceston	dep.			7 10		10 15				2 22			2 30				6 15		9 30
Lifton	„			7 18		10 23				2 30							6 24		9 38
Coryton	„			7 25		10 30				2 36							6 36		9 44
Liddaton Halt	„			7 30		10 36				2 42							6 41		9 50
Lydford §	„			7 42		10 46				2 52							6 57		10 0
Mary Tavy and Blackdown	„			7 49		10 52				2 57						7 3			10 6
Tavistock	„	6 47		8 0	8 47	11 0	1 45			3 5		4 25		6 35		7 14	8 40		10 25
Whitchurch Down Platform	„	6 50		8 3	8 50	11 3	1 48			3 8		4 28		6 39		7 17	8 43		10 28
Horrabridge	„	6 57		8 10	8 57	11 10	1 58			3 16		4 37		6 47		7 25	8 51		10 36
Yelverton	arr.	7 1		8 15	9 1	11 15	2 2			3 20		4 41		6 52		7 29	8 55		10 40
Princetown	dep.			7 35		10 30	12 8			3 55		6 0						
King Tor Halt	„			7 40		10 36	12 14			4 1		6 6						
Ingra Tor Halt	„			7 49		10 45	12 23			4 10		6 15						
Burrator Halt	„			8 1		10 57	12 35			4 22		6 27						
Dousland	„			8 6		11 3	12 41			4 28		6 33						
Yelverton	arr.			8 11		11 8	12 46			4 33		6 38						
Yelverton	dep.	7 2		8 16	9 2	11 18	1 3			3 21		4 43		6 57		7 30	8 57		10 41
Clearbrook Halt	„	7 5		8 19	9 5	11 21	1 6			3 24		4 46		7 0		7 33	9 0		10 44
Shaugh Bridge Platform	„	7 8		8 22	9 8	11 24	1 9			3 27		4 50		7 4		7 36	9 4		10 47
Bickleigh	„	7 11		8 26	9 11	11 27	1 12			3 30		4 54		7 9		7 40	9 9		10 50
Plym Bridge Platform	„	7 16		8 31		11 32	1 20					4 59		7 13					
Marsh Mills	„	7 20		8 35	9 19	11 36	1 25			3 37		5 6		7 19		7 48	9 18		10 58
Plymouth (North Road)	arr.	7 33		8 47	9 26	11 43	1 37			3 47		5 14		7 26		7 55	9 25		11 5

G.W.R. Passenger Time Table for October 6th 1947 & U.F.N.

GOODS TIMETABLE

FOR THE PERIOD COMMENCING MONDAY, 17th MAY, 1945

From the Plymouth Area GWR Goods Working Timetable

WEEKDAYS

			am	pm	pm	MWFO pm	pm		pm		pm	SUNDAYS ONLY
LAUNCESTON	...	dep.							2.50			
Lifton	...	arr.							3.05			
		dep.							3.30			
Coryton	...	arr.							3.39			
		dep.							3.55			
Lydford	...	arr.							4.12X			
		dep.							4.30			
Quarry Siding	...	dep.	9.45									
Tavistock	...	arr.	9.50						4.47			
		dep.		1.05					5.35		12.45	
Horrabridge	...	arr.		1.18X					5.48X		12.58	
		dep.	12.00	1.32	2.30				6.15		1.15	
Yelverton	...	arr.	12.07X		2.37X							
		dep.	12.17									
Stop Board	...	arr.	P	1.38P					6.22P		1.22P	
		dep.		1.41					6.23		1.25	
Bickleigh	...	arr.	12.29X						6.33X			
		dep.	12.45						6.40			
Stop Board	...	arr.									1.37P	
		dep.							P		1.38	
Marsh Mills	...	arr.	12.56X	1.59					6.51		1.49	
		dep.	1.36	2.05		5.30			7.02		1.52	
LAIRA JUNCTION	...	arr.	1.43	2.12		5.40			7.09		1.55	

Princetown Goods · *Coypool Transfer* · *Calls at Leet Siding (between Launceston and Lydford) and Mary Tavy and Blackdown as required.*

PLYMOUTH, TAVISTOCK AND LAUNCESTON.

Single Line between Marsh Mills and Launceston, worked by Electric Train Staff between Marsh Mills and Lifton, and Electric Train Token between Lifton and Launceston.
Trains can be crossed at all Stations except Mary Tavy & Blackdown and Coryton. Down Trains must not draw ahead at Bickleigh.

SPEED OF TRAINS ON THIS BRANCH NOT TO EXCEED 40 MILES AN HOUR. (See page 138.)

Down Trains. 　　　　　　　　　　　　　　　Week Days.

M.P. Mileage.		Distances from Plymouth.		STATIONS.	Ruling gradient 1 in	Point to Point times.	Allow for Stop.	Allow for Start.	Freight.¶		Pass.	Empty St. Austell Workmen.		6.35 a.m. Saltash Passenger.		Passenger.		Passenger.		Freight.		Freight.
														SX		SO						
												SO										
									K		B			B		B		B		K		K
						Mins.	Mins.	Mins.	arr.	dep.	dep.	arr.	dep.	arr.	dep.	arr.	dep.	arr.	dep.	arr.	dep.	arr. de
M	C	M	C						a.m.	a.m.	a.m.	a.m.	a.m.	a.m.	a.m.	a.m.	a.m.	a.m.	a.m.	a.m.	a.m.	a.
—	—	0	68	**PLYMOUTH**	61 R	—	—	2		5135				6148				7125				
—	—	2	62	**NORTH ROAD** ...	72 F	9	1	1			5 50	6 46	6150	6 53	7 10	6153	7 10	7129	7 45			
0	0	3	54	Laira Junction ...	143 R	2	—	—		5 25										7 50		9
0	18	3	72	Tavistock Junction ..	200 R	1	1	1	5 29		5 55		6 56	7 16		7 16		7 50	7 55		9
1	11	4	65	Marsh Mills	97 R	—	—	—	5 30		5 57	6157	—	7 17	X7 20	7 17X	7 20	7 51	7 52	7 57	X8 40	C9 43S
1	39	5	13	Plym Bridge Platform	132 R	—	—	—														
4	9	7	63	Bickleigh	60 R	12	1	2		C S		6 7		7 29	7 294	7 29	7 294	8 1	8 2	8 55X	9 15	C9 54S
5	25	8	53	Shaugh Bridge Ptfm.	58 R	—	—	—							7 33		7 33	8 6	8 64			
6	37	9	79	Clearbrook Halt	58 R	—	—	—										8 104	8 11			
7	11	11	11	YELVERTON	60 R	12	1	1				6 17		7 40	7 41	7 40	7 41	8 15	X8 16			
7	41	11	16	Stop Board ...	L.	—	—	—	5 56P	5 59												
8	77	12	51	Horrabridge ...	60 F	5	1	1		C R		6 21		7 44	7 45	7 44	7 45	8 19	8 20	9 29	P9 32	10 7 P1o
11	65	15	39	Whitchurch Down Ptfm.	60 F	—	—	—				6 26			7 50		7 50		8 25	9 39		10 18 10
12	71	16	45	TAVISTOCK ...	64 F	8	1	1	6 15	•9 5	6 29			7 524	X	7 524	X—	8 271	8 32			
14	33	18	7	Quarry Sidings	89 R	—	—	—	9 9											10 40	X1
16	23	19	77	Mary Tavy & B'kdown	66 R	9	1	1										8 881	8 391			
19	43	23	17	Lydford	64 R	9	1	1	RR	Quarry								8 46	8 46	11 25	11	
20	46	23	20	Stop Board ...	57 F	—	—	—		Sidings to											—P	
22	35	26	9	Liddaton Halt ...	55 F	—	—	—		Lydford and								8 55				
23	76	27	50	Coryton	54 R	—	—	—		back.								8 581	9 0			
27	14	30	68	Lifton	140 F	7	1	1										9 61	9 81	11 51	11 59	12
31	64	35	38	**LAUNCESTON** ..	126 R	12	—	—										9 16		12 19	12	1 0

¶—Must run strictly to time.　Not to delay 5.50 a.m. Plymouth (North Road) to Tavistock.

PLYMOUTH, TAVISTOCK AND LAUNCESTON.

Down Trains 　　　　　　　　　　　　　　　Week Days.

STATIONS	B		B		B		K	B		B		D	B		B		B		B		B	
	Passenger.		Passenger.		Passenger.		Prince-town Freight	Passenger.		Passenger.		C'ches.	Passenger.		Passenger.		Motor.		Passenger.		Passenger.	
	WFSO				SO		MW FO						SX						WO SUSPENDED		SO	
	arr.	dep.	arr.	dep.	arr.	dep.	dep.	arr.	dep.	arr.	dep.	dep.	arr.	dep.	arr.	dep.	arr.	dep.	arr.	dep.	arr.	dep.
	a.m.	a.m.	p.m.	a.m.	p.m.	p.m.	p.m.	p.m.	p m.	p.m.	p.m.	p.m.	p.m.	p.m.	p.m.	p.m.	p.m.	p.m.	p.m.	p.m.	p.m.	p.m.
PLYMOUTH																						
NORTH ROAD ...	10137	10 44	12† 0	12 7	12†39	12 48		2† 0	2 10	3† 0	3 10		5115	5 25		6114	6 23		7 40	9†27	9 30	9†27	9 30
Laira Junction ...		1050		1213		1253			2 16		3 15	3130		530			698		7 45		935		935
Tavistock Junction ..	10 51	10 52	12 14	12 15	12 54	12 54		2 17	X2 20	3 16	3 17	3 33	5 31	5 32	6 29	6 30	7 46	7 48	9 36	9 38	9 36	9 38
Marsh Mills	10 55	10 56			12 58	12 58						3134										
Lee Moor Crossing ...																						
Plym Bridge Platform	11 2	11 3	12 28X	12 30	1 4	X1 5		2 24	2 24	3 20	3 21		5 35	5 36	639X	6 40	7 57	7 58	9 47	9 48	9 47	9 48
Bickleigh	11 7	11 7	12 34	12 35	1 9	1 91		2 31	2 32	3 27	X3 31		5 42	5 44	6 44	6 45	8 2	8 3	9 52	9 53	9 52	9 53
Shaugh Bridge Ptfm.	11 11	11 12	12 40	12 41	1 14	1 14		2 36	2 37	3 35	3 351		5 48	5 49	6 49	6 50	8 7	8 8	9 57	9 58	9 57	9 58
Clearbrook Halt	11 16	X11 19	1247X	12 50	1 18X	1 19		2 414	2 424	3 391	3 40		5 53	5 54	6 54	X6 55	8 12	8 13	10 2	10 3	10 3	
YELVERTON								2 47	2 49	3 44	3 45		5 58	5 59								
Stop Board							2 5															
Horrabridge ...	11 22		12 53	12 54	1 22	1 221	P	2 52	2 521	3 48	3 49		6 2X	6 3	6 58	6 59	8 16	8 17	10 6	10 7	10 6	10 7
Whitchurch Down Ptfm.		11 28		12 59		1 271	2 12		2 57		3 54			6 8					8 22		10 12		10 12
TAVISTOCK ...	11 304		1 1	1 8	1 30			3 0	X	3 561	4 0		6 101		7 61	X7 13	8 241		10 141		10 141	X10 20
Quarry Sidings ..																						
Mary Tavy & B'kdown ..			1 141	1 151						4 61	4 7				7 191	7 211					10 271	10 34
Lydford			1 22	1 24						4 131	4 14				7 28	7 29					10 331	10 34
Stop Board				1 31							4 21					7 36					10 41	
Liddaton Halt..			1 341	1 36						4 241	4 25				7 391	7 401					10 441	10 45
Coryton			1 42	1 44						4 31	4 311				7 461	7 471					10 51	10 511
Lifton										4 39					7 55						10 59	
LAUNCESTON ...			1 52																			

LAUNCESTON, TAVISTOCK AND PLYMOUTH.

gle Line between Marsh Mills and Launceston, worked by Electric Train Staff between Marsh Mills and Lifton, and Electric Train Token between Lifton and Launceston. Trains can be crossed at all Stations except Mary Tavy & Blackdown and Coryton.

SPEED OF TRAINS ON THIS BRANCH NOT TO EXCEED 40 MILES AN HOUR. (See page 138.)

p Trains. — Week Days.

ce a- n. C.	STATIONS.	Ruling Gradient 1 in	Time Allowances for Ordinary Freight Trains. See page 55. Point to Point times.	Allow for Stop.	Allow for Start.	B Passenger.		B Passenger.		B Passenger.		K Freight.		B Passenger.		B St. Austell Workmen. SO		K Freight.		B Passenger. WFSO		K Freight. SX	
						arr.	dep.	arr.	dep.	arr.	dep.	arr.	dep.	arr.	dep.	arr.	dep.	arr.	dep.	arr.	dep.	arr.	dep.
			Mins.	Mins.	Mins.	a.m.	a.m	a.m.	a.m.	a m.	a.m.	a.m.	a.m.	a.m	a.m.	p.m.	noon	a.m.	a.m.	p.m.	p.m.	p.m.	p.m.
—	**LAUNCESTON**	—	—	—	1	....	....	—	**7 10**	....	....	....	....	—	**10 15**	....	....	....	....	....	....	....	....
50	Lifton	126 F	12	1	1	..	..	7 17½	7 18½	..	..	..	..	10 22½	10 23½	..	..	..	..	..	..	..	..
68	Coryton	140 R	7	1	1	....	....	7 24½	7 25½	....	....	....	....	10 29½	10 30½	....	....	....	....	....	....	....	....
29	Liddaton Halt	55 R	—	—	—	..	..	—	7 31	..	..	..	..	—	10 36	..	..	..	..	..	..	..	..
21	Lydford	55 R	15	1	1	....	....	7 41	7 44	....	....	....	....	—	10 46	....	....	....	....	....	....	....	....
41	Mary Tavy & B'kdown	64 F	7	2	1	..	..	—	7 50	..	..	..	..	—	10 52	..	..	..	..	..	..	..	..
31	Quarry Siding	66 F	—	—	—	....	....	—	—	....	....	—	**9 45**	—	—	....	....	....	....	....	....	....	....
73	**TAVISTOCK**	89 F	8	1	1	—	**6 47**	**7 55½**	**X8 0**	—	**8 47**	**9 50**	—	**10 57½**	**11 2**	..	..	—	11 45	—	*12 33*	..	..
79	Whitchurch Down Ptfm.	64 R	—	—	—	—	6 50	—	8 3	—	8 50			—	11 5	....	....	—	—	—	*12 36*	....	....
67	Horrabridge	60 R	11	1	1	—	6 57	8 10	8 11½	8 56½	8 57½	....	....	11 11½	11 12½	..	..	11 58	12 0	*12 43*	*12§44*	—	12 55
27	**YELVERTON**	60 R	5	1	1	**7 1**	**7 2**	**8 15½**	**X8 17**	**9 1½**	**9 2½**	..	..	**11 16½X**	**11 19½**	....	....	C	S	*12§48X*	*12 51*	1 2	1 5
35	Stop Board	60 F	—	—	—	—	—	—	—	—	—	....	....	—	—	..	..	12 7P	12 10	—	—	–P	—
39	Clearbrook Halt	60 F	—	—	—	—	7 5	—	8 20	—	9 5	..	..	—	11 23	....	....	—	—	—	*12 55*	—	—
65	Shaugh Bridge Ptfm.	58 F	—	—	—	—	7 8	—	8 23	—	9 8	....	....	—	11 26	..	..	—	—	—	*12 59*	—	—
55	Bickleigh	58 F	8	1	1	7 10½	7 11	8 25½	8 27	9 10½	X9 11	..	..	11 29	11 30	....	....	1220C X	S1230	*1 2X*	*1 5½*	1 15	1 29
66	Stop Board	58 F	—	—	—	—	—	—	—	—	—	....	....	—	—	..	..	—	—	—	—	—	—
25	Plym Bridge Platform	60 F	—	—	—	—	7 16	—	8 32	—	—	..	..	—	11 35	....	....	—	—	—	*1 10*	—	—
53	Lee Moor Crossing	132 F	—	—	—	—	—	—	—	—	—	....	....	—	—	..	..	—	—	—	—	—	—
46	Marsh Mills	97 F	9	1	1	7 19X	7 20	8 35	X8 36	9 18	9 19	..	..	11 38	11 39	—	*12 †0*	12 42	12 51	*1 13*	*1 14*	1 40	2 7
64	Tavistock Junction	200 F	1	—	—	7	21	8	37	9	20	....	....	11	40	*12*	*1*	12	53	*1*	*15*	2	9
58	Laira Junction	143 R	2	1	1	—	—	—	—	—	—	..	..	—	—	—	—	1 0	—	—	—	2 15	—
53	**NORTH ROAD**	72 R	—	—	—	**7 26**	**7†28**	**8 43**	**8†45**	**9 26**	**9†27**	....	....	**11 47**	—	*12 †8*	*12 15*			*1 21*	*1†24*		
41	**PLYMOUTH**	61 F	9	2	—	**7†32**	—	**8†49**	—	**9†31**	—	..	..					..	..	*1†28*	—	..	..

§—Two minutes later on Saturdays (not advertised).

No. 6

LAUNCESTON, TAVISTOCK AND PLYMOUTH.

p Trains. — Week Days.

STATIONS.	K Freight. SO		B Pass. SO	K Princetown Freight. MWFO		B Passenger.		B St. Austell Workmen. SX	B Truro Passenger. ¶			K Freight.			B Passenger.		B Passenger.		B Motor.		B Passenger. WO SUSPENDED		B Passenger. SO	
	arr.	dep.	dep.	arr.	dep.	arr.	dep.	dep.	arr.	dep.		arr.	dep.		arr.	dep.	arr.	dep.	arr.	dep.	arr.	dep.	arr.	dep.
	p.m.	p.m.	p.m.	p.m.	p.m.	p.m.	p.m.	p.m.	p.m.	p.m.		p.m.	p.m.		p.m.	p.m.	p.m.	p.m.	p.m.	p.m.	p.m.	p.m.	p.m.	p.m.
ICESTON	....	....	..	..	..	—	**2 22**	..	..	..	..	—	3 40	..	..	..	—	**6 15**	..	..	..	..	—	*9 30*
n	..	..	....	....	....	2 29½	2 30½	....	....	....	....	3 55X	4 32	....	....	....	6 22½	6 27½	....	....	....	....	*9 37½*	*9 38*
ton	....	....	..	..	..	—	2 36½	..	..	..	..	C	R	..	..	..	—	6 34	..	..	..	..	*9 44*	*9 44½*
aton Halt	..	..	....	....	....	—	2 42	....	....	....	....	—	—	....	....	....	—	6 41	....	....	....	....	—	*9 50*
ord	....	....	..	..	..	2 51½	2 52½	..	..	..	..	4 56	X5 10	..	..	..	6 53	6 54	..	..	..	..	*9 59½*	*10 0*
Tavy & B'kdown	..	..	....	....	....	—	2 58	....	....	....	....	—	—	....	....	....	—	7 0	....	....	....	....	—	*10 6*
rry Siding	....	....	..	..	..	—	—	..	..	..	..	—	—	..	..	..	—	—	..	..	..	..	—	—
STOCK	..	..	*1 48*	....	....	**3 3½**	**X3 5½**	....	—	**4 30**	....	5 27	5 45	....	—	**6 35**	**7 5½**	**X7 10**	—	**8 45**	—	*10 25*	*10 11½*	*X10 25*
church Down Ptfm.	....	....	*1 51*	..	..	—	3 8½	..	—	4 33	..	—	—	..	—	6 39	—	7 13	—	8 48	—	*10 28*	—	*10 28*
abridge	—	*12 55*	*1 58*	—	*2 30*	3 15½	3 16	....	—	4 41	....	5 58X	6 4	....	6 46	6 48	7 19½	7 21	8 55	8 56	*10 35*	*10 36*	*10 35*	*10 36*
ERTON	*1 2X*	*1 20*	*2 3*	*2 37*	—	**3 20**	**3 21**	..	**4 45**	**4 47**	..	C	S	..	**6 52X**	**6 57**	**7 25**	**7 26**	**9 0**	**9 1**	*10 40*	*10 41*	*10 40*	*10 41*
Board	P	—	—			—	—	....	—	—	....	6 11	P6 12	....	—	—	—	—	—	—	—	—	—	—
rbrook Halt	—	—	*2 6*	..	..	—	3 24	..	—	4 50	..	—	—	..	—	7 0	—	7 29	—	9 4	—	*10 44*	—	*10 44*
gh Bridge Ptfm.	—	—	*2 9*	....	....	—	3 27	North	—	4 53	....	—	—	....	—	7 4	—	7 32	—	9 7	—	*10 47*	—	*10 47*
leigh	*1 30*	*1 44*	*2 12*	..	..	3 29½	X3 30	Road	4 56	4 58	..	6 22X	6 41	..	7 8	7 9	7 34½	7 35	9 9½	9 10	*10 49½*	*10 50*	*10 49½*	*10 50*
Board	—	—	—	....	....	—	—	arr.	—	—	....	—P	—	....	—	—	—	—	—	—	—	—	—	—
Bridge Platform	—	—	—	..	..	—	—	4†29	—	5 3	..	—	—	..	—	7 14	—	—	—	—	—	—	—	—
Moor Crossing	—	—	—	....	....	—	—	—	—	—	....	—	—	....	—	—	—	—	—	—	—	—	—	—
sh Mills	*1 55* •	*2 23*	*2X20*	..	..	3 37	3 38	4†20	5 6	5 9	..	6 52	7 5	..	7 17	7 18	7 42	7 43	9 17	9 18	*10 57*	*10 58*	*10 57*	*10 58*
stock Junction	*2*	*25*	*2 21*	....	....	3	39	4 21	5	9½	....	7	7	....	7	19	7	44	9	19	*10*	*59*	*10*	*59*
Junction	*2 31*	—	—	..	..	—	—	—	—	—	..	7 12	—	..	—	—	—	—	—	—	—	—	—	—
TH ROAD			*2§27*	....	....	**3 45**	**3†48**	**4 35**	**5 15**	**5 23**	....			....	**7 26**	**7†28**	**7 50**	—	**9 25**	—	*11 5*	*11† 7*	*11 5*	*11† 7*
IOUTH	..	..	*2†34*	..	..	**3†52**	—				..	..	..	..	**7†32**	—					*11†11*	—	*11†11*	—

¶—Must run strictly to time to form 5.23 p.m. North Road to Truro.

§—North Road depart *2†30* p.m.

No. 6

WEEKDAYS

PLYMOUTH, TAVISTOCK AND LAUNCESTON

SINGLE LINE between Marsh Mills and Launceston, worked by Electric Train Staff between Marsh Mills and Lifton, and Electric Train Token between Lifton and Launceston.

The Crossing Places are Bickleigh, Yelverton, Horrabridge, Tavistock, Lydford and Lifton. Down trains must not draw ahead at Bickleigh.

Speed of Trains on this Branch not to exceed 40 miles per hour.

DOWN

Mile Post Mileage		Mileage from Plymouth (Millbay)		DOWN	Ruling Gradient 1 in	K	K	K	K	K	K
M	C	M	C			am	am	TTh SO am	MW FO am	Th FO PM	MW FO PM
										12.8 pm Princetown	12.35 pm Princetown
—	—	0	0	PLYMOUTH (North Road) ... dep	61 R						
—	—	0	0			9* 5					
—	—	2	30	Laira Junction ... dep	72 F	5X20		7 50			
—	—	3	41	Tavistock Jn. ... dep	143 R	5 29					
4	9	7	72	Marsh Mills ... arr	200 R	5 30	6 18	7X57			
								9 50			
7	37	11	63	Bickleigh ... arr	60 R		6 32	10 5			
							6X47	10 25			
7	9	11	7	YELVERTON ... arr	60 R	5X56	7 4	10X40	1 40	1 10 P	1 45
8	41	11	16	Horrabridge ... dep		5 59	7X24	10 43	1 45		
12	77	12	45	TAVISTOCK SOUTH ... dep	51 F	6 15		10 50	1 47	1 17 P	1 52
14	33	16	16	Stop Board ... dep	16						
19	43	18	23	Lydford ... arr	64 R		8 38				
20	46	20	50	Coryton ... arr	57 F		8 53				
23	76	23	27	Stop Board ... dep			9 4				
27	14	27	68	Lifton ... arr	55 F		9 16				
27	64	30	68	Lifton ... dep	140 F		9 25				
31	64	35	38	LAUNCESTON (W.R.) ... arr	126 R		9 5				
							10 5				

UP

Mileage from Launceston		LAUNCESTON (W.R.) UP	Ruling Gradient 1 in	MW FO am	K	K	TTho PM	MW FO PM	SO PM	TTho PM	MW FO PM	K
M	C				am		PM	PM	PM	PM	PM	
—	—	LAUNCESTON (W.R.) ... dep	126 R									
4	50	Lifton ... arr	68									
7	68	Coryton ... dep	140 F	10 0								
12	21	Lydford ... arr	55 R	10 8	9 45		1 40		1 32	1 40	2 10	
17	73	Stop Board ... dep	58 F		9 50							
18	31	Tavistock Jn. ... dep	58 F									
22	67	Horrabridge ... dep	60 R	11 30								
24	27	YELVERTON ... arr	60 R	11 43	9 50	12X55	2 35			1 47	2 17	
24		Quarry Siding ... arr	89 F	12 0		12X55						
31	64	TAVISTOCK SOUTH ... arr	66 F	12 33			2 40		1 45	1 56		
34	50	Marsh Mills ... arr	200 R	12 56		12X56						
35		Bickleigh ... dep	58 F	12 10		1 15	2 48	1 47	2 55			
		Stop Board ... dep	60 F	12P 7		1P 2		1X19 P				
		Laira Junction ... dep	143 R	10 8			2 42	2 45			5 13	
		PLYMOUTH (North Road) ... arr	72 R	10 8			2 48	1 0			5 20	

N—Must run strictly to time. Not to delay 5.50 am Plymouth (North Rd.) to Tavistock.
Q Quarry Sdgs to Lydford and back

BRITISH RAILWAY WESTERN OPERATING AREA, WORKING TIME TABLE OF FREIGHT TRAINS, PLYMOUTH DISTRICT, 19th SEPTEMBER, 1955 to 10th JUNE, 1956 & U.F.N.

D49

PASSENGER TIMETABLE
FOR THE PERIOD COMMENCING MONDAY, 10th SEPTEMBER, 1962
From the WR Public Timetable

WEEKDAYS ONLY		PSC	PB	PB	SX	SO	SO			pm	pm	pm	PB	SO PB
		am	am	am	am	am	pm			pm	pm	pm	pm	pm
PLYMOUTH ...	... dep.	5.45	7.10	7.40	10.40	10.40	12.45	.	2.10	3.05	5.25		6.20	8.40
Tavistock South ...	... arr.	6.25	7.56	8.22	11.24	11.24	1.32	.	2.57	3.54	6.11		7.03	9.22
	dep.	.	8.00	.	.	11.35	.	.	.	4.00	.		7.12	9.30
LAUNCESTON	... arr.	.	8.43	.	.	12.15	.	.	.	4.39	.		7.55	10.10

		PB		PB			SO			PB	SO PB
		am	am	am	am	pm	pm	pm	pm	pm	pm
LAUNCESTON	... dep.	.	7.05	.	10.15	.	12.40	.	5.40	.	8.35
Tavistock South ...	... arr.	.	7.56	.	10.58	.	1.25	.	6.31	.	9.17
	dep.	6.40	8.00	8.45	11.04	12.40	1.33	4.30	6.40	7.10	9.30
PLYMOUTH ...	... arr.	7.22	8.48	9.26	11.51	1.25	2.17	5.17	7.25	7.50	10.10

PSC—Does not call at Plym Bridge Platform, Shaugh Bridge Platform and Clearbrook Halt.
PB—Does not call at Plym Bridge Platform.

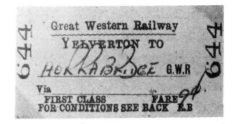

GOODS TIMETABLE FOR THE PERIOD
COMMENCING 17th JUNE, 1963
from the WR Plymouth Division working timetable

			am	noon	pm
TAVISTOCK SOUTH ...	dep.		.	12.00	.
Quarry Sidings	...	...	.	P	.
LYDFORD	...	... arr.	.	12.25	.
		dep.	8.40	.	2.00
Stop Board ...	...	...	P	.	P
Coryton	...	...	.	.	.
LIFTON ...	...	... arr.	9.00	.	2.20

			am	am	pm
LIFTON ...	...	... dep.	10.05	.	3.05
Coryton	...	...	.	.	.
LYDFORD	...	... arr.	10.29	.	3.29
		dep.	.	10.45	.
Quarry Sidings	...	...	.	.	.
TAVISTOCK SOUTH ...	arr.		.	11.00	.

P—Stops only to pin down or pick up wagon brakes.

G. W. R.

Plymouth, Crownhill
and Roborough Village
(for the Moors),

via Derry's Clock, Mutley Plain, Compton Lane End and Tor Lane.

Commencing October 1st, 1911, and until further notice, the service will be as under (condition of roads and circumstances permitting.)

		WEEK DAYS.										SUNDAYS.		
		NIGHT	A.M.	A.M.	A.M.	P.M.		P.M.	P.M.	P.M.		A.M.	A.M.	P.M.
LONDON (Paddington)	dep.	12X0	5 30	10 30	11 50	1 30	..	3 30	4 15	..	..	12 30	9 20	12 45
BRISTOL	,,	6 15	8 40	10B23	1 10	3 0	....	4 18	8 33	...	...	6 45	12 30	3 40
				P.M.		P.M.								P.M.
EXETER	,,	8 37	11 30	12B32	2 55	4 55	..	6 35	8 12	8 25	..	9 47	2 40	6 40
				F.M.										
PLYMOUTH (Millbay)	arr.	9FD54	12 10	2F37	4 55	6F25	..	8 23	9 45	10 45	..	12 8	4§ 40	8 15
		A.M.	A.M.	A.M.	P.M.	P.M.		P.M.		P.M.		A.M.		P.M.
PENZANCE	dep.	6 35	10 0	10 35	1 15	2 0	..	4 35	..	6 20	..	8 20	..	5 0
														P.M.
TRURO	,,	7 45	10 55	11 50	2 11	4 15	....	6 2	..	8 0	..	9 36	..	6 5
				P.M.										
PLYMOUTH (Millbay)	arr.	10 0	12F25	1F40	3F52	6 36	..	8 16	..	10 28	..	11 48	..	8 16
		A.M.	P.M.	P.M.	P.M.	P.M.		P.M.	P.M.	P.M.		P.M.	P.M.	P.M.
MILLBAY STATION	dep.	10 *0	1 15	3 0	5 15	7 0	..	8S30	9 8 45	11K 0	..	2 15	4 35	8*20
CROWNHILL	arr.	10 30	1 45	3 30	5 45	7 30	....	9B 0	10S 15	11K50	..	2 45	5 5	8 50
PLYM BRIDGE LANE	,,	10 40	1 55	3 40	5 55	7 40		....	....	....	..	2 55	5 15	9 0
(For Convalescent Home)														
GEORGE HOTEL	,,	10 45	2 0	3 45	6 0	..	..	....	....	....	..	3 0	5 20	..
ROBOROUGH VILLAGE	,,	10 50	2S 5	3 50	6 5	..	..	....	...	....	..	3 5	5 25	..
		A.M.	P.M.	P.M.	P.M.	P.M.		P.M.	P.M.			P.M.	P.M.	P.M.
ROBOROUGH VILLAGE	dep.	10 55	*S10	4 10	6 10	..	..	—	—		..	3 10	5 30	—
GEORGE HOTEL	,,	11 0	2 15	4 15	6 15	..	..	—	—		..	3 15	5 35	—
PLYM BRIDGE LANE	,,	11 2	2 17	4 17	6 17	7 45	..	—	—		..	3 17	5 37	9 0
(For Convalescent Home.)														
CROWNHILL	,,	11 15	2 30	4 30	6 30	7 55	..	9S 0	10S 15	11K30	..	3 30	5 50	9 10
MILLBAY STATION	arr.	11 45	2 45	4 55	6 55	8 20	..	9S25	10S 40	11K 55	..	3 55	6 15	9 35
		P.M.	P.M.	P.M.	P.M.	P.M.					A.M.	P.M.	P.M.	NIGHT
PLYMOUTH (Millbay)	dep.	12F32	4F 0	5 40	7 20	9 10	..	..	..		12 10	6 10	8 10	12 10
EXETER	arr.	2A10	5 22	7C25	9 50	11M40	..	..	..		1§45	8 33	10 3	1 45
						A.M.								A.M.
BRISTOL	,,	3A50	7 31	9 45	12 10	..	..	..	..		3§37	..	12 5	3 37
LONDON (Paddington)	,,	4 45	8 40	..	3 30	..	..	..	..		6§45	..	3 30	6 45
		P.M.	P.M.	P.M.	P.M.	P.M.								
PLYMOUTH (Millbay)	dep.	12 25	2F55	5 10	7 55	..	..	..	..		....	..	..	..
TRURO	arr.	2 17	5 5	7 33	10 16	..	..	..	..		....	..	..	..
PENZANCE	,,	3 35	7 0	9 3	11 20	..	..	..	..		....	..	..	..

* Awaits arrival of Up Train on request being made to Station Master at Devonport.
‡ Mutley passengers join Road Motor Mutley Plain.
§ Saturday nights (Sunday Mornings) excepted.
A Bristol and Exeter Passengers travel by 12.32 p.m. train ex Millbay.
B Arrive Plymouth 2.17.
C Millbay depart 5.0 p.m.

D Car will wait for passengers Mutley Plain (Baptist Chapel) on request being forwarded to Station Master at Millbay.
F North Road
K Wednesdays, Fridays and Saturdays only.
M One class only.—Newton Abbot to Exeter.
S Saturdays only.
§ Monday Mornings excepted.

SINGLE FARES:—

FROM		TO							
		Millbay Station.	G.W.R. Town Office.	Compton Lane End.	Tor Lane.	Crownhill.	Plym Bridge Lane.	George Hotel.	Woolwell Cottages.
		S. D.	S. D.	S. D.	S. D.	S. D.	S. D.	S. D.	S. D.
G.W.R. TOWN OFFICE	... ...	0 2							
COMPTON LANE END	... ...	0 2	0 2						
TOR LANE	... ...	0 3	0 2	0 2					
CROWNHILL	... ...	0 4	0 3	0 2	0 2				
PLYM BRIDGE LANE (and Convalescent Home)		0 5	0 4	0 3	0 3	0 2			
GEORGE HOTEL	... ...	0 6	0 5	0 4	0 3	0 2	0 2		
WOOLWELL COTTAGES	... ...	0 7	0 6	0 5	0 4	0 3	0 2	0 2	
ROBOROUGH VILLAGE	... ...	0 8	0 6	0 5	0 5	0 4	0 3	0 2	0 2

BOOKS OF 24 TICKETS at reduced scale of charges can be obtained at the Booking Offices at Millbay Station at the following prices :—Books of 24 Tickets at 2d...3/6.
Books of 24 Tickets at 3d.....5/3.   Books of 24 Tickets at 4d.....7/-.   Books of 24 Tickets at 5d.....8/9.   Books of 24 Tickets at 6d.....10/6.
Books of 24 Tickets at 8d.....14/-.

Special Cars for the Conveyance of Private Parties can be provided at reasonable charges.
Seats may be retained.

The Company have Agents for the receipt of Goods and Parcels Traffic, Luggage in Advance, &c., as follows :—Crownhill—Mr. F. Partridge, Exchange Office ; George Hotel—Mr. H. Hammand ; Roborough Village—Mr. H. Treasure, Lope's Arms.

For Parcels Rates, General Notices and Regulations relating to the Company's Road Motor Cars, see separate bill or announcement in Company's Time Table, or apply to Mr. C. Aldington, Paddington Station, or the Stationmaster at Plymouth (Millbay).

PADDINGTON, September, 1911.

JAMES C. INGLIS, General Manager.

WYMAN & SONS, Ltd., Printers, Fetter Lane, London, E.C., and Reading.—2596a.

GWR Bus service time table for October 1911 and UFN for buses between Millbay, Crownhill, Plymbridge Lane
Author's collection

									O								B	
	*a.m.	a.m.	*a.m	a.m.	noon	p.m.		p.m.	p.m.	p.m.	p.m.	p.m.	p.m.	p.m.				p.m.
Plymouth—dep. (St. Andrew's Church)	7-45	9-0	10-0	11-0	12-0	1-0	2-0	3-0	3-30	4-0	5-0	6-0	7-0	8-0	9-0	10-0		11-0
Crownhill	8-0	9-15	10-15	11-15	12-15	1-15	2-15	3-15	3-45	4-15	5-15	6-15	7-15	8-15	9-15	10-15		11-15
Roborough	8-14	9-29	10-29	11-29	12-29	1-29	2-29	3-29	3-59	4-29	5-29	6-29	7-29	8-29	9-29	10-29		11-29
Yelverton	8-29	9-44	10-44	11-44	12-44	1-44	2-44	3-44	4-14	4-44	5-44	6-44	7-44	8-44	9-44	10-44		11-44
Saddler's Shop	8-34	9-49	10-49	11-49	12-49	1-49	2-49	3-49	4-19	4-49	5-49	6-49	7-49	8-49	9-49	—		11-49
Cemetery	8-52	10-7	11-7	12-7	1-7	2-7	3-7	4-7	4-37	5-7	6-7	7-7	7-8	8-7	9-7	10-7		—	12-7
Tavistock—arr.	9-0	10-15	11-15	12-15	1-15	2-15	3-15	4-15	4-45	5-15	6-15	7-15	8-15	9-15	10-15	—		12-15

								O								O		
	*a.m.	a.m.	*a.m.	a.m.	p.m.	p.m.		p.m.	p.m.	p.m.	p.m.	p.m.	p.m.	p.m.	p.m.		p.m.	p.m.
Tavistock—dep. (Bedford Square)	8-0	9-15	10-30	11-30	12-30	1-30	2-0	2-30	3-30	4-30	5-30	6-30	7-30	8-15	9-15	10-0	—
Cemetery	8-9	9-24	10-39	11-39	12-39	1-39	2-9	2-39	3-39	4-39	5-39	6-39	7-39	8-24	9-24	10-9	—
Saddler's Shop	8-26	9-41	10-56	11-56	12-56	1-56	2-26	2-56	3-56	4-56	5-56	6-56	7-56	8-41	9-41	10-26	—
Yelverton	8-31	9-46	11-1	12-1	1-1	2-1	2-31	3-1	4-1	5-1	6-1	7-1	8-1	8-46	9-46	10-31	10-55
Roborough	8-45	10-0	11-15	12-15	1-15	2-15	2-45	3-15	4-15	5-15	6-15	7-15	8-15	9-0	10-0	10-45	11-9
Crownhill	9-0	10-15	11-30	12-30	1-30	2-30	3-0	3-30	4-30	5-30	6-30	7-30	8-30	9-15	10-15	11-0	11-24
Plymouth—arr. (St. Andrew's Church)	9-15	10-30	11-45	12-45	1-45	2-45	3-15	4-45	4-45	5-45	6-45	7-45	8-45	9-30	10-30	11-15	11-39

Buses marked * do not run on Sundays. B—Saturdays only.

Return Tickets are available to either Devonport or Plymouth.

For additional services to and from Yelverton, see pages 12 and 21.

Passengers to and from Tavistock via Horrabridge and Whitchurch change at Sadler's Shop except where marked "O" which do not connect. For Times see page 11.

TAVISTOCK AND LAUNCESTON (showing connections from Plymouth).

	Week-days.						Sundays.			Fares from Tavistock.
	a.m	C.a.m.	p.m.	p.m.	A.p.m.	B.p.m.	a.m.	p.m.	p.m.	
Plymouth (St. Andrew's Church)—dep.	7-45	9-0	1-0	4-0	7-0	8-0	9-0	2-0	8-0	—
Tavistock (Bedford Square)—arrive	9-0	10-15	2-15	5-15	8-15	9-15	10-15	3-15	9-15	—
Tavistock (Bedford Square)—depart	9-30	10-30	2-20	5-30	8-15	9-15	11-15	3-30	9-15	—
Lamerton (Blacksmith's Arms)	9-45	10-45	2-35	5-45	8-30	9-30	11-30	3-45	9-30	5d.
Fuel Down Cross Roads	9-54	10-54	2-44	5-54	8-39	9-39	11-39	3-54	9-39	9d.
Milton Abbot Post Office	10-0	11-0	2-50	6-0	8-45	9-45	11-45	4-0	9-45	11d.
Dunterton Cross	10-9	—	2-59	6-9	8-54	9-54	11-54	4-9	9-54	1/1
Greystone Bridge	10-19	—	3-9	6-19	9-4	10-4	12-4	4-19	10-4	1/3
Bennets Arms	10-25	—	3-15	6-25	9-10	10-10	12-10	4-25	10-10	1/6
Launceston (The Square)—arrive	10-40	—	3-30	6-40	9-25	10-25	12-25	4-40	10-25	1/9

LAUNCESTON AND TAVISTOCK (showing connections to Plymouth).

	Week-days.						Sundays.			Fares from Launceston.
	a.m.	C.a.m.	p.m.	p.m.	A.p.m.	B.p.m.	a.m.	p.m.	p.m.	
Launceston (The Square)—depart	8-0	—	1-0	4-0	6-45	8-0	9-15	2-15	8-0	—
Bennets Arms	8-15	—	1-15	4-15	7-0	8-15	9-30	2-30	8-15	5d.
Greystone Bridge	8-21	—	1-21	4-21	7-6	8-21	9-36	2-36	8-21	8d.
Dunterton Cross	8-31	—	1-31	4-31	7-16	8-31	9-46	2-46	8-31	9d.
Milton Abbot Post Office	8-40	11-0	1-40	4-40	7-25	8-40	9-55	2-55	8-40	11d.
Fuel Down Cross Roads	8-46	11-6	1-46	4-46	7-35	8-46	10-1	3-1	8-46	1/1
Lamerton (Blacksmith's Arms)	8-55	11-15	1-55	4-55	7-40	8-55	10-10	3-10	8-55	1/4
Tavistock (Bedford Square)—arrive	9-10	11-30	2-10	5-10	7-55	9-10	10-25	3-25	9-10	1/9
Tavistock (Bedford Square)—depart	9-15	11-30	2-30	5-30	8-15	9-15	11-30	3-30	9-15	—
Plymouth (St. Andrew's Ch.)—arrive	10-30	12-45	3-45	6-45	9-30	10-30	12-45	4-45	10-30	—

A—Fridays only. B—Saturdays only. C—Wednesdays & Fridays only.

Cheap Return Tickets, available for 3 days, between Plymouth & Launceston, 5/6; Tavistock & Launceston 2/9.

TAVISTOCK, WHITCHURCH and HORRABRIDGE.

		‡		‡								
	a.m.	a.m.	a.m.	p.m.	p.m.	p.m.	p.m.	p.m.	p.m.	p.m.	p.m.	p.m.
TAVISTOCK—depart	8-0	9-15	10-30	11-30	12-30	1-30	2-30	3-30	4-30	5-30	6-30	7-30	9-15
Whitchurch	8-6	9-21	10-36	11-36	12-36	1-36	2-36	3-36	4-36	5-36	6-36	7-36	9-21
Horrabridge	8-16	9-31	10-46	11-46	12-46	1-46	2-46	3-46	4-46	5-46	6-46	7-46	9-31
Saddler's Shop—arrive	8-20	9-35	10-50	11-50	12-50	1-50	2-50	3-50	4-50	5-50	6-50	7-50	9-35
Saddler's Shop—depart	8-26	9-41	10-56	11-56	12-56	1-56	2-56	3-56	4-56	5-56	6-56	7-56	9-41
PLYMOUTH—arrive	9-15	10-30	11-45	12-45	1-45	2-45	3-45	4-45	5-45	6-45	7-45	8-45	10-30

HORRABRIDGE, WHITCHURCH and TAVISTOCK.

		‡		‡									
	a.m.	a.m.	a.m.	a.m.	noon	p.m.	p.m.	p.m.	p.m.	p.m.	p.m.	p.m.	p.m.
PLYMOUTH—depart	7-45	9-0	10-0	11-0	12-0	1-0	2-0	3-0	4-0	5-0	6-0	7-0	9-0
Saddler's Shop—arrive	8-34	9-49	10-49	11-49	12-49	1-49	2-49	3-49	4-49	5-49	6-49	7-49	9-49
Saddler's Shop—depart	8-34	9-56	10-56	11-56	12-56	1-56	2-56	3-56	4-56	5-56	6-56	7-56	9-56
Horrabridge	8-38	10-0	11-0	12-0	1-0	2-0	3-0	4-0	5-0	6-0	7-0	8-0	10-0
Whitchurch	8-48	10-10	11-10	12-10	1-10	2-10	3-10	4-10	5-10	6-10	7-10	8-10	10-10
TAVISTOCK—arrive	9-14	10-16	11-16	12-16	1-16	2-16	3-16	4-16	5-16	6-16	7-16	8-16	10-16

‡—Not Sundays. Passengers to and from Plymouth change at Saddler's Shop.

Fares—Tavistock to Chollacott Lane, 2d. ; Whitchurch P.O., 3d. ; Horrabridge Village, 5d. ; Saddler's Shop, 6d. ; Chollacott Lane to Whitchurch Post Office, 2d. ; Horrabridge, 4d. ; Saddler's Shop, 5d. ; Whitchurch P.O. to Horrabridge, 2d. ; Saddler's Shop, 4d. ; Horrabridge School to Saddler's Shop, 2d.

	X			
	a.m.	a.m.	p.m.	p.m.
PLYMOUTH—depart	9- 0	11- 0	2- 0	5- 0
Tavistock—arrive	10-15	12-15	3-15	6-15
Tavistock—depart	10-15	12-30	3-15	6-30
Mary Tavy	—	12-50	3-35	—
Brentor	10-35	1- 5	3-50	6-50
Lydford (Manor Hotel)	10-44	1-17	4- 2	7- 2
Lydford Gorge	10-51	1-24	4- 9	7- 9
Dartmoor Inn	10-57	1-30	4-15	7-15
Fox & Hounds	—	—	—	7-20
OKEHAMPTON—arrive	—	—	—	7-52

	X			
	a.m.	a.m.	p.m.	p.m.
OKEHAMPTON—depart	8-30	10-35S.O.		
Fox & Hounds	9- 5	11-10S.O.		
Dartmoor Inn	9-10	11-15	2-15	5-15
Lydford Gorge	9-16	11-21	2-21	5-21
Lydford (Manor Hotel)	9-24	11-29	2-29	5-29
Brentor	9-35	11-40	2-40	5-40
Mary Tavy	—	11-55	2-55	5-55
Tavistock—arrive	9-55	12-13	3-13	6-13
Tavistock—depart	10-30	12-30	3-30	6-30
PLYMOUTH—arrive	11-45	1-45	4-45	7-45

Excursion Plymouth to Lydford, 4/9 return.

X—Not Sundays.   S.O.—Sundays only.

OKEHAMPTON, LAUNCESTON and CALLINGTON.

WEEK DAYS ONLY.

			Sats. only.			Weds. and Sats.	Fares from Oke-hampton.
				A			
	a.m.	p.m.	p.m.	p.m.	p.m.	p.m.	
Okehampton—arr.	9- 0	1- 0	—	4-15	—	—	—
Bridestowe School	9-35	1-35	—	4-50	—	1/-
Lew Down	9-55	1-55	—	5-10	—	1/8
Lifton	10-10	2-10	—	5-25	—	2/-
Launceston—arr.	10-30	2-30	—	5-45	—	2/6

						Fares from Launceston.
Launceston—dep.	10-30	—	2-30	5-45	7- 0	Launceston.
S. Petherwin	10-39	—	2-39	5-54	7- 9	4d.
Congdon Shop	10-55	—	2-55	6-10	7-25	8d.
Coad's Green	11- 2	—	3- 2	6-17	7-32	10d.
Bray Shop	11-17	—	3-17	6-32	7-47	1/1
Stoke Climsland P.O.	11-29	—	3-29	6-44	7-59	1/6
Kelly Bray Station	11-37	—	3-37	6-52	8- 7	1/10
Callington Golding's Hotel.	11-45	—	3-45	7- 0	8-15	2/-

A—Through Bus to Liskeard.

CALLINGTON, LAUNCESTON and OKEHAMPTON.

WEEK DAYS ONLY

			Sats. only.		Weds. &Sats.	Fares from Callington.
	a.m.	noon	p.m.	p.m.	p.m.	
Callington Golding's Hotel.	10- 0	12- 0	—	4-30	8-15	—
Kelly Bray Station	10- 8	12- 8	—	4-38	8-23	3d.
Stoke Climsland P.O.	10-16	12-16	—	4-46	8-31	6d.
Bray Shop	10-28	12-28	—	4-58	8-43	11d.
Coad's Green	10-43	12-43	—	5-13	8-58	1/3
Congdon Shop	10-50	12-50	—	5-20	9- 5	1/5
S. Petherwin	11- 6	1- 6	—	5-36	9-21	1/9
Launceston—arr.	11-15	1-15	—	5-45	9-30	2/-

						Fares from Launceston.
Launceston—dep.	11-15	—	2-30	6B 0	9-30	Launceston.
Lifton	11-35	—	2-50	6-20	9-50	9d.
Lew Down	11-50	—	3- 5	6-35	10- 5	1/1
Bridestowe School	12-10	—	3-25	6-55	10-25	1/6
Okehampton—arr.	12-45	—	4- 0	7-30	11- 0	2/6

B—Not Wednesdays and Saturdays.

PLYMOUTH, TAVISTOCK, LYDFORD and OKEHAMPTON.

	a.m.	a.m.	p.m.	p.m.	p.m.	p.m.	p.m
Plymouth—dep. (St. Andrew's Church).	9- 0	11- 0	12- 0	2- 0	4- 0	8- 0	—
Crownhill	9-15	11-15	12-15	2-15	4-15	8-15	—
Roborough	9-29	11-29	12-29	2-29	4-29	8-29	—
Yelverton	9-44	11-44	12-44	2-44	4-44	8-44	—
Horrabridge	9-49	11-49	12-49	2-49	4-49	8-49	—
Cemetery	10- 7	12- 7	1- 7	3- 7	5- 7	9- 7	—
Tavistock—arrive	10-15	12-15	1-15	3-15	5-15	9-15	—

Tavistock—dep.	10-15	12-30	1-15	3-15	5-15	9-25	—
Mary Tavy	10-35	12-50	1-35	3-35	5-35	9-45	—
Lydford	10-53	—	1-53	—	5-53	10- 3	—
Bridestowe	10-58	—	1-58	—	5-58	10- 8	—
Sourton	11-11	—	2-11	—	6-11	10-21	—
Okehampton—arr. (West Bridge)	11-30	—	2-30	—	6-30	10-40	—

OKEHAMPTON, LYDFORD, TAVISTOCK and PLYMOUTH.

	a.m.	a.m.	p.m.	p.m.	p.m.	p.m.	p.m.
Okehampton—dep. (West Bridge)	8- 0	—	12-45	—	4-15	—	7- 0
Sourton	8-22	—	1- 7	—	4-37	—	7-22
Bridestowe	8-35	—	1-20	—	4-50	—	7-35
Lydford	8-40	—	1-25	—	4-55	—	7-40
Mary Tavy	8-57	11-55	1-42	2-55	5-12	5-55	7-57
Tavistock—arr.	9-15	12-13	2- 0	3-13	5-30	6-13	8-15

Tavistock—dep.	9-15	12-30	2- 0	3-30	5-30	6-30	8-15
Cemetery	9-24	12-39	2- 9	3-39	5-39	6-39	8-24
Horrabridge	9-41	12-56	2-26	3-56	5-56	6-56	8-41
Yelverton	9-46	1- 1	2-31	4- 1	6- 1	7- 1	8-46
Roborough	10- 0	1-15	2-45	4-15	6-15	7-15	9- 0
Crownhill	10-15	1-30	3- 0	4-30	6-30	7-30	9-15
Plymouth—arr. (St. Andrew's Church).	10-30	1-45	3-15	4-45	6-45	7-45	9-30

TAVISTOCK to PRINCETOWN

	a.m.	a.m.	p.m.	p.m.	Sats. & Suns. only. p.m.	Fares from Tavistock
TAVISTOCK—depart	10- 0	11–45	2–30	5–30	9–30	—
Taviton	10- 6	11–51	2–36	5–36	9–36	3d.
Moorshop	10–15	12- 0	2–45	5–45	9–45	6d.
Merrivale	10–33	12–18	3- 3	6- 3	10- 3	9d.
Foggentor	10–45	12–30	3–15	6–15	10–15	1/-
Rundlestone	10–50	12–35	3–20	6–20	10–20	1/3
PRINCETOWN—arrive	10–58	12–43	3–28	6–28	10–28	1/6

PRINCETOWN to TAVISTOCK.

	a.m.	a.m.	p.m.	p.m.	Sats. & Suns. only. p.m.	Fares from Princetown.
PRINCETOWN—depart	8–20	11- 0	1–15	4–30	6–45	—
Rundlestone	8–28	11- 8	1–23	4–38	6–53	3d.
Foggentor	8–30	11–10	1–25	4–40	6–55	6d.
Merrivale	8–36	11–16	1–31	4–46	7- 1	9d.
Moorshop	8–48	11–28	1–43	4–58	7–13	1/-
Taviton	8–52	11–30	1–47	5- 2	7–17	1/3
TAVISTOCK—arrive	8–57	11–37	1–52	5- 7	7–22	1/6

*—Not on Sundays.   Special Return Fare Tavistock and Princetown, 2/6.

PLYMOUTH, YELVERTON (Crapstone Corner), DOUSLAND (for Burrator).

	a.m.	a.m.	a.m.	p.m.	p.m.	p.m.	p.m.	p.m.	Sats. only. p.m.
PLYMOUTH—depart	7–15	8–30	10–30	12–30	2–30	4–30	6–30	8–30	10- 0
Yelverton (Rock Hotel)	7-59	9–14	11–14	1–14	3–14	5–14	7–14	9–14	10–44
Dousland arrive	8- 4	9–19	11–19	1–19	3–19	5–19	7–19	9–19	10–49

DOUSLAND, YELVERTON and PLYMOUTH.

	a.m.	a.m.	a.m.	p.m.	p.m.	p.m.	p.m.	p.m.	Sats. only. p.m.
DOUSLAND—depart	8–10	9–25	11–25	1–25	3–25	5–25	7–25	9–25	10–50
Yelverton (Rock Hotel,	8–15	9–31	11–31	1–31	3–31	5–31	7–31	9–31	10–55
Plymouth—arrive	9- 0	10–15	12–15	2–15	4–15	6–15	8–15	10–15	11–39

*—Not Sundays.

FARES—Plymouth to Rock Hotel, 1/- single.   1/9 return.

„   Dousland, 1/3 „   2/- „

For additional Services to YELVERTON, see pages 12 and 21.

Pages 145 to 147

A selection of Devon Motor Transport time tables for October 1926 showing the competing road services to the railway with connecting times in and out of various towns and villages along the line.

Although the railway survived another 35 years after this the seeds of its destruction were already sown.

CITY CENTRE—YELVERTON—DOUSLAND—MEAVY
ROUTE IN PLYMOUTH:—Via Tavistock Road, Mutley Plain and Crownhill).

WEEKDAYS — **SUNDAYS**

Bus Station (Breton Side)	dep	N 6 55	Sch	8 45	...	1125	11 5	2 45	Sch 4	15 5 45	...	8 15	1015	...	9 40	1125	...	1 10	2 45	...	4 15	5 50	...	8 15	...	1015
Royal Parade	,,	6 57	8 47	...	1127	1 17	2 47	...	4 17	5 47	...	8 17	1017	...	9 42	1127	...	1 12	2 47	...	4 17	5 52	...	8 17	...	1017
Crownhill	,,	5 18 7 12	9 2	...	1142	1 32	3 2	...	4 32	6 2	...	8 32	1032	...	9 57	1142	...	1 27	3 2	...	4 32	6 7	...	8 32	...	1032
George Hotel	,,	5 23 7 17	9 7	...	1147	1 37	3 7	...	4 37	6 7	...	8 37	1037	...	10 2	1147	...	1 32	3 7	...	4 37	6 12	...	8 37	...	1037
Lopes Arms	,,	5 26 7 20	9 10	...	1150	1 40	3 10	...	4 40	6 10	...	8 40	1040	...	10 5	1150	...	1 35	3 10	...	4 40	6 15	...	8 40	...	1040
Yelverton (Roundabout)	arr	6 0	7 30	...	9 20	...	12 0	1 50	3 20	...	4 50	6 20	...	8 50	1050	...	1015	12 0	...	1 45	3 20	...	4 50	6 25	...	8 50	...	1050
Yelverton (Roundabout)	dep	6 0	7 30 8 12	9 26	1126	12 0	1 52	3 26	3 39 4 52	6 26	...	8 52	1055	...	1020	12 0	...	1 45	3 23	...	4 52	6 25	7 38	8 52	...	1055
Walkhampton	,,	7 36 8 18	...	1232	...	3 45	...	6 32	...	8 58	11 1	...	12 6	...	...	6 31	...	8 58	...	11 1	...
Dousland	,,	6 6 7 42	9 32	1132	1212	1 58	3 32	...	4 58	6 38	...	9 4	11 7	...	1026	1212	...	1 51	3 29	...	4 58	6 37	7 44	9 4	...	11 7
Meavy	arr	7 46	...	1216	...	...	6 42	...	9 8	...	1216	...	...	6 41	...	9 8	...

		NS C	NS Sch					NS Sch																
Meavy	dep	7 48	...	1222	...	6 48	9 22	...	1219	...	6 41	...	9 17	...
Dousland	,,	6 6 7 52	9 32	1132	1226	1 58	3 32	...	4 58	6 52	9 26	11 7	...	1032	1223	...	1 51	3 29	...	4 58	6 45	7 44	9 21	...	11 7
Walkhampton	,,	7 58	...	8 18	1232	...	3 45	...	6 58	9 32	...	1229	...	6 51	...	9 27	...
Yelverton (Roundabout)	arr	6 11 8 4	8 24 9 38	1138	1238	2 4	3 38	3 51 5	47	4 9	38	1113	...	1038	1235	...	1 57	3 35	...	5 4	6 57	7 50	9 33	...	1113
Yelverton (Roundabout)	dep	6 11 8 4	9 58	1238	2 4	3 43	3 48	...	5 14 7	14	4 48	1113	...	1038	1245	...	2 7	3 45	...	5 14 7 7	...	8 0	9 48	...	1123
Lopes Arms	,,	6 21 8 14	8 28	9 58	1248	2 14	3 48	...	5 14 7 14	...	4 48	1113	...	1048	1245	...	2 7	3 45	...	5 14 7 7	...	8 0	9 48	...	1123
George Hotel	,,	6 24 8 19	8 28	10 3	1253	2 19	3 53	...	5 19 7 19	9 53	1128	...	1053	1250	...	2 12	3 50	...	5 19 7 12	...	8 5	9 53	...	1128
Crownhill	,,	6 29 8 24	8 33	10 8	1258	2 24	3 58	...	5 24 7 24	9 58	1133	...	1058	1255	...	2 17	3 55	...	5 24 7 17	...	8 10	9 58	...	1133
Bus Station (Breton Side)	arr	6 55 8 39	8 48	1023	...	1 13	2 39	4 13	...	5 39 7 39	1013	E	...	1113	1 10	...	2 32	4 10	...	5 39 7 32	...	8 25	1013	...	1148

B—Via St. Levan Road and Devonport.   **C**—Via Clearbrook dep. 8.15 a.m. and 9.50 a.m.   **E**—To Milehouse Garage via Peverell.   **N**—From Plymouth Station dep. 5.5 a.m.   **NS**—Not Saturdays.   **Sch**—Operated during School Terms only.

CITY CENTRE—YELVERTON—BUCKLAND MONACHORUM—MILTON COMBE
ROUTE IN PLYMOUTH:—Via Tavistock Road, Mutley Plain and Crownhill.

WEEKDAYS — **SUNDAYS**

Bus Station (Breton Side)	dep	N 5 45	6 50	S 9 15	1015	...	9 15	1015	C	...	4 20	5 47	...	...	9 55	...	2 15	...	5 45	...	8 25	...
Royal Parade	,,	5 47	6 52	9 17	1017	...	2 20	...	4 22	5 49	...	9 57	...	2 17	...	5 47	...	8 27	...
Crownhill	,,	5 18	6 7	7 7	9 32	1032	...	2 35	...	4 37	6 4	...	1012	...	2 32	...	6 2	...	8 42	...
Roborough (George Hotel)	,,	5 23	6 7	7 12	9 37	1037	...	2 40	...	4 42	6 9	...	1017	...	2 37	...	6 7	...	8 47	...
Roborough (Lopes Arms)	,,	5 26	6 10	7 15	9 40	1040	...	2 43	...	4 45	6 12	...	1020	...	2 40	...	6 10	...	8 50	...
Yelverton (Rock Shelter)	,,	5 34	6 18	7 23	9 48	1048	...	3 3	...	5 5	6 30	...	1028	...	2 48	...	6 18	...	8 58	...
Yelverton (Roundabout)	arr	7 25	9 50	1050	...	3 3	...	5 5	6 32	...	1030	...	2 50	...	6 20	...	9 0	...
Yelverton (Roundabout)	dep	7 27	8 24	9 50	1050	12 0	1 0	6 3	3	...	3 51	4 55	6 3	7 50	8 50	10 10	1030	12 0	1242	...	2 50	3 42	6 20	...	9 2	1020
Yelverton (Rock Shelter)	,,	5 34	6 18	7 29	8 26	9 52	1052	12 2	1 8	3 5	...	3 53	4 57	5 8	6 5	7 52	8 52	2 12	1244	...	2 52	3 44	6 22	...	9 4	1022
Crapstone (Memorial)	,,	5 38	6 22	7 33	8 30	9 56	1056	12 6	1 12	3 9	...	3 57	5 0	1012	1036	12 6	1248	...	2 56	3 48	6 26	...	9 8	1026
Buckland Monachorum (Institute)	,,	5 40	6 24	7 35	8 32	9 58	1058	12 8	1 14	3 11	...	3 59	3 46	5 8	1014	1038	12 8	1250	...	2 58	3 50	6 28	...	9 10	1028
Buckland Monachorum (Netherton Cross)	,,	8 34	10 0	11 0	1210	...	1 15	5 6	4 20	8 8	1024	1048	1252	...	3 0	3 52	6 30	...	...	1030
Milton Combe	arr	5 45	6 29	7 40	8 42	10 8	11 8	1218	1 19	3 21	...	4 9	5 13	6 50	8 8	1024	1048	1213	1 0	...	3 8	4 0	6 38	...	9 15	1038

		S																							
Milton Combe	dep	5 45	6 30	7 42	8 42	1015	1115	1 8	1220	1 20	3 21	...	4 15	5 15	6 50	8 15	9 15	1025	11 0	1215	1 15	...	3 15	4 15	7 15	...	9 15	1038
Buckland Monachorum (Netherton Cross)	,,	5 53	6 38	7 50	8 50	1023	1116	1228	1 283	29	...	4 23	5 23	6 58	8 23	9 23	11 8	1223	1 23	...	3 23	4 23	7 23	...	9 23	1046
Buckland Monachorum (Institute)	,,	5 55	6 40	7 52	8 54	1027	1120	1230	11 30 3	30	...	4 25	5 25	7 0	8 25	9 25	1030	1110	1125	1 25	...	3 25	4 25	7 25	...	9 25	1048
Crapstone (Memorial)	,,	5 57	6 42	7 54	8 54	1027	1120	1232	12 32 3	32	...	4 27	5 27	7 2	8 27	9 27	1032	1112	1127	1 27	...	3 27	4 27	7 27	...	9 27	1050
Yelverton (Rock Shelter)	,,	6 4	6 7	5 8	58	1034	1124	1236	1 36 3	37	...	4 31	5 31	7 6	8 31	9 31	1036	1116	1231	1 31	...	3 31	4 31	7 31	...	9 31	1054
Yelverton (Roundabout)	arr	6 6	4 88	0 9	0	1033	1126	1238	1 38 3	39	...	4 33	5 33	7 8	8 33	9 33	1038	1118	1233	1 33	...	3 33	4 33	7 33	...	9 33	1056
Yelverton (Roundabout)	dep	6 11	6 48	...	9 10	1033	...	1 38	...	4 35	3 35	...	1038	...	1 35	...	4 35	...	...	1056
Yelverton (Rock Shelter)	,,	6 13	6 50	...	9 12	21035	...	1 40	...	4 35	4 3	...	1040	...	1 35	...	4 35	...	11 6	1058
Roborough (Lopes Arms)	,,	6 21	6 58	...	9 10	1043	...	1 48	...	4 43	4 43	...	1048	...	1 43	...	4 43	...	11 6	1106
Roborough (George Hotel)	,,	6 24	7 0	8 ...	9 15	1048	...	1 51	...	4 48	4 46	...	1053	...	1 48	...	4 48	...	1111	
Crownhill	,,	6 29	7 12	9 20	1053	...	1 58	...	4 53	5 53	...	1053	...	1 53	...	4 53	...	1116	
Bus Station (Breton Side)	arr	6 55	7 28	...	9 35	11 8	...	2 13	...	5 8	6 8	...	1113	...	2 8	...	5 8	...	D	

S—Saturdays only.   **N**—From Plymouth Station dep. 5.5 a.m.   **B**—Via St. Levan Road and Devonport.   **D**—To Milehouse Garage.   **G**—From Glenholt dep. 7.4 a.m.
C—Via Clearbrook dep. 2.50 p.m. and 6.19 p.m.

Plymouth Joint services Timetable for 1963, showing the two services serving Clearbrook by routes 45 and 46 for each direction.

*A GWR omnibus en route for
the Dartmoor village of Chagford
during the Summer of 1906.
Originating from
Mortonhampstead,
it was typical of the
scene between
Tavistock, Princetown
and Postbridge.
Chapman & Son*

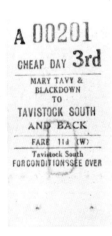

*Bridge weight restriction notice
recovered from Coryton,
restored by author and
now at GWR Museum
Didcot
A.R. Kingdom*

ENGINEERING AND OPERATING DATA

a) Pages 152 to 171 are reproduced from South Devon Railway Instruction No 59, dated 29 April 1876 by kind permission of British Rail, Public Records Office, Kew.

b) Pages 174 to 188 are reproduced from the Appendix to No 6 Section of the Service Time Tables, GWR - April 1939; Alterations and Additions to Appendix No 6 Section of the Service Time Tables, Supplements No 1 & 7, GWR Instructions, Plymouth Division; No's 2353 dated July 1939, 2470 dated February 1944, and GWR Notice No B828 dated 13 September 1943.

c) Pages 188 to 190 are reproduced from British Railways, Western Region, Service Time Tables, Plymouth to and from Ashburton Junction & Penzance, dated 27 September 1948 and until further notice. In addition updating is reproduced from British Railways, Western Operating Area, working Time Table of Freight Trains, Plymouth District, dated 19 September 1955 to 10 June 1956 or until further notice.

d) Pages 191 to 204 are reproduced from the Sectional Appendix to the Working Time Tables and Books of Rules and Regulations, BR (WR) Plymouth Traffic District, June 1960, plus supplement No 1 dated August 1965.

e) Page 234 is reproduced from GW Engine Sheds 1837-1947 by E Lyons - OPC.

f) Pages, 230 to 233 are reproduced from GW Stations, Vol II by R H Clark - OPC.

g) Pages 205 to 218 are Signal Box and G.F. Diagrams of stations on the branch. They are prepared for this book by members of the Signalling Records Society and Derek Butler from data by Larry Crosier.

Photographs of luggage labels and tickets used are on various pages throughout the book.

Items 'a' to 'd' in this chapter are reproduced by kind permission of British Railways Board and, irrespective of dates, remain its exclusive copyright.

The original lettering as fully restored by the author prior to its departure to Saltram House museum in 1978.

A.R. Kingdom

The BR station signboard at Lydford as its existed since modified in 1948

L. Crosier

SOUTH DEVON RAILWAY.

OPENING OF THE
MIXED GAUGE

BETWEEN

LIDFORD & PLYMOUTH.

Instructions to Station Masters, Inspectors, Signalmen, Engine Drivers, Guards, and Others concerned in Working the Line between Lidford and Plymouth.

The London and South Western Railway Company's Narrow-Gauge Trains will commence running between Lidford, Plymouth, and Devonport, on   day, the   day of May, 1876.

The Line from Lidford Junction to Marsh Mills is Single.

From Marsh Mills to Plymouth Station (North Road), and thence to Devonport, the Line is Double.

The Line from Lidford to Marsh Mills will be worked under the Train Staff and Ticket System, the Block Telegraph being used in addition, as described on page 16 to 20 inclusive.

DISTANCE FROM	TO	MILES.	CHAINS.	LENGTH OF CROSSING PLACE.
Lidford Junction ...	Mary Tavy Station	3	19	800 feet
,,	Tavistock Station	6	49	1,050 ,,
,,	Horrabridge Station	10	44	400 ,,
,,	Yelverton (crossing place only)	12	2	650 ,,
,,	Bickleigh Station	15	32	700 ,,
,,	Marsh Mills Station	19	22	} Double line.
,,	Mutley Station	22	3	
,,	Plymouth (North Road) Station	22	26	,,
,,	Devonport L. and S. W. R. Station ...	23	42	,,

Each Station Junction is provided with a Signal Hut, in which all Signals, Switch Levers, are connected.

LIST OF GRADIENTS BETWEE LIDFORD AND PLYMOUTH,
(North Road Station.)

		MILES.	CHAINS	TOTAL DISTANCE.
Immediately after leaving... ...	**Lidford Junction for Mary Tavy.**			Lidford Station to Mary Tavy. Miles, Chains. 3 ... 19
	The Line falls about 1 in 122 for	½	—	
	,, ,, ,, 1 in 77 for ...	2½	—	
	Level at the Station for	—	5	
Immediately after leaving... ...	**Mary Tavy for Tavistock.**			Mary Tavy to Tavistock. Miles, Chains. 3 ... 30
	The Line falls about 1 in 80 for	2	53	
	,, rises 1 in 114 for	—	9	
	,, is then level ... ... }		45	
	at Tavistock Station for			
Immediately after leaving... ...	**Tavistock for Horrabridge.**			Tavistock to Horrabridge. Miles, Chains. 3 ... 75
	The Line is level for	—	35	
	,, then rises 1 in 165 for ...	—	40	
	,, level for	—	10	
	,, then rises 1 in 64 for ...	—	60	
	,, ,, 1 in 105 for	—	8	
	,, ,, 1 in 396 for ...	—	12	
	,, falls 1 in 60 for	—	32	
	,, level for	—	26	
	,, then rises 1 in 60 for	0	4	
	,, is level at Horrabridge Station for	—	10	
Immediately after leaving... ...	**Horrabridge for Yelverton.** (CROSSING PLACE.)			Horrabridge to Yelverton. Miles, Chains. 1 ... 38
	The Line rises 1 in 60 for	—	4½	
	,, is level for	—	7	
	,, rises 1 in 60 for	—	34	
	,, rises 1 in 104 for	—	6	
	,, level for	—	4	
	,, rises 1 in 60 for	—	21	
	,, rises 1 in 110 for	—	30	
	,, is level at Yelverton for	—	14	

	MILES.	CHAINS	TOTAL DISTANCE.
Immediately after leaving... ... **Yelverton for Bickleigh.**			Yelverton to Bickleigh. Miles, Chains.
The Line falls 1 in 66 for	1	5	
,, is level for	—	10	
,, falls 1 in 58 for	2	2	
,, is level	—	10	3 ... 30
at the Station for			
Immediately after leaving... ... **Bickleigh for Marsh Mills.**			Bickleigh to Marsh Mills. Miles, Chains.
The Line falls 1 in 60 for	1	14	
,, ,, 1 in 528 for	—	8	
,, ,, 1 in 60 for	—	49	
,, ,, 1 in 528 for	—	10	
,, is level for	—	7	3 ... 70
,, falls 1 in 60 for	—	44	
,, ,, 1 in 322 for	—	22	
,, is level for	—	4	
,, rises 1 in 188 for	—	10	
,, level for	—	10	
,, falls 1 in 97 for	—	16	
,, is level for	—	10	
,, falls 1 in 100 for	—	26	
at Marsh Mills Station is level for ...	—	3	

The Main Line of the South Devon Railway is reached immediately after leaving Marsh Mills.

The Gradients from Marsh Mills to Plymouth (North Road Station), are as follows:

	MILES.	CHAINS	TOTAL DISTANCE.
Immediately after leaving... ... **Marsh Mills for Plymouth, (North Road Station.)**			Marsh Mills to North Road Station. Miles, Chains.
The Line falls 1 in 528 for	—	9	
,, is level for...	—	60	
,, falls 1 in 85 for...	—	8	3 ... 4
,, then rises 1 in 80 for	1	30	
,, is level for...	—	8	
,, then falls 1 in 81	—	33	
to North Road Station			

Trains leaving **Lidford** for **Plymouth** are called **Down Trains.** Trains leaving **Plymouth** for **Lidford** are called **Up Trains.**

LOOP LINES AT STATIONS.

Up and **Down** Trains and Engines must run to the proper, or, **left** hand Line at Stations.

LIDFORD STATION.

This Station is protected by Semaphore Signals as follows :—

DOWN SIGNALS.

A Down Broad Gauge Distant Signal fixed about ¼-Mile, Launceston **End** of the Station.

A Down Broad Gauge Signal fixed near the facing Points, Launceston End of the Station.

A Down Starting Signal for Broad Gauge Trains fixed at the 6-foot space.

A Down Starting Signal for Narrow Gauge Trains fixed near the Facing Points leading to the Main Line.

A Down Advance Starting Signal for Narrow and Broad Gauge Trains fixed ¼-Mile from the Station.

UP SIGNALS.

Two Up Distant Signals on one Pole, fixed nearly ½-Mile from the Station; the Left arm is for **Broad** Gauge Trains and Engines, and the **Right** arm for **Narrow** Gauge Trains and Engines.

Two Up Home Signals, on one Pole, fixed near the facing Points ; the Left arm is for **Broad** Gauge Trains and the **Right** arm for **Narrow** Gauge Trains.

An Up Broad Gauge Starting Signal fixed at the 6-foot space at the Launceston End of the Station.

An Up Broad Gauge advance Starting Signal fixed ¼-mile Launceston, End of the Station.

All Up and Down Goods Trains must stop " dead " at Lidford Station, and the Head Guard must consult the Driver as to how many breaks it is necessary to apply at that Station, to ensure the Trains being kept under control in decending the inclines, and to ensure their being stopped at the Signals at Coryton and Mary Tavy, if necsssary. The Guards must put down the number of Breaks at Lidford Station which may be stated to be required by the Driver.—*See page* 13, *Rules* 1 *and* 2.

When Down through Trains or Engines have left Bridestow 2 double Beats on the Telegraph Gong thus, ○ ○   ○ ○ will be given to Lidford, and be repeated to the South Devon Signalman at Lidford, to prepare him for the approaching Train.

MARY TAVY STATION.

ThisStation is protected by semaphore signals as follows :—

DOWN SIGNALS.
A Down Distant Signal fixed about ½-Mile from the Station
A Down Home Signal fixed near the Facing Points.
A Down Starting Signal fixed at the 6-foot space.

UP SIGNALS.
An Up Distant Signal fixed about ½-Mile from the Station.
An Up Home Signal fixed near the Facing Points.
An Up Starting Signal fixed at the 6-foot space.
An Up Advance Starting Signal fixed ¼-Mile from the Station.

There is a Ground Disc in the Siding at Mary Tavy Station. Drivers on the Main Line must not take any notice of this Disc, but Drivers in the Siding must not attempt to pass the Disc when it is standing at Danger, as, if they do, their Engines will be thrown off the Line at the Throw-off Switch.

☞ Drivers of Down Trains or Engines must approach this Station very Cautiously, and have their Trains or Engines under complete control, so as to prevent the possibility of accidents from the Trains running beyond the six-foot space at the Station, and coming into collision with an Up Train which may be approaching.

All Down Goods Trains must stop "dead" at Mary Tavy Station, and the Head Guard must consult the Driver as to how many Brakes is necessary to apply to ensure the Trains being kept under control in decending the incline, and to ensure their being stopped at the Signals at Tavistock, if necessary. The Guards must put down the number of Breaks at Mary Tavy Station which may be required by the Driver.—*See page* 13, *Rules* 1 *and* 2.

Immediately after Up Narrow Guage Trains, or Engines, have left Mary Tavy for Lidford 2 Double Beats on the Gong, thus ○ ○   ○ ○ must be sent to Lidford, and be repeated there to the South Western Company's Signal Hut. This in addition to the usual Beats on the Gong announcing the departure of Trains, &c.

The two Double Beats on the Gong must be acknowledged by **one** Beat on the Gong.

TAVISTOCK STATION.

This Station is protected by semaphore signals, worked in Two Signal Huts as follows :—

DOWN SIGNALS.

A Down Distant Signal fixed about ¼-Mile from the Station.

A Down Home Signal fixed near the Facing Points.

A Down Starting Signal fixed at the 6-foot space

A Down Advance Starting Signal fixed ¼-Mile from the Station.

UP SIGNALS,

An Up Distant Signal fixed about ½-Mile from the Station.

An Up Home Signal fixed near the Facing Points.

An Up Double Starting Signal at the 6-foot space, between the Up and the Down Lines, Lidford end of the Station. The **Top** Arm being for Trains starting from the Goods Shed Line. The **Lower** Arm being for Trains starting from the Up Passenger Platform Line.

An Up Advance Starting Signal fixed about ¼-Mile from the Station.

There are Ground Discs at Tavistock in the several Sidings. Drivers on the Main Line must not take any notice of these Discs, but Drivers in the Sidings must not pass them when they shew danger, as, if they do so, their Engines will be thrown off the Line at the Throw-off Switches.

There is an Iron Scotch fixed on the Rail of the Centre Line, Plymouth end of Station, to prevent Trucks running out. Drivers must not go out of the Centre Line when the Disc is against them ; neither may Trucks or Engines be shunted into the Siding without the sanction of the Signalman.

HORRABRIDGE STATION.

This Station is protected by the following semaphore signals :—

DOWN SIGNALS.

A Down Distant Signal fixed about ½-Mile from the Station.

A Down Home Signal fixed near the Facing Points.

A Down Starting Signal fixed at the 6-foot space.

UP SIGNALS.

An Up Distant Signal fixed about ½-Mile from the Station.

An Up Home Signal fixed near the Facing Points.

An Up Starting Signal fixed at the 6-foot space.

☞ There are Ground Discs in the Sidings. Drivers on the Main Line must not take any notice of them, but Drivers in the Sidings must not attempt to pass the Discs when at Danger, as, if they do so, their Engines will be thrown off the Line at the Throw-off Switches.

Drivers of Up Trains must approach this Station very cautiously, as the Line falls rapidly from Yelverton towards Horrabridge.

YELVERTON (Crossing Place.)

This is protected by the following semaphore signals :—

DOWN SIGNALS.

A Down Distant Signal fixed about ½-Mile from the Station, Horrabridge side of the Tunnel.

A Down Home Signal fixed at the Facing Points of Loop Line.

A Down Starting Signal at the 6-foot space, Plymouth End of the yard.

UP SIGNALS.

An Up Distant Signal fixed about ¾-Mile from the Station.

An Up Home Signal at Facing Points of Loop Line.

An Up Starting Signal at the 6-foot space, Horrabridge End of the yard.

All Up and Down Goods Trains must stop "**dead**" at Yelverton Crossing Place, and the Head Guard must consult the Driver as to how many Breaks it is necessary to apply at that Station, to ensure the Trains being kept under control in descending the inclines, and to ensure their being stopped at the Signals at Horrabridge and Bickleigh if necessary. The Guards must put down the number of Breaks at Yelverton Crossing Place which may be required by the Driver.—*See page 13, Rule 1.*

BICKLEIGH STATION.

This Station is protected by the following semaphore signals :—

DOWN SIGNALS.

A Down Distant Signal fixed about ½-Mile from the Station.
A Down Home Signal fixed near the Facing Points,
A Down Starting Signal fixed at the 6-foot space.

UP SIGNALS.

An Up Distant Signal fixed ¼-Mile from the Station.
An Up Home Signal fixed near the Facing Points.
An Up Starting Signal fixed at the 6-foot space.

There are Two Ground Discs or Point Indicators at this Station—one in the Up Siding, and one in the Down Siding. Drivers on the Main Line must not take any notice of these Discs. Drivers in the Sidings must not attempt to Pass them to come out on the Main Line, as if they do so, their Engines will be thrown off the Line at the Throw-off Switches.

☞ Drivers of Down Trains or Engines must approach Bickleigh Station very cautiously, and have their Trains or Engines under complete control, so as to prevent the possibility of accidents from the Train running beyond the 6-foot space at the Station, and coming into collision with Up Trains which may be approaching. The Line falls rapidly from Yelverton to Bickleigh, and beyond it for about three miles.

All Down Goods Trains must stop " dead " at Bickleigh Station, and the Head Guard must consult the Driver as to how many Breaks it is necessary to apply at that Station, to ensure the Trains being kept under control in decending the inclines, and to ensure their being stopped at the Signals at Lee Moor Level Crossing, or Marsh Mills if necessary. The Guards must put down the number of Breaks at Bickleigh Station which may be required by the Driver.—*See Rules 1 and 2, page 13.*

☞ There is a self-acting throw-off switch near the 6-foot space on the Up Line at the Southern or Plymouth side of the Bickleigh Station. Guards and Drivers must be very careful to see when running their Engines or Trucks against it, that the points are held over for the Main Line. Neither Carriages nor Trucks may be allowed to stand on the Southern or Plymouth side of this Throw-Off Switch.

LEE MOOR LEVEL CROSSING, ABOUT 3 MILES PLYMOUTH END OF BICKLEIGH STATION.

This Level Crossing is protected by the following Signals (Discs and Cross Bars.)

DOWN SIGNALS.

A Down Signal fixed about ¼ mile from the Level Crossing.

UP SIGNALS.

An Up Signal fixed about 1/8 mile from the Level Crossing.

☞ Drivers of Up and Down Trains must approach this Level Crossing cautiously and have their Trains and Engines under such control as to be able to stop at the Down Signal if necessary.

MARSH MILLS STATION.

This Station is protected by the following Semaphore Signals :—

DOWN SIGNALS.

A Down Distant Signal fixed about ¼-Mile from the Station.

A Down Home Signal near the Facing Points of the Double Line.

A Down Starting Signal fixed in the 6-foot space, Tavistock Junction side of the Bridge.

UP SIGNALS.

An Up Home Signal fixed near the Bridge, Tavistock Junction side of it.

An Up Starting Signal fixed at the 6-foot space near the End of the Up Platform.

☞ Drivers of Down Trains or Engines must approach Marsh Mills very cautiously, and have their Trains or Engines under complete control as they must stop dead at the Station.

TAVISTOCK JUNCTION.

This is protected by the following signals :

DOWN SIGNALS.

A Down Junction Semaphore Signal a short distance from the South Devon Main Line.

A Down Advance Starting Semaphore Signal for Main Line and Branch Trains fixed by the side of the Main Line about ¼-Mile from the Tavistock Junction. towards Laira

A Down Distant Signal (Disc and Cross Bar) fixed about ¼-mile from the Junction towards Plympton.

A Home Signal (Disc and Cross Bar) fixed near the Junction on the Main Line.

UP SIGNALS.

An Up Semaphore Distant Signal fixed by the side of the Up South Devon Main Line about ¼-Mile from Tavistock Junction.

An Up Semaphore Home Signal, on a Double Bracket, fixed near the Facing Points, the Left Arm being for Trains going on the Tavistock Branch, and the Right Arm for Main Line Trains.

An Up Advance Main Line Starting Signal (Disc and Cross Bar) fixed nearly ¼ mile from the Junction.

No Down Train or Engine must be permitted to leave Marsh Mills Station after an Up South Devon Main Line Train or Engine has been Signalled " off" Laira, until after such Up Train or Engine has passed the Tavistock Junction.

No Down Train or Engine must be permitted to leave Marsh Mills Station, after a Down South Devon Main Line Passenger Train or Engine has been Signalled " off" Plympton, until such Down Train has passed Laira, and Line has been reported " clear" from Laira to Tavistock Junction.

Should a Down Train or Engine be at Marsh Mills ready to start for Plymouth, when an Up Branch Train or Engine has been Signalled "off" Laira, the Down Train may be started from Marsh Mills, provided Line Clear has been obtained from Laira.

When a Down Goods Train has left Plympton for Plymouth, and a Down Passenger Train is at, or near, Marsh Mills, the Down Goods Train must be stopped at Tavistock Junction to allow the Passenger Train to proceed, but the latter must never be started from Marsh Mills, unless the Down Goods Train has come to a stop clear of the Branch Lines at the Junction.

LAIRA JUNCTION.

This is protected by the following Signals :—

DOWN SIGNALS.

A Down Distant Signal about ½-Mile from the Junction.

A Down Home Signal on a Double Bracket, the Right Hand Arm being for the Main Line, and the Left Arm for the Laira Branch.

UP SIGNALS.

An Up Distant Signal about ¼-Mile from the Junction.

An Up Home Signal near the Junction.

An Up Distant Signal fixed nearly ¼ mile from the Junction on the Laira Branch.

An Up Branch Home Signal Laira side of the Level Crossing.

There are Ground Discs in the Up Main Line Shunt Siding, and in the Siding on the Branch leading on to the Main Line. Engines in the Sidings must not pass the Discs when they show Danger.

NORTH ROAD STATION—EAST CABIN.

DOWN SIGNALS.

A Double Down Signal, fixed near the Facing Points at the East End of the North Road Station. The Right Arm being for Trains running to No. 3 Platform. The Left Arm being for Trains running to No. 4 Platform.

UP SIGNALS.

There are 2 Up Starting Signals fixed at the 6-foot space, at the East End of the Station. The Left Hand Signal being for Trains starting from No. 1 Platform. The Right Hand Signal being for Trains starting from No. 2 Platform.

There is a Point Indicator in the Siding, East End of the Station. Drivers of Trains or Engines on the Main Lines must not take any notice of this Point Indicator, but Drivers in the Siding must not attempt to pass the Disc when standing at Danger: if they do so, their Engines will be thrown off the Line at the Throw-off Switch.

NORTH ROAD STATION—WEST CABIN.

DOWN SIGNALS.

There are 2 Down Starting Signals at the 6-foot space, West End of Down Platforms. The Right Hand Signal being for Down Trains starting from No. 3 Down Platform. The Left Hand Signal being for Down Trains starting from No. 4 Down Platform.

There is also a Double Down Signal fixed near the Facing Points. The Right Arm being for Trains running over the Loop Line towards Devonport. The Left Arm being for Trains running towards Plymouth (Mill Bay) Station.

UP SIGNALS.

An Up Home Signal fixed at the 6-foot space for South Devon Trains from Plymouth.

An Up Home Signal, fixed at the 6-foot space, for Trains coming over the Loop Line.

There is also an Up Double Signal fixed near the Facing Points, at the West End of the Station. The Left Arm being for Trains running to No. 1 Platform. The Right Arm being for Trains running to No. 2 Platform.

CORNWALL JUNCTION.

This is protected by the following Semaphore Signals :—For Trains starting from, and going to Plymouth (Millbay) Station.

DOWN SIGNALS.

A Down Home Main Line Signal fixed near the North Road Bridge, for Trains going to Plymouth (Milbay) Station.

A Down Signal fixed near the Junction, worked by the Plymouth Switchman at the Engine-Shed Cabin. It must, as a rule, stand at Danger, and only be turned to admit Trains from Cornwall or North Road Station.

When Trains are approaching Cornwall Junction, the Signalman there must ring the Telegraph Gong twice to call attention.

UP SIGNALS.

An Up Double Signal fixed near the Junction Facing Points. The Right Arm being for Up Trains going in the direction of **Exeter**. The Left Arm being for Down Trains going in the direction of **Devonport**.

An Up Home Signal fixed near the Bridge, at the Cornwall Junction, for Trains going to Millbay Station.

There is also a **Point Indicator** at the **Throw-off Switch** in the Shunt Siding. Drivers of Trains or Engines on the Main Lines, must not take any notice of this Point Indicator ; but Drivers in the Sidings, must not attempt to pass it when standing at danger : if they do so, their Engines will be thrown off the Line at the Throw-off Switch.

DEVONPORT JUNCTION.

DOWN SIGNALS.

There is a Double Down Signal fixed at the 6-foot space, on the Cornwall Railway, at the West end of the Loop Line. The Right Arm being for Down Trains running over the Loop Line from North Road Station. The Left Arm being for Down Trains running from Plymouth (Millbay Station) into Cornwall, on the Cornwall Line.

A Down Double Signal fixed near the Facing Points on the Cornwall Main Line. The Right Arm being for Trains going into Cornwall. The Left Arm being for South Western Trains going to their Devonport Station.

The Down Double Signal fixed on the Devonport Branch near the Junction, is for Narrow Gauge Trains and Engines only, the Left Arm is for Goods' Trains, and the Right Arm for Passenger Trains. All Down Trains and Engines will draw within this Signal, even when it is showing Danger.

UP SIGNALS.

There is an Up Distant Signal fixed a short distance East of **Devonport** Station, on the Cornwall Line. This will also be used as a Starting Signal for **Trains** leaving the Devonport (Stoke) Station.

There is an Up Distant Signal fixed on the Devonport Branch of the South Western Railway, about ¼-mile from the Junction.

An Up Double Home Signal, fixed at the 6-foot space at the Junction. The Right Arm, being for Narrow Gauge Trains coming off the South Western Branch for North Road Station. The Left Arm, being for Up Trains from Devonport, on the Cornwall Line.

An Up Double Signal fixed near the Facing Points, leading to the Loop Line, and to the Plymouth (Millbay) Station. The Right Arm, being for Trains running into Plymouth Station (Mill Bay). The Left Arm being for Trains running over the Loop Line, towards the North Road Station.

☞ After an Up Train has left Devonport Station, on the Cornwall Railway, for Millbay, no Up Train must be allowed to pass the Up Home Signal on the South Western Company's Devonport Branch, or a Down Train be allowed to pass the Down Signal at the West End of the Loop, relating to Trains leaving North Road over the Loop Line until the Up Train from the Cornwall Line has passed clear of the Devonport Junction and the Loop Lines.

☞ After an Up Train has left the South Western Company's Station, Devonport Branch, no Up Train must be allowed to leave Devonport Station on the Cornwall Line, or a Down Train from Millbay for the Cornwall Line be allowed to pass the Down Signal at the West End of the Loop Line, until the Up Train from the South Western Branch has passed the Devonport Junction and clear of the Cornwall Line.

☞ After a Down Train from Millbay for the Cornwall Line has passed the Cornwall Junction, no Down Train from North Road must pass the Signal at the West of the Loop Line, or an Up Train pass the Home Signal on the South Western Devonport Branch, until the Down Train from Millbay has passed clear of the Devonport Junction.

☞ After a Down Train has left the North Road Station over the Loop for the Cornwall Line, no Down Train from Millbay must pass the Signal at the West End of the Loop, or an Up Train from the South Western Company's Branch pass the Home Signal, nor an Up Train be allowed to leave Devonport Station on the Cornwall Line for Millbay, until the Down Train from North Road for the Cornwall Line has passed clear of the Main Lines leading to the Devonport Branch.

☞ After a Down Train has left North Road Station for the South Western Branch, no Down Train from Millbay must pass the Signal at the West End of the Loop Line, or an Up Train for Millbay leave Devonport Station (Cornwall Line), until the Down Train from North Road for the South Western Branch has passed clear of the Cornwall Line at the Devonport Junction.

☞ After an Up Train has been Signalled off the Devonport Junction for Millbay Station, no Down Train from the North Road Station for Millbay must be allowed to leave that Station, or an Up Train from Millbay be allowed to pass the Up Main Line Signal fixed near the Engine shed, until the Up Train from Cornwall has passed the Cornwall Junction.

63. After a **Down** Train has left North Road Station for Millbay, no **Up** Train must be allowed to leave Devonport Junction for Millbay, until the **Down** Train from North Road has passed the Cornwall Junction.

64. After an **Up** Train has been Signalled off the Devonport Junction for North Road, no **Up** Train from Millbay must pass the **Up** Main Line Signal fixed at the East End of the Loop Line, until the **Up** Train from Devonport Junction has passed and is clear of the Junction at North Road Station. In like manner, after an **Up** Main Line Train has been Signalled off Cornwall Junction for North Road, no **Up** Train must pass the Inner Signal at the East End of the Loop Line, until the **Up** Main Line Train from Cornwall Junction has passed and is clear of the Junction at North Road Station.

65. After an **Up** Main Line Train from Millbay has been Signalled off Cornwall Junction, no **Down** Train must leave North Road Station for the Loop Line, until after the **Up** Train from Millbay has passed and is clear of the Junction at the North Road Station.

66. After a **Down** Train has left the North Road Station for the Loop Line no **Up** Train from Millbay must pass the Main Line Signal at the East End of the Loop Line, until the **Down** Train from North Road for the Loop Line has passed and is clear of the Junction at North Road.

The following Special Whistles must be given by Drivers of Trains and Engines at the undermentioned places :—

DOWN JOURNEY.		Whistles of South Devon Company's Engines must be Sounded	Whistles of London and South Western Company's Engines must be Sounded
Before starting	From Lidford for Mary Tavy	Once ...	Twice
When approaching	Laira Junction for Plymouth	Once ...	Once
,, ,,	Do. for Sutton Harbour	Twice ...	3 Times
,, ,,	North Road for (No. 3) Platform	Once ...	Once
,, ,,	Do. for (No. 4) Platform	Twice ...	Twice
Before starting	From North Road for the Loop Line	Twice ...	Twice
,, ,, ...	Do. for Plymouth (Millbay)	Once ...	—
When approaching	Devonport Junction for Cornwall Line	Once ...	Once
,, ,, ...	Do. for Devonport Branch	—	Twice

UP JOURNEY.			
When approaching	Cornwall Junction (from Millbay Station) for North Road ...	Once ...	—
,, ,,	Do. for Cornwall	Twice ...	—
,, ,,	Devonport Junction for Plymouth (Millbay)	Once ...	—
,, ,,	Do. for the Loop Line	Twice ...	Twice
,, ,,	North Road for (No. 1) Platform	Once ...	Once
,, ,,	Do. for (No. 2) Platform	Twice ...	Twice
Before starting	From North Road from (No. 1) Platform	Once ...	Once
,, ,, ...	Do. from (No. 2)	Twice ...	Twice
When approaching	Tavistock Junction for Plympton	Once ...	—
,, ,,	Do. for Tavistock	Twice ...	3 Times
,, ,,	Lidford Station	Once ...	Twice

163

GENERAL INSTRUCTIONS AS TO BRAKE POWER, OUT-DOOR SIGNALLING, &c., AND AS TO HEAD, SIDE, and TAIL LAMPS.

1.—Before descending the steep inclines,

From Lidford to Coryton	From Yelverton to Horrabridge
„ Lidford to Mary Tavy	„ Yelverton to Bickleigh
„ Mary Tavy to Tavistock	„ Bickleigh to Marsh Mills

all Goods and Mineral Trains must be brought to a stand, and it will be the duty of the Head Guard to consult the Driver as to how many Brakes it is necessary to apply, and the Driver will say what number of Brakes, in his opinion, should be put down. This, however, will not relieve the Guard from any responsibility if, in his opinion more Brakes should be put down than the Driver considers necessary; and he (the Guard) must watch the Train while decending the incline, and apply the Brakes if necessary.

2.—Goods and Mineral Trains must not be started from Stations with more Trucks than the Engines can take up the inclines without dividing; but in the event of such a Train coming to a standstill in ascending the inclines, it must be divided, and one part taken to the top of the incline at a time, care being taken that the hinder part is properly secured with Sprags and Brakes before the foremost part of the Train is disconnected; and in the case of two Guards being with the Train, the senior Guard must remain with the portion of the Train left behind, and the junior Guard go up with the first portion of the Train to the top of the incline. When there is only one Guard with the Train, he must remain with the portion of the Train left behind, and the first portion of the Train must be taken up under the charge of the Engineman amd Fireman.

3.—Each Guard must carry a Sprag placed so as to have it ready for instant use in case of necessity.

.4—**When the Section ahead** is blocked, the Signalman must keep all **his Signals** for the Line referred to **at Danger**, so as to bring the Train to a **dead stop at the Home Signal.** When an Engine-man finds a Distant Signal exhibiting Danger, he must immediately shut off steam, blow the Brake Whistle, put on his Brake, and reduce the speed of his Train, so as to be able to stop at the Distant Signal.

5.—**No Engine or Train can leave or pass a Station until the Section ahead is Clear,** and the Starting Signal has been lowered to show " All Right."

6.—The action of the Signals must frequently be tried, and the Wires must be kept at the proper length by means of regulating screws or links so as to compensate for the expansion and contraction caused by variations of temperature. The greatest promptness must also be observed in the use of them; and in the case of an approaching Train or Engine, the Signal must be put on as soon as the Engine has passed it.

7.—When a Home Signal has been lowered for the passing of a Train or Engine, it must not be again placed at Danger, until such Train or Engine has passed within such Home Signal; but it must be placed at **Danger** immediately afterwards. Distant Signals must be put at Danger immediately they are passed by Engines or Trains.

8.—Signalmen must be very careful not to attempt to turn **Facing Points** when Trains are running against them. They must wait until all the Vehicles have passed over such Points. The object of this order, is to prevent Vehicles running on different Lines, from the Points being altered too soon.

9.—**Locking Bolts to cross over roads must never be pulled off** by a Signalman unless all his out-door Signals for both lines are at Danger, and he must never release the Points when a Train is running in the Section towards his Station in either direction.

10.—**Signals out of Repair, &c.**—If a Signal Light is not burning when it ought to be, or a Signal has been blown down, or is evidently not in proper working order, it is to be regarded by Enginemen as a Danger or Stop Signal. Enginemen who have observed any defects in Signals, should always report the circumstance at the next Station, and Guards should also report both specially and on their journal.

11.—**Signal Lamp Trimming.**—Station Masters are requested to give this their attention; and whenever a lamp fails to keep alight, the Station Master must examine it in order to ascertain whether it has been well trimmed or not, and if the cause is owing to bad trimming, or want of proper cleaning, the party in fault will be dealt with severely.

12.—When Vehicles are detached from Trains at Stations, and have to be shunted into Sidings, steps must be at once taken to apprise the Signalman of the fact, in order that the Signals may continue to be exhibited for the protection of the Line; and, at night, in addition, a Red Light must be hung upon the rear end of the Vehicles, until they are safely placed in the Sidings.

The following Head, Side, and Tail Signals will be **carried on Trains and** Engines working between Lidford and Plymouth :—

ENGINE HEAD DAY SIGNALS.

South Devon Engines will carry a Board on the leading Buffer Beam with two White Diamonds painted upon it.

South Western Engines will carry two White Discs, one at the foot of the Funnel, and the other on the centre of the Buffer Beam.

ENGINE HEAD LIGHTS.

South Devon Engines will carry a Green Head Light.

South Western Engines will carry two Green Head Lights, one at the foot of the Funnel, and the other on the centre of the Buffer Beam.

SIDE LAMPS, (By night).

South Devon Trains will carry two Side Lamps on the last Carriage or Van in the Train, showing white Lights in front and Red Lights behind.

South Western Passenger Trains will not carry Side Lamps, but their Goods Trains will do so.

TAIL SIGNALS, (By day).

South Devon Trains will carry a Tail Lamp on the Last Vehicle.

South Devon empty Engines will carry a Board on the Trailing End with a Red Diamond painted upon it.

South Western Trains, and empty Engines will carry a Tail Lamp on the rear end.

When a Special Train or Engine is to follow a South Devon Train or Engine, the preceding Train or Engine will carry a Double Red Target.

When a Special Train or Engine is to follow a South Western Train or Engine, the preceding Train or Engine will carry a Red Board, with S. T. Marked upon it.

South Devon Special Trains or Engines will carry a Red and Green Target

Engines returning from assisting Trains will carry a Board with a Red Diamond painted upon it.

South Western Special Trains or Engines will carry a Green Tail Board with S. T. marked upon it.

TAIL SIGNALS, (By night).

South Devon and and South Western Trains will carry a Red Tail Light.

When a special Train or Engine is to follow another Train, the preceding South Devon or South Western Train or Engine, will carry a Double Red Light at the rear end of the last Vehicle.

South Devon and South Western Special Trains, or Special empty Engines will carry a Red and Green Tail Light, when the previous Train has been Targetted for Special Train or Engine to follow.

Empty Engines returning by night from assisting Trains, will carry a Red Light only, at the rear end.

C. E. COMPTON,

Superintendent.

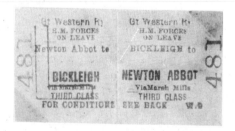

SOUTH DEVON RAILWAY.

INSTRUCTIONS FOR WORKING THE SINGLE LINE

BETWEEN

LIDFORD & MARSH MILLS

UNDER THE

TRAIN STAFF AND TICKET SYSTEM,

The Block Telegraph being used in addition to the Train Staffs and Tickets.

TO COMMENCE ON   MAY, 1876.

The Train Staff and Ticket Regulations are as under :—

1.—In all cases, either a Train Staff or a Train Staff Ticket is to be carried with each Train or Engine to and fro, and without this Staff or Ticket no Train or Engine is to be allowed to travel over the Line.

2.—No Train or Engine must be permitted to leave any Train Staff Station unless the Staff for the portion of the Line over which it is to travel is then at the Station, and not even then unless the Block Telegraph Regulations have been complied with.

3.—The Officer in charge of the Station for the time is the sole person authorized to receive and deliver the Staff or Ticket.

4.—Upon a Train or Engine being ready to start from a Station, and no second Train or Engine being intended to follow it, it is the duty of the Officer in charge of the Station to give the Staff to the Engineman, after ascertaining from the Signalman that the Line is clear, and that the Block Telegraph Regulations have been carried out.

5.—If other Trains or Engines are intended to follow in succession before the Staff can be returned, a Train Ticket, stating "Staff will follow," will be given to the Engineman of the leading Train or Engine, *The Staff being shown to him*, and so on with any other, except the last Train or Engine, the Staff itself being given to the Engineman of the last Train or Engine, as directed in Clause 4; but in every case the Block Telegraph Regulations must be carried out.

After the Staff has been sent away, no other Train or Engine can leave the Station, under any circumstances whatever, until its return.

6.—The Train Tickets are to be kept in a Box, fastened by an inside spring, the key to open the Box being attached to the Train Staff, so that a Ticket cannot be obtained without the Train Staff.

7.—The Train Staffs have engraved metal plates on them, showing between what points they are to work, and the Ticket Boxes are marked with the names of the different sections. The inside spring on the Boxes and the keys on the Staffs are so arranged that the Round Staff cannot open the Box of the Square Staff, and so on. The Train Tickets for the different Sections are printed in different colours, and numbered consecutively, and will correspond in shape with the Train Staffs.

8.—An Engineman with a Train or single Engine must not leave a Station until he has received the Staff or Ticket, which he is not to take from any other person than the Officer in charge of the Station for the time, as explained in Clauses 3, 4, and 5. After receiving the Staff or Ticket, he must not start until the usual signal has been given by the Guard, who must receive his authority from the Officer in charge of the Station, that the business of the Train is completed. On arriving at the Station to which the Staff or Ticket extends, such Staff or Ticket must be immediately given up to the Officer in charge of the Station, who will be held responsible for the Tickets being *at once* cancelled and forwarded to the Divisional Superintendent's Office at Plymouth, at the end of the day, so as to prevent the possibility of their being used a second time.

9.—An Engineman will render himself liable to severe punishment if he, under any circumstances, leaves the Station without the Train Staff or Ticket, as above explained.

10.—Enginemen must also be extremely careful not to take the Staff or Ticket beyond the Station at which it ought to be left.

11.—The Guard in charge of the Train must not give the signal to start from a Station until the Engineman has shown him the Staff or Ticket, and he (the Guard) has obtained the authority of the Officer in charge of the Station to the Train leaving.

12.—Whenever a Special Train is to run, the usual Special **Train Tail** Signal must be used for the guidance of the Platelayers and Gatekeepers upon the Line.

13.—When a BALLAST TRAIN has to WORK on the Line, the Train Staff is to be given to the Engineman, so as to close the Line whilst the Ballast Train is at work. The Ballast Train must proceed afterwards to one of the Terminal Stations of the Staff, to open the Line before the ordinary traffic can be resumed, and the Block Telegraph Regulations must also be strictly carried out.

14.—When the Trains are assisted by a Pilot Engine, the Pilot Engine, if in front, must carry the staff or Ticket. When the Pilot Engine is at the rear of the Train, it must carry the Train Staff or Ticket.

15.—In the event of an Engine or Train breaking down between two Stations, the Junior Guard, if there are two Guards to the Train, or the Fireman, if there be only one Guard, is to take the Train Staff to the Station in the direction whence assistance may be expected, that the Staff may be at the Station on the arrival of an Engine. Should the Engine that fails be in possession of a Train Ticket instead of the Staff, assistance must only come from the Station at which the Staff has been left ; but in cases where assistance can be more readily obtained at a Station other than the one at which the Staff is resting, immediate steps must be taken to have the Staff transferred to the other end of the "Block." The Guard or Fireman is to accompany the assistant Engine to the place where he has left his own Engine, which must not be moved under any circumstances, until the Fireman or Junior Guard has returned.

16.—Should the accident be of such a nature as to block the road, and the traffic is likely to be stopped for any considerable time, special arrangements must be made for working the Trains to and from the point of obstruction on either side. The Train Staff Regulations must be carried out on that side where the Staff happens to be at the moment of the accident ; and on the other side, the Traffic must be conducted by a Pilotman to be appointed in writing, in accordance with the Company's Instructions, dated, 15th February, 1876, and the Officer in charge of the Station at each Staff Terminal must have a copy of the notice.

17.—When the road is again Clear, no Train must be allowed to pass the point of obstruction *without the Staff and the Pilotman*. The Pilotman is to accompany *the Train carrying the Staff* to the Staff Terminal, when the Traffic will be conducted according to the usual Staff Regulations.

THE TRAIN STAFFS AND TICKETS WILL WORK AS UNDER:

Form of Staff and Ticket	Colour of Ticket.	Working Between.
ROUND.	YELLOW.	LIDFORD and MARY TAVY.
SQUARE.	PINK.	MARY TAVY and TAVISTOCK.
TRIANGULAR.	GREEN.	TAVISTOCK and HORRABRIDGE.
SIX-SIDED.	WHITE.	HORRABRIDGE and YELVERTON.
OBLONG.	BLUE.	YELVERTON and BICKLEIGH.
HALF-ROUND.	BROWN.	BICKLEIGH and MARSH MILLS.

Instructions for Working the Block Telegraph between Lidford and Marsh Mills, as an auxiliary to the Train Staff and Ticket System.

The Disc Block Telegraph Stations are Lidford, Mary Tavy, Tavistock, Horrabridge, Yelverton, Bickleigh, and Marsh Mills.

1.—The " Block," or Signal Instruments are to be used exclusively for the purpose of ascertaining if the Line is clear between Station and Station. The authority to work them is entrusted solely to the Station Masters or Signalmen in charge of the Instruments, without whose authority no Signal whatever is to be passed.

2.—Each Station has its own independent Block Telegraph circuit to the next Station on either side, Up and Down.

3.—Under no circumstances may a Train be permitted to leave, or pass a Station (except both Telegraphs are out of order, and then only, as provided in Rule 19), unless the Signal " *Line clear* " has been obtained immediately before, from the Station next in advance.

4.—In order to make the following instructions clearly intelligible, the Station from which the Train is to start, is called Station **A**, and the Station next in advance, Station **B**.

5.—Immediately before starting the Train from Station **A** for Station **B**, the needle of the Block Telegraph Instrument must be moved steadily to and fro—" Left, Right, Left, Right " —and this must be continued until replied to in like manner by Station **B**. Station **A** will then give three steady and distinct beats with his needle to the right, which will ask the question, " *Is Line clear* ? "

6.—If the Line is clear, Station **B** will reply to Station **A**, by repeating three steady and distinct beats with his needle, also to the right, which will indicate, " *Yes, Line clear* ? "

7.—On receiving such reply, Station **A** must signal to Station **B**—" *Train will Start.*" This signal will be made by giving three steady and distinct beats with his needle to the left for a Passenger Train, and five steady and distinct beats to the left for a Goods Train. Station **B** will then place the brass peg in the handle of the instrument, and block the needle to the words on the Dial—" *Train on Line.*" Station **A** may start the Train as soon as Station B has blocked the needle to " *Train on Line*," in answer to the message, " *Train will Start.*"

169

8.—Immediately on arrival of the Train at Station B (but not until the Signalman has satisfied himself that the whole of the Train has arrived, by seeing the Tail Lamp or special Train Target or lamp on the last vehicle), the peg must be removed from the handle of the instrument, and Station B must call Station A, and give one beat with the needle to the right, which will indicate "Train has arrived," and which Station A must acknowledge to Station B in the same manner.

9.—If the Line is not clear from Station A to Station B when Station A asks the question in the manner described, the reply to that effect must be immediately returned by Station B to Station A by giving eight steady and distinct beats to the left, and the needle at B must then be blocked over to the left, and it must remain in that position until the Line is clear, when the peg must be removed from the handle, and the instrument be left free for a repetition of the enquiry.

10.—On Station A receiving the reply from Station B, as above, it will be the duty of the person in charge of the instrument at Station A to watch it until the needle is restored to its upright position. The question, "*Is Line clear?*" must then be repeated by Station A to B ; and under no circumstances whatever, (other than as described in Rule 19) is the Train to be started until the reply is received at A " *Yes, Line clear*" (as provided in Rule 6), and Station B has in reply to the signal, " *Train will start*" (indicated as provided in Clause 7), blocked his needle over to " *Train on Line.*"

11.—Before the Train is permitted to pass or start from Station B for Station C, Station B must ask Station C the question, "*Is Line clear?*" (as provided in Rule 5.) If the Line is clear, Station C must give "*Line clear,*" and block his instrument (as provided in Rule 7), before the Train may pass or leave Station B, and the same regulations apply from Station to Station throughout the journey.

12.—The time at which "*Line clear*" is received, time of departure of the Train, and time of receipt of the signal, " *Train has arrived,*" must be carefully entered in the "Line Clear Book," kept at the Stations, and the signature of the Station Master or Signalman must be placed opposite the entries. The book must always be left open in a convenient position near the instrument.

13.—Should anything occur at or between Stations, by which the Line is blocked, so as to prevent, or render dangerous, the passing of a Train, the Stations on both sides the block must be immediately advised thereof by first calling attention, and then giving eight distinct beats of the needle to the left, and the needles must then be blocked over to " *Train on Line*" until the obstruction has been removed, when the brass pegs must be taken out of the handles and the needles restored to their upright position.

14.—The person Telegraphing the state of the Line, must at all times satisfy himself before he replies "*Line clear,*" that, in addition to the ordinary or special Trains, the line is also clear from any Trucks, &c., which may have been sent out during the Engineer's occupation. He must also be assured, as provided in Clause 8, that no Train has been divided, and only part of it brought into the Station, the remainder being left on the Line, as may occasionally occur with heavy Trains.

15.—Should it ever happen that the Block Telegraph instrument is out of order, the Station in advance must be signalled to on the Single Needle instrument, when the following rules must be observed :—

(1.) When a Train is ready to leave the question to the next Station will be thus, "*Is Line clear?*"

(2.) If the Line is clear, the answer in this case must be " *Yes, clear.*" Both the above questions and answers must be sent in full, entered in the Book kept for that purpose, and timed before the Train is allowed to proceed.

170

(3.) As soon as a Train has started, after the receipt of "*Yes, clea*■." "*T*■*ain Off,*" must be telegraphed to the next Station. The Officer in charge of the Station to which the Train is running must, as soon as he has satisfied himself that the whole of the Train has arrived, telegraph back "*Up T*■*ain In,*" or "*Down T*■*ain In,*" as the case may be.

(4.) Should the Line **not** be clear the answer in this case must be "**No, Blocked!**" and the Train must **not** be permitted to start or pass. When the message "*Line clea*■." is received from the Station that returned "*No, Blocked!*" the question "*Is Line clea*■ *?*" must be again asked, and, if "*Line clea*■" is received the Train may be sent on.

16.—When a Ballast Engine, Ballast Train, or other plant, leaves Station **A**, after Station **B** has given "*Line clea*■" to **A**, and does **not go so** far as **Station B**, but **returns to** Station **A**, Station **B** must be informed of the return of the Ballast Engine, Ballast Train, or other plant, to Station **A**, by means of the Single Needle Telegraph Instruments, and Station **B** may then release the Telegraph Needles at **A** and **B** from "*Train on Line*" to their upright position.

The same regulation must be adopted when any other Train started from **A** fails to reach **B**, but returns to **A**.

17.—Every Message **affecting the working of the line,** is to be entered in the " Telegraph Message Book" before the Message is sent, and the Receiving Station must Repeat it to the Forwarding Station as a proof of its Receipt and correct transmission, and the time of such repetition is to be entered in the Telegraph Message Book, both by the Forwarding and Receiving Stations. Such Messages and Repeats are to bear the special prefix "S. R." (Repeated Messages) which will entitle them to take precedence of all others, except "**D. G's.**" (Danger Messages).

18.—In the event of the Block and Speaking Telegraph Instruments being out of order, the Trains must be worked on the Train Staff and Ticket System only.

Special Notices.

19.—All Drivers of Special Engines or Special Trains must be furnished before leaving the Terminal Station with a Dispatch Note, carefully filled up with the description and time of the Train or Engine, signed by the Station Master (or, in his absence, by the person in charge) issuing the same, showing the destination of the Train or Engine.

20.—The Guards before starting from a Block Telegraph Station, must ascertain from the Station Master, or man in charge, that the Line is clear to to the next Station.

21.—The Station Masters must each morning carefully examine the entries of the previous day in the Line Clear Books, and attach their Signature at the foot thereof, in proof of such examination. Should they discover any omission, or incorrect entry, a full report of the same must at once be made to the Superintendent of the South Devon Line.

These Telegraph Instructions cancel those previously issued to Stations between Marsh Mills and Lidford.

C. E. COMPTON,
Superintendent South Devon Railway.

29th April, 1876.

The late E.J. Thomas senior, a member of Yelverton Station staff for 45 years
(and his dog, a member for a little less time!)
Courtesy Mrs. E.J. Thomas

The late E.J. Thomas junior, former lad porter and signalman for Yelverton with
Les Allen, relief signalman at Horrabridge Station.
Courtesy Mrs. E.J. Thomas

Launceston Station Staff, thought to have been taken shortly before World War II.
They are from left to right:
Rear Row: Jim Walters District Inspector, Oscar Kitts, Passenger Guard (GWR), Sid Webber Passenger Guard (GWR), Jack Osborne Parcel Porter, Harry Nelder Signalman, Fred Coombe Porter, Dick Parkhouse Goods Porter, Jack Endacott Clerk (Chaplins), Albert Vodden Goods Guard, Bill Manning Relief Signalman, Ted Andrews Checker, Fred Wright Porter, Jack Chilcott Goods Guard, Mr. Passmore W.H. Smith Bookstall Manager, Mr. Palk Cattle Inspector (District).
Front Row: Hughie Godbeer Signalman, Horace Martin Shunter, Harry Bishop Porter, Fred Manning Goods Clerk, Francis Parkhouse Goods Clerk, Walter Greenslade Station Master, Claude Sowden Booking Clerk, Monty Phillips Booking Clerk, Tiny (Dog), Sydney Mitchell Parcels Porter, Charlie Bradford Checker, Wesley (Ginger) Sleep Porter
C. Barrett Collection

LAUNCESTON BRANCH.

Motor Trolley System of Permanent Way Maintenance.

The instructions on pages 65-68 of the General Appendix apply :—
Telephones and key boxes are fixed as under :—

Group 1 (one key)			Group 2 (one key)			Group 3 (one key)		
	m.	ch.		m.	ch.		m.	ch.
Marsh Mills	0	19	Bickleigh	4	8	Yelverton	7	35
Lee Moor Crossing	1	9	Key Box No. 3	5	17	Key Box No. 5 ..	8	29
Key Box No. 1 ..	2	10	Key Box No. 4	6	33	Horrabridge	8	77
Key Box No 2 ..	3	10	Yelverton	7	35			
Bickleigh	4	8						

Group 4 (one key)			Group 5 (one key)			Group 6 (one key)		
	m.	ch.		m.	ch.		m.	ch.
Horrabridge	8	77	Tavistock	12	69	Lydford ..	19	40
Key Box No. 6 ..	9	70	Key Box No. 9	13	66	Key Box No. 15	20	10
Key Box No. 7 ..	10	53	Key Box No. 10	14	52	Key Box No. 16	20	60
Key Box No. 8 ..	11	60	Key Box No. 11	15	38	Key Box No. 17	21	44
Tavistock	12	69	Marytavy	16	23	Key Box No. 18	22	28
			Key Box No. 12	17	10	Key Box No. 19	23	12
			Key Box No. 13	17	73	Coryton ..	23	76
			Key Box No. 14	18	56	Key Box No. 20	24	60
			Lydford	19	40	Key Box No. 21	25	43
						Key Box No. 22	26	27
						Lifton	27	14

Group 7 (one key)		
	m.	ch.
Lifton	27	14
Key Box No. 23	27	65
Key Box No. 24	28	40
Key Box No. 25	29	27
Key Box No. 26	30	11
Key Box No. 27	31	0
Launceston	31	67

NOTE.—The telephones communicate with the following Signalmen :—
Groups 1 and 2 with Bickleigh.
Group 3 with Yelverton.
Groups 4 and 5 with Tavistock.
Group 6 with Lydford.
Group 7 with Launceston.

Three Gangs are employed, and the Home Stations and sections of lines for which they are responsible are:—

Home Station.			Section.
Yelverton	..	..	Marsh Mills to Horrabridge (inclusive).
Tavistock	..	..	Horrabridge to Lydford (inclusive).
Lifton	..	..	Lydford to Launceston.

MARSH MILLS.

The Regulations on page 35, under "Shunting at Stations," apply.

Shunting towards Tavistock Junction.

As far as possible, shunting operations must not involve fouling the Main Line, and the traffic on the trains must be so arranged to admit of the operations taking place to and from the Shunt Spur. In the event of it being necessary to occupy the Main Line towards Tavistock Junction, the permission of the Marsh Mills Signalman must first be obtained. When the work is completed and the train is ready to leave, it may start from the Siding on receipt of verbal instructions or hand signal from the Marsh Mills Signalman.

An engine and not more than fifteen wagons may be worked from Marsh Mills to Tavistock Junction without a brake van in the rear, provided in all cases the engine is at the Plymouth end, and the provisions of Rule 153 (b) are carried out. Before the train leaves Marsh Mills a proper understanding must be arrived at by the Signalman at Marsh Mills and Tavistock Junction, and also between the Trainmen.

Catch Points.

Catch points have been fixed at the Bickleigh end of the Down Loop, and act as a trap point to Down trains. The points are connected to the Box, and the Signalman must not reverse the Loop Facing points, neither must the Single line be fouled for shunting purposes, until he has received "Train out of Section" from Bickleigh and the "Blocking back outside Home Signal" signal has been offered to and accepted by Bickleigh Box.

Dartmoor China Clay Co.'s Sidings.

The Sidings are on a rising gradient of 1 in 40 from Marsh Mills, and the engine working the traffic must be at the Marsh Mills end of the trucks in all cases.

A notice board is fixed at the point marked "X" on the sketch below, and engines may proceed up to "X" with inwards traffic. Outwards loaded traffic will be picked up from the Siding marked "E".

The points at "B" have been coupled to the Catch point "Z," with normal position for the Siding "C," in which position they will be padlocked, and before a train leaves Marsh Mills for the Sidings. the Porter must obtain the key of padlock from the Signal Box, place the points referred to in the reverse position, and, after satisfying himself that all is clear for the train to proceed to the Sidings, give the necessary hand signal to the Guard. The Porter will be responsible for seeing the points are again locked in the normal position when the train leaves for Marsh Mills.

When propelling wagons to the Sidings, the Guard must ride on the leading vehicle, and keep a sharp look-out. He must not detach the engine until he has properly secured the trucks.

The speed of the train when being propelled, must not exceed five miles per hour, and the load must not exceed ten wagons.

A spring Catch point worked by hand lever is provided for the protection of the Marsh Mills Yard, and the Guard, before closing this Catch point for the passage of a train from the Dartmoor China Clay Co.'s Sidings to our Sidings, must satisfy himself that all is clear in the Yard for the train to proceed.

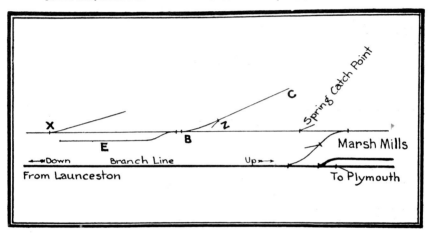

Traffic to and from Plym Bridge Platform.

On Bank Holidays and other days authorised by special notice, rail auto cars may work from Marsh Mills to Plym Bridge Platform and back under the following instructions.

1. The rail car may enter the Marsh Mills-Bickleigh Electric Train Staff Section, in accordance with Electric Train Token Regulation 8A.

2. The Loop points at Marsh Mills must remain set for the Down Loop and the Catch point remain open until the return rail car comes to a stand at the Up Home Signal, after which the Loop points may be set for the Up Loop.

3. Whilst the rail car is in the Marsh Mills–Bickleigh Section, the Down Home Signal for Marsh Mills must be kept at Danger until any Down train has been brought to a dead stand at the signal, when the signal may be lowered to admit the train to the platform.

It is essential that all concerned should come to a complete understanding.

LEE MOOR LEVEL CROSSING.

Situate between Marsh Mills and Bickleigh Stations.

1. A Gateman will be on duty at this crossing (week days only) from the passing of the first until the passing of the last train of Tram Wagons. He may be absent for meals in accordance with his duty paper.

2. An electric indicator and bell are fixed at Lee Moor Level Crossing Signal Box, to shew when a train has left Bickleigh or Marsh Mills, as the case may be.

3. After the indicator shews "Up train on line," or "Down train on line," no Tram wagons or vehicles of any kind, nor any animals, must, under any circumstances, be allowed to pass over or foul the line of railway until after such train has passed.

4. Before Tram Wagons, or horses, are allowed to pass over, or foul the railway at Lee Moor, the Up and Down Signals worked from Lee Moor Level Crossing must be placed at "Danger," and be so kept until the line is again clear.

5. Before the Gateman at the crossing leaves duty, the crossing gates must be locked across the Tramway, and all signals be put to show "All right." The Signal Box must be locked up, and the key of it kept in the custody of the level crossing Gateman.

BICKLEIGH.
Traffic to and from Shaugh Bridge Platform.
On Bank Holidays and other days authorised by special notice, rail auto cars may work from Bickleigh to Shaugh Bridge and back, and may enter the Bickleigh-Yelverton Electric Train Staff Section, in accordance with Electric Train Token Regulation 8A. It is essential that all concerned should come to a complete understanding.

YELVERTON.
Shunting Princetown Trains.
1. At Yelverton the engine must be run around the coaches of the Princetown train in the following manner :—
2. After the passengers have left the coaches the train must be pushed towards Dousland, clear of the Siding leading to the turntable.
3. The train must then be stopped, and after the coaches have been secured by means of the brake, the engine must be detached and run into the Turntable Siding. The coaches may then be allowed to drop down to the platform clear of the points leading to the turntable, where they must stand until the engine is attached to them.
4. During the time the coaches are being moved in the manner described, the points must be set for the Dead End, so that the coaches cannot foul the Main line.
5. When shunting Mixed trains and trains of unusual length, the points must be set for the Main line, instead of the Dead End, before dropping the train down to the platform, and the Guard must not drop the train down before he has asked for and received a signal from the Signalman that the points are right, and the line is clear.
6. As the line falls rapidly towards the junction, it is of the utmost importance that the coaches should be let down to the platform very cautiously, and the Guard of the Princetown Branch trains will be held responsible for carrying out this work.

Down Shunt Siding.
The Down Refuge Siding at Yelverton is for the purpose of putting away Divided Down trains, also when a train is assisted in the rear by a second engine intended to travel with the train beyond Yelverton, for such train to be backed into the Siding, while the assistant engine is run to the head of the train either on the Up or Down line, also for Goods traffic for and from Princetown Branch.

Conveyance of Goods Traffic to Princetown.
If to facilitate the transit of important General Goods traffic to Princetown it should be necessary to put wagons off at Yelverton the following arrangements must be followed :—
The traffic must be confined to the Tavistock Goods ex Laira, to go forward by the first available Mixed train from Yelverton. When the Tavistock Goods is assisted by a Bank engine in the rear, the wagons must be formed next to the train engine, but when the train is worked by one engine the wagons must be formed next to and in front of the brake van, and the van shunted on to the Princetown Branch line to stand before any other work is performed.
When the latter arrangement is made, the traffic for Princetown will be dealt with as follows :—
The person in charge of Yelverton must take care that no more wagons are put off in the Refuge Siding than can be conveyed by the Mixed train.
When there is traffic to be picked up from the Refuge Siding at Yelverton, the traffic on the train for Princetown must be placed on the Princetown Branch line attached next to the brake van, and the Guard must see that the wagons, together with the brake van, are properly secured by brakes and sprags before detaching the front part, and going back to pick up the traffic in the Refuge Siding. When the latter traffic has been attached to the engine, etc., the wagons must be drawn out of the Siding and propelled with caution against the train standing on the Princetown Branch. The whole of the train except the van must then be set back, traffic for the Princetown Branch must be placed in the Refuge Siding, and, after the van on the Princetown Branch line is attached, the Freight train may proceed on its journey.
A Goods brake van will work from Princetown on the first available train from that station, and the engine of that train must pick up the wagons in the Refuge Siding on arrival at Yelverton and form them in the Mixed train thence.

Working of Through Coaches Plymouth to Princetown.
The following instructions must be observed in dealing with Through Coaches for Princetown which are put off Down trains at Yelverton :—
1. The coach or coaches must be detached on the Down Loop line at Yelverton, the brake of the coach being put on or vehicle properly secured before it is detached.
2. The Princetown train must then be backed out from the Branch line, drawn through the Up Loop, and backed to the coach, which must be coupled to the train. The engine must then push the train over the Down Loop until clear of the Branch points, when it can be drawn to the Branch platform or despatched direct, as may be necessary.

HORRABRIDGE.
Horse boxes, carriage trucks, and other vehicles must not be detached at this station, or left on the Main line, unless they are properly secured from running down the incline.

Shunting Freight Trains.
When any shunting is being done at Horrabridge, in connection with a Down Freight train, the points for the Down Shunt Siding must always be set for that Siding, and no wagon or part of a train is to be allowed to stand on the Tavistock side of the Siding points.
On arrival at Horrabridge Station all Up Freight trains must be shunted into the Shunt Siding before being uncoupled to do station work.

TAVISTOCK.

Quarry Sidings, between Tavistock and Mary Tavy.

These Sidings are situated between the $14\frac{1}{4}$ m.p. and $14\frac{1}{2}$ m.p. on the Launceston Branch on Up side of the line with facing connection to Down trains. The points are worked from a Ground Frame locked by key on the Electric Train Staff Tavistock-Lydford Section.

There are four Sidings adjoining the Main line, and traffic will be worked to and from Tavistock by Special Engineering Department trains or otherwise. One Siding must be left clear for running round purposes. Shunter to accompany train.

A train proceeding to the Sidings will be signalled forward, and a staff withdrawn under Electric Train Token Regulation 8, and, on arrival, after the train has been drawn into the Sidings clear of the Main line, the points must be set for the trap dead end, as the Sidings are on a falling gradient towards the Main line. All vehicles not being shunted must be properly secured to prevent them moving towards the Main line, and the Shunter must properly secure all wagons left in the Sidings by brakes, and, if necessary, sprags. He must see that the points are in their proper position before giving any hand signal to the Enginemen. The Guard to assist in the shunting operations. The Main line may be fouled in connection with the shunting operations in the Sidings provided the engine is at the Tavistock end.

The load of a train proceeding to the Sidings must not exceed 20 wagons.

Occupation Level Crossing leading to Pitts Cleave Quarry between Tavistock and Mary Tavy (14m. 17ch.)

1. A telephone has been provided at the above level crossing for the use of Messrs Hoare Bros., in connection with the passage of road traffic to and from the Quarry.

2. Before motor lorries or other heavy vehicles are allowed to pass over the crossing, Messrs. Hoare Bros will telephone to the Tavistock Signalman asking whether the crossing can be used, and if the Tavistock-Lydford Section is clear, and permission has not been given for a Down train to leave Tavistock, or an Up train to leave Lydford, the Signalman, provided the "Blocking Back" signal has been sent to and accepted by Lydford, in accordance with Electric Train Token Regulation 16, Clause (*b*) Exception (ii), may give the necessary authority by replying "Crossing may be used." If the Signalman is not in a position to allow the crossing to be used, the reply must be "No" on the telephone.

3. When the crossing operation has been completed, and the gates again closed across the roadway, Messrs. Hoare Bros. must telephone to the Tavistock Signalman and advise him that the line is clear. The "Obstruction removed" signal must then be sent to Lydford, and ordinary working resumed.

4. Trains to and from Quarry Sidings.—The Guard or Shunter on the Train proceeding from Tavistock to the quarry under Electric Train Staff Regulation 8, must, after the train has arrived in the Sidings, so advise the Tavistock Signalman on the telephone provided at the Ground Frame. Should a request be received by the Tavistock Signalman for permission to use the level crossing whilst a train is in the Quarry Sidings, authority may be given, and Clause 2 of these instructions will not then apply. When the train is ready to return from the Quarry Sidings, the Guard or Shunter, before allowing it to come out on to the Branch line, must telephone to the Tavistock Signalman for permission to do so, and this may only be given if the crossing is not in use. Permission must not be given for the level crossing to be used, whilst a train is returning from Quarry Sidings to Tavistock.

LYDFORD.

The line falls towards Mary Tavy and towards Coryton. All Up and Down Freight trains upon arrival, and before any shunting is performed, must be placed in the Refuge Siding clear of the Running lines.

The Guard of any Freight train conveying wagons for the Southern Railway Sidings, must first obtain the padlock key which unlocks the points leading to the Sidings, from the Signalman, and upon the completion of the work, must return the key to the Signalman.

The Guard is responsible for seeing that all wagons are left clear of adjoining lines and securely braked.

This station is an authorised transfer place with the Southern Railway.

LIFTON.

Level Crossing Gates.

The following regulations must be observed for opening and closing the level crossing gates at Lifton :—

When trains are not expected, the normal position of the gates must be across the railway, and when trains are expected the arrangement must be as follows :—

For Passenger trains coming from Launceston, when one Signalman only is on duty, the gates must be closed across the public road three minutes after "Train entering Section" has been received, and when two men are on duty, the gates must be placed across the public road five minutes after "Train entering Section" has been received.

For Passenger trains coming from Lydford, when one Signalman only is on duty, the gates must be placed across the public road ten minutes after "Train entering Section" has been received, and when two men are on duty twelve minutes after this signal has been received.

When there are two men on duty, and a train is expected, one must go to the level crossing gates, and when the Signalman in the Box signals to him that the gates are to be closed, the man in charge of the level crossing gates must at once close them.

Leet Siding.

Is entered by points facing to Down trains, and the points are controlled by a Ground Frame, locked by Annett's Key on the Electric Train Staff. Guards who have to do work at this Siding, must be careful that all wagons for the Siding are put inside the Catch points.

Up Freight trains only will call at this Siding.

Incline situated between	Length of Incline.	Gradient one foot in	Falling towards	Places at which Notice Boards have been fixed and at which trains must stop to put down brakes.	Modifications of or additions to the Standard Instructions for working Inclines.
Branches—*continued.* Marsh Mills and Bickleigh	4 m.	60	Marsh Mills ..	At the Plymouth end of Bickleigh Up platform, 4m. 6ch. Brakes must be picked up at Marsh Mills	**Ascending.**—Assisting engines must be placed behind Down Freight trains at Marsh Mills Station and push them to Yelverton, uncoupled. When such assisting engines are going beyond Yelverton, they must be placed in front of the trains at Yelverton. **Descending.**—Freight trains must not descend these inclines at a higher speed than 20 miles an hour.
Bickleigh and Yelverton ..	3¼ m.	58	Bickleigh ..	At the Plymouth end of Yelverton Up platform, 7m. 32ch.	
Yelverton and Horrabridge	1¾ m.	60	Horrabridge ..	At the Horrabridge end of Yelverton Down platform, 7m. 42ch. Trains must stop to pick up brakes at Horrabridge	Freight trains must not descend this incline at a higher speed than 20 miles an hour.
Horrabridge Station and Walkham Viaduct	1¾ m.	60	Tavistock ..		
Walkham to Grenofen Tunnel and Tavistock	½ m.	60	Horrabridge ..		
Grenofen Tunnel and Tavistock ..	1¾ m.	64	Tavistock ..		
Tavistock and Lydford ..	6 m.	Max. 63 with varying lengths of lesser gradients	Tavistock ..		**Ascending.**—Assisting engines must be placed behind Down Freight trains at Tavistock Station and push them thence to Lydford uncoupled. When such engines are going beyond Lydford they must be placed in front of the trains at that station. **Descending.**—Freight trains must not descend this incline at a higher speed than 20 miles an hour.
Lydford and Coryton ..	4¾ m.	55	Coryton ..	At the Coryton end of Lydford Down platform, 19 m. 45 ch. Trains must stop to pick up brakes at Coryton	
Branches—*continued.* Coryton and 29 mile post ..	4¾ m.	Max. 157 with varying lengths of lesser gradients	Launceston ..		**Ascending.**—Assisting engines must be placed behind Up Freight trains at Lifton Station, and push them thence to Lydford uncoupled. When such engines are going beyond Lydford, they must be placed in front of the trains at that station.
29 mile post and Launceston	2¾ m.	Max. 125 and varying lengths of lesser gradients	Lifton ..		

Launceston Branch.

GROUND FRAMES AND INTERMEDIATE SIDINGS.

Name of Station or Siding.	Where Situated.	By whom Attended.	How Locked.
Lee Moor	Between Marsh Mills and Bickleigh	Crossing Keeper	Tramway Crossing only. Box locked when not in use.
Quarry Siding	Between Tavistock and Mary Tavy	Guard of Train or Shunter	Annett's Key on E.T.S.
Mary Tavy	At Station	"	"
Coryton	"	"	"
Leet	Between Lifton and Launceston	" or Porter	" Box locked when not in use.
Launceston	At Station	" " or Porter	Bolt locked. Box locked when not in use.
Dousland	" "	Signalman or Porter-Signalman	Electrically locked from Signal Box. Standard Key of Cabin kept in Signal Box.
Swell Tor	Between Dousland and Princetown	Guard of Train	Annett's Key on E.T.S. Box locked when not in use by Annett's Key.
Tavistock Junction	Crossover Road, West End	Shunter	Electrically locked from Signal Box. Standard Key of Cabin kept in Signal Box.

WORKING OF SINGLE LINES.

FROM	TO	Description of Staff, etc. Colour.	Description of Staff, etc. Shape.	Where Electric Train Token or Train Staff and Tickets are kept.	Persons at Station or Junction responsible for exchanging Token or Ticket when on duty.	Person responsible when aforesaid man is not on duty.	REMARKS.
Marsh Mills	Bickleigh	Electric Staff	—	Signal Box, Marsh Mills	Signalman	Porter Signalman	
Bickleigh	Yelverton	"	—	Signal Box, Bickleigh	"	"	
Yelverton	Horrabridge	"	—	Signal Box, Yelverton	"	"	
Horrabridge	Tavistock	"	—	Signal Box, Horrabridge	"	"	
Tavistock	Lydford	"	—	Signal Box, Tavistock	"	"	
Lydford	Lifton	"	—	Signal Box, Lydford Booking Office Lifton	"	"	
Lifton	Launceston	"	—	Signal Box, Launceston	S.R. Signalman	"	

COUPLING AND UNCOUPLING OF ENGINES OF PASSENGER TRAINS EXCEPT WHERE OTHERWISE SHOWN.

The following arrangements will apply to the coupling and uncoupling of engines in the Plymouth Division.

Station.	Work performed by Fireman.	Work performed by Traffic Department.
Yelverton	Main Line and Branch Departure	
Tavistock	Departure	Arrival and Shunting.
Launceston	Departure	
North Road	Arrival and Departure	Shunting.
Millbay	Departure (Loaded or Empty)	Arrival and Shunting.

WHISTLING AT LEVEL CROSSINGS.

Drivers of all trains must sound their whistles when approaching the following places :—

Where Whistles **must** be sounded.	Position, and whether Whistle Boards provided.
Launceston Branch.	
Marsh Mills	Whistle Board for Down trains.
Horrabridge Station	Whistle Board for Down trains.
Pitts Cleave Crossing	Between Tavistock and Mary Tavy.

STATIONS AT WHICH LOOSE SCREW COUPLINGS ARE KEPT—PLYMOUTH DIVISION.

Referring to page 145 of the General Appendix, Emergency Loose Screw Couplings are provided at the following Stations :—

Station.	Number of Couplings.			Station.	Number of Couplings.		
		Type.				Type.	
	4	5	6		4	5	6
Yelverton	—	1	—				
Princetown	1	—	—				
Horrabridge	—	1	—				
Tavistock	1	5	4				
Lydford	1	—	—				
Lifton	1	—	—				
Coryton	—	1	—				
Launceston	—	2	—				
North Road	—	6	6				
Millbay	5	6	—				

INSTRUCTIONS AND RESTRICTIONS WITH REGARD TO WORKING OF 70 FOOT STOCK.

Station.	Line over which 70 foot stock must not pass.	Line over which 70 foot stock must pass with caution.
	Launceston Branch.	
Marsh Mills	Messrs. Hoares Sidings.	
Horrabridge	Back Shunt from Up Refuge.	
Tavistock	Crossover Up Loop to Down Platform	Down Main to Goods Shed (north end).
Lydford	Transfer Shed.	Down Shunt to No. 2 Siding.

Between what Stations.		Up or Down Lines	Where situated.	If connected with and worked from the Signal Box.	Gradient 1 in	Signal Box. when Lever Clip and Padlock are kept.
From	To					
			Tavistock Branch.			
At Marsh Mills	Bickleigh ..	Down Loop	Bickleigh end of Down Loop ..	Yes	100	Marsh Mills
At Bickleigh ..		Down Loop	Opposite Signal Box and Yelverton end of Down Loop.	No	60	Bickleigh.
At Yelverton ..		Down	Bickleigh end of Down Loop ..	Yes	66	Yelverton.
At Horrabridge		Up	Yelverton end of Up Loop ..	Yes	104	Horrabridge.

STATIONS IN PLYMOUTH DIVISION WHERE RE-RAILING RAMPS ARE KEPT.

Station.	Where stored.
Tavistock Junction	In Lamp Room.
Yelverton	Under stairs, Down Platform.
Tavistock	In Weighbridge House.
Launceston	In Guard's Room.
Laira	Shunting Truck.
North Road	West end of No. 7 Platform.
Millbay	One in receptacle of Yard Shunting Truck, and one at Passenger Station near Lamp Room.

LIST OF PUBLIC LEVEL CROSSINGS.

Name of Crossing.	Where Situated.		Whether Block Post.	If not a Block Post whether Gatekeeper Indicators, or Bells are provided.	Whether there are signals.	Whether the Gates are interlocked with the Signals.
	Between	And				
Launceston Branch.						
Horrabridge ..	At Horrabridge Station		,,	—	,,	,,
Lifton	At Lifton Station..		,,	—	,,	,,

PROVISION OF ASSISTING ENGINES.

Where Stationed.	Points between which Assisting Engines may be used.	Up or Down Trains.	Special Instructions.
	Launceston Branch.		
Laira	Marsh Mills and Yelverton ..	Down	See page 21.
,, ...	Tavistock and Lydford	Down	See page 21.
,, ...	Lifton and Lydford..	Up	See page 21.

Stations in the Plymouth Division where Engines can take Water

Station.	Where Cranes, etc., are situated.
Bickleigh	Down Platform.
Yelverton..	Down Platform and Princetown Branch Line.
Princetown	Locomotive Engine Shed.
Horrabridge	Up and Down Platforms.
Tavistock	Up and Down Platforms and Turntable.
Lydford	Up and Down Platforms.
Launceston	Locomotive Engine Shed.

HALTS AT WHICH STAFF IS NOT KEPT.

The following are the halts where staff is not kept, and the supervision of these halts comes under the Station Master at the Station shown below. The Station Master must visit the halts from time to time, to see that the premises are in proper condition, and that gates, notice boards, shelters, seats, etc., are in order :—

Name of Halt.	Station supervising Halt.
Plym Bridge	Bickleigh.
Shaugh Bridge	Bickleigh.
Clearbrook	Yelverton.
Liddaton	Coryton.
Burrator	Yelverton.

HALTS, CLEANING, LIGHTING, Etc.

The Engineering Department will see that the Halts and Platforms where no staff are employed are kept clean, and the Platforms sprinkled with sand when necessary. Guards will be held responsible for calling attention to any cases where these places are dirty, or to any unusual circumstance such as damaged lamp glasses, disfigured notice boards, etc.

ENGINE TURNTABLES.

Station.	Diameter.		Where situated.
	Ft.	In.	
Laira	65	0	In Engine Shed.
North Road West	65	0	In triangle.
Princetown	23	6	In Engine Shed.
Yelverton	23	6	Near South end of Station (Princetown Branch).
Tavistock	45	0	South end of Yard.
Launceston	45	0	Entrance to Engine Shed.

PERMANENT WAY TROLLIES.

Trollies going through the undermentioned tunnels must be signalled in accordance with Regulation 9 of the Block Telegraph Instructions :—

Tunnel.	Situated between.
Yelverton..	Yelverton and Horrabridge (Launceston Branch).
Grenofen	Horrabridge and Tavistock (Launceston Branch).

HEAD LAMPS FOR G.W. TRAINS TRAVELLING OVER SOUTHERN RAILWAY.

Add :

When it is necessary to divert G.W. Company's trains, irrespective of Class, over the Southern Company's line between Exeter (St. David's) and Plymouth (North Road) or Plymouth (Millbay) via Lydford and/or between Exeter (St. David's) and Wadebridge via Lydford and Launceston, distinctive head lamps must be carried as shewn below :—

1. Between Exeter (St. David's) and Plymouth (North Road) or Plymouth (Millbay) via Lydford in both directions.

2. Between Exeter (St. David's) and Wadebridge via Lydford and Launceston in both directions.

Before entering upon the Southern Railway maintenance the head lamps should be altered as follows :

DOWN TRAINS.

Down trains leaving Exeter (St. David's) for Southern Railway to carry head lamps in accordance with the above instructions.

The standard head lamps applicable to the train concerned must be changed or restored, as the case may be, at Lydford and Launceston.

UP TRAINS.

Up trains leaving Wadebridge for the Southern Railway must carry head lamps in accordance with the above-mentioned instructions. Up trains leaving Plymouth (Millbay) or Plymouth (North Road) must carry the standard head lamps applicable to the train concerned when travelling over G.W. Company's maintenance. The standard head lamps applicable to the train concerned must be changed or restored, as the case may be, at Launceston, Lydford and Exeter (St. David's).

ARRANGEMENT OF INSPECTORS DISTRICTS.

Amend :

Totnes...... Mileage of 222 miles 23 chains to read 222 miles 20 chains.

WORKING OF SINGLE LINES.

Amend :

From	To	Description of Staff, etc.		Where Electric Train Token or Train Staff and Tickets are kept	Persons at stations or Junction responsible for exchanging Token or Ticket when on duty	Person responsible when aforesaid man is not on duty	Remarks
		Colour	Shape				
Lifton	Launceston	—	Electric Token	Booking Office, Lifton. Signal Box, Launceston	Signalman S.R. Signalman	— —	An auxiliary Token Instrument is provided at Launceston near the "From S.R. line to Up G.W Line" Starting Signal. (See page 84.)

LAUNCESTON.

Insert :

Connection between Great Western and Southern Company's Lines.

The facing points (to the G.W. Company's Down Branch trains) at 31 m. 33¼ ch., also the catch point in the connection at the G.W. end, are worked from Launceston Signal Box and are operated by motor.

An Auxiliary Electric Train Token Instrument has been provided for the Launceston—Lifton Token Section and is situated in a hut between the G.W. single line and the connection to the S.R. line at the "From S.R. line to Up G.W." Starting signal.

The Electric Train Token for Down and Up G.W. trains, also for trains passing over the connection to the S.R. line is dealt with by the Signalman. When, however, a G.W. train from the S.R. line has to stand at the "From S.R. Line to G.W. Up" Starting signal waiting "Line Clear" the Fireman must obtain a Token from the Auxiliary Instrument in accordance with the instruction shewn on page 43 of the General Appendix to the Rule Book.

The following alterations and additions to No. 6 Appendix will apply and the necessary corrections and additions must be made on the pages indicated:

GROUND FRAMES AND INTERMEDIATE SIDINGS

Page 4

Name of Siding	Where situated	By whom attended	How locked
Add : Tavistock Gas Co. Siding	Bewtween Whitchurch Down and Tavistock	Guard of train or shunter	Annett's key on E.T.S.

INCLINES STEEPER THAN 1 in 200

Incline situated between	Falling towards	Modification of or additions to Standard Instructions for working inclines
Page 15 Hemerdon and Tavistock Junction	Plympton	Descending—The instruction that " Freight trains must not descend the incline at more than 20 miles per hour ", will apply to " K ", " J " and " H " Head-lamp trains only.
Page 21 Launceston Branch. Marsh Mills and Bickleigh	Marsh Mills	Ascending—Instructions amended as follows : "Assisting engines must be coupled to rear of Down Freight trains at Marsh Mills Station and assist to Yelverton. When such assisting engines are going beyond Yelverton, they must be placed in front of the trains at Yelverton.

TAVISTOCK.

Page 84.

Add :

Gas Company's Private Siding.

The private siding for the Tavistock Gas Company is situated at 12m. 49½c. between Whitchurch Down Platform and Tavistock and has trailing connection to Down trains. It accommodates 10 wagons and the following working arrangements apply :

1. The points are worked from a two-lever ground frame locked by Key on the Electric Train Staff for the Horrabridge—Tavistock section.

2. Traffic at the siding will be dealt with to and from Tavistock in accordance with E.T.T. Regulation 8A

3. Not more than 10 wagons may be propelled to the siding from Tavistock without a brake van and at a speed not exceeding 5 miles per hour. Guard or Shunter to ride on leading or nearest most suitable vehicle and keep a sharp lookout. Not more than 10 wagons may be drawn from the siding to Tavistock Station without a brake van in accordance with Rule 153(b).

4. The engine must be kept at the Tavistock end of the vehicles and whilst in the section the points at Tavistock must be kept set for the middle siding until the engine or engine and vehicles have returned and have been brought to a stand at the Down Home signal.

5. The siding must not be worked during darkness nor during fog or falling snow.

J. H. PARKER,

Plymouth, July 17th, 1939   198—4,300.   **District Traffic Manager.**

GREAT WESTERN RAILWAY

(For the use of the Company's Employees only)

PLYMOUTH DISTRICT

LAUNCESTON—

Signal Alterations and bringing into use New Connection between Great Western and Southern Companies Lines.

SUNDAY, SEPTEMBER 19th, 1943.

A new connection will be brought into use between the Great Western and Southern Companies lines as shewn on the attached sketch.

The following new signals will be brought into use :

Form	Description	Position	Distance from Box yards
A	From S. R. Line to G.W.R. Up Main Starting.	Up side of Up S.R. Line	601
B	1. Down Main Home. 2. Down Main to S.R. Line Home.	Down side of Down Main Line.	730
C	Up Main Outer Advanced Starting.	Down side of Up Main Line.	982

The existing Down Main Home signal will become the Down Main Intermediate Home signal.

An Auxiliary Token Instrument for the Launceston-Lifton Section will be provided in a suitable hut, situated between the Up and Down Main Line and the new S.R. Line at the Up S.R. Line to Up G.W. Line Starting signal.

TELEPHONES.

Telephonic communication will be provided between Launceston Signal Box and the Auxiliary Token Instrument and the Down Main Home signals.

TRACK CIRCUITS.

The following track circuits will be brought into use on Sunday, September 19th, 1943:

Line	Length and Position of Track	Position of Diamond Shaped Sign	Signals Locked When Track Circuit Occupied	Whether Block controlled	Whether Vehicle on Line Switch provided
Up & Down G.W. and from S.R. Line	110 yards through facing connections Track No. 11T.	—	G.W. Up Advanced Starting. From S.R. to G.W. Up Starting. G.W. Down Home. From G.W. to S.R. Home. (Approach locks from S.R. to G.W. Up Starting. G.W. Down Home. From G.W. to S.R. Home)	No	No
From S.R. to G.W.	341 yards to rear of From S.R. to G.W. Up Starting. Track No.3.A.T.	On signal	From G.W. to S.R. Home.	No	No
Up & Down G.W. Line	272 yards between Down G.W. Homes and Up Outer Advanced Starting. Track No. 16.A.T.	On Signal	G.W. Up Advanced Starting. From S.R. to G.W. Up Starting.	No	No

The existing Launceston East Ground Frame will be taken out of use.

Occupation of the Locking Frame will be required for the purpose of testing interlocking between the G.W. and S.R. Lever Frames.

This work will be carried out between the hours of 7.0 a.m. and 6.0 p.m. on Sunday, September 19th, 1943, or until completed, and all arrangements for safe working, including the appointment of handsignalmen, will be made by District Inspector Selley.

ALL CONCERNED TO PLEASE NOTE AND ACKNOWLEDGE RECEIPT

J. S. P. PEARSON,
District Traffic Manager.

Plymouth, September 13th, 1943.   301—1,400

Received District Traffic Manager's Notice No. B.828 re Launceston Signal Alterations, etc.

Γate................... Station.................... Signature.................

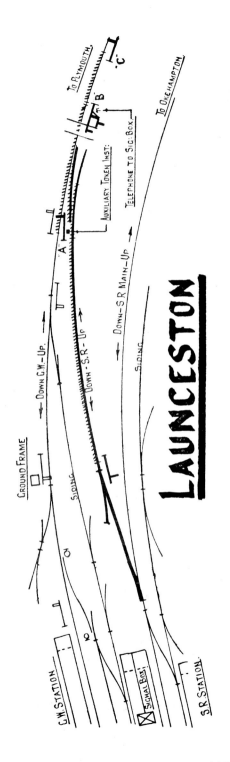

SINGLE LINE LOOPS AT STATIONS.

Station.	Length in feet.		Station.	Length in feet.	
	Up.	Down.		Up.	Down.
Launceston Branch.					
Bickleigh	980	904			
Yelverton	719	719			
Horrabridge	397	442			
Tavistock	946	962			
Lydford	567	595			
Lifton	510	604			

REFUGE SIDINGS AND RUNNING LOOPS.

Station.	Up or Down.		Number of Wagons Siding holds in addition to large Engine and Van.		When closed and not available for use.
	Down.	Up.	Down.	Up.	
Bickleigh	1	1	24	21	
Yelverton	1	–	25	—	
Horrabridge	1	1	35	44	‡ Between Catch Points 59.
Lydford	1	1	26	43	

142 No. 6

Engine Restrictions—continued.
BRANCHES—continued.

Section of Line.	Engines Authorised.	Prohibitions.
Yelverton	Connection to Princetown Branch ..	28XX, 30XX, 42XX, 52XX, 72XX, Austerity 2–8–0, L.M.R. 2–8–0.
Yelverton, exclusive, to Launceston.	Uncoloured	—
	" Yellow " 2–6–2T	2251 Class.
	45XX specially authorised ..	—
Tavistock Jct. to Yelverton, inclusive.	All classes except 60XX and 47XX..	**Marsh Mills—Clay Works Siding.**—No engine heavier than 45XX permitted, or 94XX.

138 No. 6

Speed of Trains through Junctions and at other Specified Places—continued.

NAME OF PLACE.	DIRECTION OF TRAIN.		Miles per Hour.
	From	To	
Tavistock and Launceston Branch.			
The speed of all Up and Down trains between 45 miles per hour and for the remainder of	Lifton and Launceston, 27¼ m.p. and 31¼ m.p., must not exceed Branch 40 miles per hour, with the following further restrictions :—		
Tavistock Junction	Main Line	Branch Line	10
Tavistock Junction	Branch Line	Main Line	10
Bickleigh	All Up Trains	.. ..	20
Yelverton	All Up Trains	.. ..	20
Horrabridge	All Down Trains	.. ..	20
Tavistock	All Up and Down Trains ..	.. ..	20
Lydford	All Up Trains	.. ..	20
Lydford and Coryton (between 19m. 40c. and 22 m.p.)	All Up and Down Trains	.. ..	35

STANDARD LOADS OF PASSENGER, PARCELS, MILK AND FISH TRAINS FOR ENGINE WORKING PURPOSES—continued,

BRANCH LINES.

SECTION.		CLASS OF ENGINE.								
From	To	10XX, 100,111 4000, 4016, 4032, 4037 4073- 4099 5000- 5099 70XX	4003- 4072 (except 4016, 4032 and 4037) 39XX, 49XX, 59XX, 69XX, 68XX.	29XX 78XX 43XX 53XX 63XX 73XX 93XX 31XX 41XX 51XX 61XX 81XX 56XX 66XX	4400–4410, 4500–4599, 5500–5574.	3335–3455	90XX 2200– 2299. 32XX 0–6–2T "B" Group.	0–6–0 and 0–6–0T. 0–6–2T. "A" Group.	2–4–0T Metro. 0–4–2T 14XX 58XX 844– 896	0–4–2T. 3574 3575 3577 1334 1335 1336
		Tons	Tons	Tons	Tons	Tons	Tons	Tons	Tons	Tons
Plymouth ...	Yelverton ...	325	285	240	220	220	—	190	—	—
Yelverton ...	Launceston ...	—	—	—	240	—	—	190	—	—
Launceston ...	Yelverton ...	—	—	—	220	—	—	170	—	—
Yelverton ...	Plymouth ...	420	390	240	220	220	—	170	—	—

LIST OF SIGNAL BOXES.

Distance Box to Box.		NAME OF BOX.	TIMES DURING WHICH BOXES ARE OPEN.					Whether Provided with Switch.
			Week Days.			Sundays.		
			Opened.		Closed at	Opened at	Closed at	
			Mondays.	Other Days.				
—	—	Launceston	—	—	—	—	—	
4	53	Lifton	7. 0 a.m.	7. 0 a.m.	8. 0 p.m. V	As requ|ired	—	No.
7	48	Lydford						
6	54	Tavistock	5.50 a.m.	5.50 a.m.	9. 0 p.m. M 10.40 p.m. M	As requ|ired.	—	No.
3	72	Horrabridge	5.45 a.m.	5.45 a.m.	9.10 p.m. M 10.45 p.m. M	As requ|ired.	—	No
1	42	Yelverton	5.30 a.m.	5.30 a.m.	9.20 p.m. M 11. 0 p.m. M	As requ|ired.	—	No.
—	—	Princetown	7. 0 a.m.	7. 0 a.m.	8.0 p.m.	—	—	No.
8	65	Dousland	7. 0 a.m.	7. 0 a.m.	8.0 p.m.	—	—	No.
1	47	Yelverton		See above.		—	—	No.
3	27	Bickleigh	5.20 a.m.	5.20 a.m.	9.30 p.m. L 11.15 p.m. M	As requ|ired.	—	No.
3	69	Marsh Mills	5.20 a.m.	5.20 a.m.	9.30 p.m. L 11.15 p.m. M	As requ|ired.	—	No.

J—Or until the 6.55 p.m. North Road has entered the Section.   **N**—Or until 7.20 p.m. Penzance clears section.
K—9.35 p.m. Saturdays.   **V**—11.10 p.m. Saturdays.
L—Saturdays excepted.   ‡—10.15 p.m. on Saturdays.
M—Saturdays only.   ¶—10.35 p.m. on Saturdays.

VACUUM-FITTED BALLAST TRAINS.

TAVISTOCK QUARRY TO LAIRA AND KEYHAM.

	Point-to-Point time.	Start.	Stop.
Quarry to Tavistock	3	1	1
Tavistock to Horrabridge	9	1	1
Horrabridge to Yelverton	6	1	1
Yelverton to Bickleigh	7	1	1
Bickleigh to Marsh Mills	7	1	1
Marsh Mills to Laira	2	1	1
Marsh Mills to Keyham	12	1	1

WORKING LOADS. — MAXIMUM ENGINE LOADS.

BRANCH.

X — See page 158 for Engine Loads on these sections for ungrouped engines and group "A" engines having less than 165 lbs. boiler pressure.

ASSISTED TRAINS.—See page 154.

From	To	Maximum number of wagons to be conveyed except for Trains specially provided for in the Service Book or by arrangement.	For Group A Engines.				For Group B Engines.				For Group C Engines.				For Group D Engines.				For Group E Engines.			
			Class 1 Traffic.	Class 2 Traffic.	Class 3 Traffic.	Empties.	Class 1 Traffic.	Class 2 Traffic.	Class 3 Traffic.	Empties.	Class 1 Traffic.	Class 2 Traffic.	Class 3 Traffic.	Empties.	Class 1 Traffic.	Class 2 Traffic.	Class 3 Traffic.	Empties.	Class 1 Traffic.	Class 2 Traffic.	Class 3 Traffic.	Empties.
LAUNCESTON.																						
Launceston	Lydford	45	13	16	20	26	15	18	23	30	16	19	24	32	58	28	70	88				
Lydford	Tavistock	45	35	42	53	60	40	48	60	80	44	53	66	85	70	35	100	84				
Tavistock	Yelverton	45	14	17	21	28	40	20	24	34	44	24	26	38	100	46	84	100				
Yelverton	Laira	45	14	42	53	60	40	48	60	80	44	53	66	85	100	34	100	42				
Laira	Yelverton	45	17	18	23	30	40	20	24	34	44	23	29	38	23		56					
Yelverton	Tavistock	45	15	42	53	60	17	48	60	80	19	53	66	85								
Tavistock	Lydford	45	13		23	30	40	20	26	34	44	23	29	38								
Lydford	Launceston	45																				

D66

Time Allowances for Freight Trains—continued

PLYMOUTH, TAVISTOCK AND LAUNCESTON

DOWN	Allow for Stop. Mins.	Allow for Start. Mins.	Point-to-Point Times. Mins.	UP	Allow for Stop. Mins.	Allow for Start. Mins.	Point-to-Point Times. Mins.
Plymouth	—		—	Launceston S.R.	—		—
Laira Junction	—	2	9	Lifton	—		12
Tavistock Junction	—	—	2	Coryton	—		7
Marsh Mills	—	—	1	Lydford	—	—	15
Bickleigh	—	—	12	Mary Tavy and Blackdown	—	—	7
Yelverton	—	—	12	Tavistock South	—	—	8
Horrabridge	—	—	5	Horrabridge	2	—	11
Tavistock South	2	—	8	Yelverton	—	2	5
Mary Tavy and Blackdown	—	—	9	Bickleigh	—	—	8
Lydford	—	—	9	Marsh Mills	—	—	9
Coryton	—	—	9	Tavistock Junction	—	—	8
Lifton	—	—	7	Laira Junction	—	—	2
Launceston W.R.	—	2	2	Plymouth	—	—	9

TAVISTOCK JUNCTION TO LAUNCESTON (Launceston Branch)

PASSENGER STOCK RESTRICTIONS IN RAiLWAY SIDINGS.

The following instructions apply to the working of Passenger Stock on this Branch:—

STOCK.	SIDING, CROSSOVER, ETC.	PROHIBITED OR DETAILS OF RESTRICTION.
Marsh Mills.		
70 ft. in length and over	Messrs. Hoares Sidings	Prohibited.
Horrabridge.		
70 ft. in length and over	Back Shunt from Up Refuge	Prohibited.
Tavistock South.		
70 ft. in length and over	Crossover Up Loop to Down Platform	Prohibited.
70 ft. in length and over	Down Main to Goods Shed (North End)	Must pass with caution.
Lydford.		
70 ft. in length and over	Transfer Shed	Prohibited.
70 ft. in length and over	Down Shunt to No. 2 Siding	Must pass with caution.

Instructions and Restrictions in regard to Rolling stock in certain Sidings on the Launceston Branch.

Owing to insufficient clearance headroom, etc., covered wagons or open wagons with exceptional loads must not be allowed to work in the following Sidings:—

STATION OR PLACE.	DESCRIPTION OF SIDING.	REASON FOR PROHIBITING.
Marsh Mills ..	Messrs. E.C.L.P. & Co., Siding ..	Insufficient headroom.

MARSH MILLS.

SHUNTING.

When it is necessary for shunting to take place between the Main line and Sidings the men engaged in the shunting must perform the necessary coupling and uncoupling from the space between the Main line and the Station sidings and must not stand between the two running lines.

The signals for controlling shunting operations will be given by means of whistles, and the standard code of audible signals in accordance with Rule 117 will apply.

SHUNTING TOWARDS TAVISTOCK JUNCTION.

As far as possible, shunting operations must not involve fouling the Main Line, and the traffic on the trains must be so arranged to admit of the operations taking place to and from the Shunt Spur.   In the event of it being necessary to occupy the Main Line towards Tavistock Junction, the permission of the Marsh Mills Signalman must first be obtained.   When the work is completed and the train is ready to leave, it may start from the Siding on receipt of verbal instructions or hand signal from the Marsh Mills Signalman.

CATCH POINTS.

Catch points have been fixed at the Bickleigh end of the Down Loop, and act as a trap point to Down trains.

MESSRS. ENGLISH CLAYS LOVERING POCHIN & CO. LTD., PRIVATE SIDINGS.

A diagram showing the layout of the sidings is given below:—

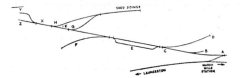

The line between "A"—"Y" and "Z", the loop "E", and the siding "F" are on a rising gradient of 1 in 40 from Marsh Mills and the engine must in all cases be at the Marsh Mills end of the wagons.

The normal position of the points " C " is for the siding " D ", in which position they must be kept clipped and padlocked.

The normal position for the points of the loop " E " is for the line " A "—" Y " and " Z ".

Wheel stops are provided on siding " F " and at the Marsh Mills end of loop " E " and these must normally be kept across the rail.

The normal position of points " G " and " H " is for the Shed Siding and these points must normally be maintained in that position.

Telephone communication has been provided between Marsh Mills signal box, points " C " and the Foreman's Office at the Works.

A diesel locomotive is normally used by the Clay Company for positioning wagons in the various sidings, situated between the points marked " C ", " Y " and " Z ", but traffic will be worked to and brought from the Private Sidings by the Commission's engine and the following instructions must be observed by all concerned:—

INWARDS TRAFFIC.

1.   Before a train leaves Marsh Mills the Signalman must telephone the Works Foreman and obtain his assurance that:

(*a*)   There are no wagons or cattle on the line between " C " and " H " and any wagons which may be between " H " and " Y " or " Z " are fully braked and scotched and points " H " and " G " are set for the Shed Siding.

(*b*)   Any wagons in the loop are fully braked and scotched, the points set normal and the wheel stop at the Marsh Mills end is in position over the rail.

(*c*)   Any wagons in siding " F " are fully braked, the wheel stop is in position over the rail, and the points set for a movement in the direction of " G ".

(*d*)   The diesel engine is in the Shed Siding and clear of the line between " C " and " H ".

2.   On receiving these assurances the Signalman must arrange for a Porter to proceed to points " C ", unclip and reverse them for the train to proceed from " A " towards " X ". When this has been done he must telephone the Signalman accordingly.

3.   The Signalman may then give permission for the train to proceed and until he does so the Guard must not give the " right away " signal to the Driver.

4.   The Guard must ride on the leading vehicle, or the nearest suitable vehicle thereto, and keep a sharp look-out. The standard instructions regarding " Shunting into Private Sidings " must be complied with.

5.   The speed of the train must not exceed five miles per hour and the maximum loads from Marsh Mills Station to the siding are:—

GROUP A ENGINES.				GROUP B ENGINES.				GROUP C ENGINES.			
1	2	3	E	1	2	3	E	1	2	3	E
8	11	16	20	9	12	18	23	10	13	20	25

6.   The train must be brought to a stand well to the rear of points " G ", after which the diesel engine may draw out wagons from the Shed Siding towards " Y " or " Z ", and when that movement comes to a stand and the wagons have been fully braked, the inwards wagons may be propelled beyond points " G " or " H ", as the case may be, where they must be fully braked prior to the Commission's engine being detached and set back clear of those points to enable the inwards wagons to gravitate to or be positioned in the Shed Siding by the diesel engine.

7.   The Commission's engine must not proceed beyond the notice board fixed at " X ", and it must not enter the loop, sidings " F " and " D ", or the connections thereto.

8.   Wagons may be propelled into siding " F " provided there is sufficient number of wagons attached so that the engine will not have to enter the siding or traverse the connection thereto.

OUTWARDS TRAFFIC.

1.   Outwards traffic will be picked up at " X " or the loop siding.   Insofar as the latter is concerned a sufficient number of wagons must be attached so that the engine will not have to enter the siding or traverse the connection thereto.

2.   The standard incline instructions must be complied with, so far as they apply, before descending the incline between " X " and " B ".

3.   The maximum load from the siding to Marsh Mills Station will be the equivalent of 17 Class 1 traffic.

4.   After the train or engine has passed points " C " the Porter will be responsible for seeing that the points are replaced, clipped and padlocked in the normal position.

5.   The train must be brought to a stand at the spring catch point worked by hand lever at " B " and the Guard, before closing the catch point for the train to proceed, must satisfy himself that all is clear in the Marsh Mills Yard.

     When, however, the volume of traffic is such that clauses 1 to 8 shown above under the heading of Inwards Traffic cannot be complied with, the Outwards Traffic must be taken from the sidings to Marsh Mills Station before the Inwards Traffic is berthed.   In this event the following instructions will apply to Outwards Traffic in place of clause 1 above:—

6.   The Outwards Traffic may be positioned between " C " and " G ".

7.   The employees of Messrs. E.C.L.P. & Co. Ltd., will be responsible for seeing that such wagons are fully braked and scotched.

8.   The Porter who unclips the points of " C " to permit the Commission's engine to enter the sidings must before doing so ascertain the exact position of the wagons standing between " C " and " G " and pilot the engine to the wagons.

     In the event of the diesel locomotive not being available to perform the shunting owing to failure or other cause, Messrs. English Clays Lovering Pochin & Co. Ltd., will give prior notice to the Marsh Mills Station Master who must arrange for the Commission's engine to carry out the work, subject to the restrictions shown in the aforementioned instructions, and any wagons to or from the shed siding via points " G " or " H " as the case may be, must be fully braked and scotched when left on the incline before the engine is detached.

HORRABRIDGE.

     Horse boxes, carriage trucks and other vehicles must not be detached at this station or left on the Main line unless they are properly secured from running down the incline.

SHUNTING FREIGHT TRAINS.

     When any shunting is being done at Horrabridge, in connection with a Down Freight train, the points for the Down Shunt Siding must always be set for that Siding, and no wagon or part of a train is to be allowed to stand on the Tavistock South side of the Siding points.

     On arrival at Horrabridge Station all Up Freight trains must be shunted into the Shunt Siding before being uncoupled to do station work.

PITTS CLEAVE QUARRY SIDINGS BETWEEN TAVISTOCK SOUTH AND MARY TAVY.

The Sidings are situated between the 14¼ m.p. and 14½ m.p. on the Launceston Branch on the Up side of the line with facing connection to Down trains. The points are worked from a Ground Frame locked by a key on the Electric Staff Tavistock South—Lydford Section.

There are four sidings adjoining the Main line and whenever possible one siding must be left clear for running round purposes. Traffic will be worked to and from Tavistock South by Special Engineering Department train or otherwise and wagons may be propelled from Tavistock South to the Sidings, but in no circumstances must the load of a train proceeding to the Sidings exceed 20 wagons and brake van.

A Porter stationed at Tavistock South will accompany all special trains proceeding to the Sidings and will assist the Guard in shunting operations.

On arrival of the train at the Sidings, after it has been drawn or propelled into the Sidings clear of the Main line, the points must be set for the trap dead-end, as the Sidings are on a falling gradient towards the Main line. All vehicles not being shunted must be properly secured to prevent them moving towards the Main line and the Guard must properly secure all wagons left in the Sidings by brakes and, if necessary, sprags. He must see that the points are in their proper position before giving any handsignal to the Enginemen. The Main line may be fouled in connection with the shunting operations in the Sidings, provided the engine is at the Tavistock South station end.

OCCUPATION LEVEL CROSSING LEADING TO PITTS CLEAVE QUARRY BETWEEN TAVISTOCK SOUTH AND MARY TAVY (14m. 17ch.).

1.   A telephone has been provided at the above level crossing for the use of Messrs. Hoare Bros. in connection with the passage of road traffic to and from the Quarry.

2.   Before motor lorries or other heavy vehicles are allowed to pass over the crossing, Messrs. Hoare Bros. will telephone to the Tavistock South Signalman and obtain his permission.

3.   Trains to and from Quarry Sidings.—The Guard or Shunter on the train proceeding from Tavistock South to the quarry, must, after the train has arrived in the Sidings, so advise the Tavistock South Signalman on the telephone provided at the Ground Frame. When the train is ready to return from the Quarry Sidings, the Guard or Shunter, before allowing it to come out on to the Branch line, must telephone to the Tavistock South Signalman for permission to do so.

LYDFORD.

The line falls towards Mary Tavy and towards Coryton. All Up and Down Freight Trains upon arrival and before any shunting is performed must be placed in the Refuge Siding clear of the Running lines.

The Guards of any Freight train conveying wagons for the Southern Region Sidings must first obtain the padlock key which unlocks the points leading to the Sidings from the Signalman and upon the completion of the work must return the key to the Signalman.

This station is an authorised transfer place with the Southern Region.

LIFTON.

LEVEL CROSSING GATES.

The following regulations must be observed for opening and closing the level crossing gates at Lifton:—

When trains are not expected, the normal position of the gates must be across the railway, and when trains are expected the arrangement must be as follows:—

For Passenger trains coming from Launceston, when one Signalman only is on duty, the gates must be closed across the public road three minutes after " Train entering Section " has been received, and when two men are on duty, the gates must be placed across the public road five minutes after " Train entering Section " has been received.

For Passenger trains coming from Lydford when one Signalman only is on duty the gates must be placed across the public road ten minutes after " Train entering Section " has been received and when two men are on duty twelve minutes after the signal has been received.

When there are two men on duty, and a train is expected, one must go to the level crossing gates, and when the Signalman in the Box signals to him that the gates are to be closed, the man in charge of the level crossing gates must at once close them.

LAUNCESTON.

CONNECTION BETWEEN THE WESTERN REGION AND SOUTHERN REGION'S LINE.

The Facing points (to the Western Region's Down Branch trains) at 31 miles 33½ chains also the catch point in the connection at the W.R. end are worked from Launceston Signal Box and are operated by motor.

The Electric Token for Down and Up W.R. trains, also for trains passing over the connection to the S.R. line is dealt with by the Signalman.

TABLE J1   INCLINES STEEPER THAN 1 IN 200.

Incline situated between.	Length of Incline.	Ruling Gradient— One in.	Falling towards.	Modifications of, or additions to, the General Instructions for Working Inclines.
TAVISTOCK JUNCTION TO LAUNCESTON.				
Marsh Mills and Bickleigh ..	4 m.	60	Marsh Mills	Ascending page 51
Bickleigh and Yelverton ..	3½ m.	58	Bickleigh ..	Descending page 55
Yelverton and Horrabridge ..	1½ m.	60	Horrabridge	
Horrabridge Station and Walkham Viaduct	1¼ m.	60	Tavistock Sth	
Walkham and Grenofen ..	½ m.	60	Horrabridge	
Grenofen Tunnel and Tavistock South	1¾ m.	60	Tavistock Sth	
Tavistock South and Lydford ..	6 m.	Maximum 64 with varying lengths of lesser gradients	Tavistock Sth	Ascending page 51
Lydford and Coryton	4¼ m.	55	Coryton ..	Ascending page 51 Descending page 55
Coryton and 29 mile post ..	4½ m.	Maximum 140 with varying lengths of lesser gradients	Launceston	
29 mile post and Launceston ..	2¾ m.	Maximum 126 and varying lengths of lesser gradients	Lifton	

MOTOR TROLLEY SYSTEM OF MAINTENANCE.

Referring to the above and the standard instructions in respect of the Motor Trolley System of maintenance, the following is a list of places where telephones and Occupation Key Boxes are fixed.

BRANCHES.

	Miles.	Chains.	Remarks.
Tavistock Junction to Launceston.			
Group No. 1 (One Key).			
Marsh Mills	0	19	The telephones communicate with the Signal-
Lee Moor Crossing	1	9	man at Bickleigh.
Key Box No. 1	2	10	Engineering Department Gang stationed at
Key Box No. 2	3	10	Yelverton.
Bickleigh	4	8	
Group No. 2 (One Key).			
Bickleigh	4	8	The telephones communicate with the Signal-
Key Box No. 3	5	17	man at Bickleigh.
Key Box No. 4	6	33	Engineering Department Gang stationed at
Yelverton	7	35	Yelverton.
Group No. 3 (One Key).			
Yelverton	7	35	This telephone communicates with the Signal-
Key Box No. 5	8	29⎫	man at Bickleigh.
Horrabridge	8	77⎭	These telephones communicate with the Signal-man at Horrabridge.
			Engineering Department Gang stationed at Yelverton.
Group No. 4 (One Key).			
Horrabridge	8	77	The telephones communicate with the Signal-
Key Box No. 6	9	70	man at Tavistock South.
Key Box No. 7	10	53	Engineering Department Gang stationed at
Key Box No. 8	11	60	Tavistock South.
Tavistock South	12	69	

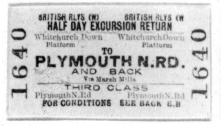

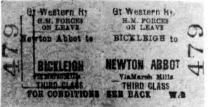

	Miles.	Chains.	Remarks.
Group No. 5 (One Key).			
Tavistock South	12	69	The telephones communicate with the Signal-
Key Box No. 9	13	66	man at Tavistock South.
Key Box No. 10	14	52	Engineering Department Gang stationed at
Key Box No. 11	15	38	Tavistock South.
Mary Tavy	16	23	
Key Box No. 12	17	10	
Key Box No. 13	17	73	
Key Box No. 14	18	56	
Lydford	19	40	
Group No. 6 (One Key).			
Lydford	19	40	The telephones communicate with the Signal-
Key Box No. 15	20	10	man at Lydford.
Key Box No. 16	20	60	Engineering Department Gang stationed at
Key Box No. 17	21	44	Lifton.
Key Box No. 18	22	28	
Key Box No. 19	23	12	
Coryton	23	76	
Key Box No. 20	24	60	
Key Box No. 21	25	43	
Key Box No. 22	26	27	
Lifton	27	14	
Group No. 7 (One Key).			
Lifton	27	14	The telephones communicate with the Signal-
Key Box No. 23	27	65	man at Launceston.
Key Box No. 24	28	40	Engineering Department Gang stationed at
Key Box No. 25	29	27	Lifton.
Key Box No. 26	30	11	
Key Box No. 27	31	0	
Launceston	31	67	

TABLE N.

TROLLEYS GOING INTO OR THROUGH TUNNELS.

The following is a list of Tunnels to which Rule 215 (1) and Block Regulation 9 apply:—

Tunnel.	Between.	Length.	
		Miles.	Yards.
TAVISTOCK JUNCTION TO LAUNCESTON.			
Yelverton	Yelverton and Horrabridge ..	—	641
Grenofen	Horrabridge and Tavistock South..	—	374

Table A: List of Signal Boxes, Running Lines etc.

Description of Block Signalling on Principal Running line. Dots indicate Block Posts	Stations, Signal Boxes, etc.	Distance from Signal Box next above M.	Yds.	Running lines Additional UP	Principal	Additional DOWN	Loops and Refuge Sidings Description	Standage Wagons E. & V.	Runaway Catch Points— Spring or unworked Trailing Points Line	Position	Gradient (Rising unless otherwise shown) 1 in.	Engine Whistles L—long s—short DOWN Main	Relief or Goods	UP. Main	Relief or Goods	Remarks C—crow
	TAVISTOCK JUNCTION TO LAUNCESTON															
●	Tavistock Junction															
●	**Marsh Mills**		660						Down Loop	C.W. Bickleigh end of Down Loop	100					
●	**Plym Bridge Platform**															
●	Bickleigh	3	1518				DRS URS CL	24 21 41	Down Loop Down Loop	C.W. Marsh Mills end of Down Loop C. Yelverton end of Down Loop	60 60					
	Shaugh Bridge Platform															
	Clearbrook Halt															
	Yelverton															
●	Horrabridge	4	1518				DRS URS CL	35 44 14	Up Loop	C.W. Yelverton end of Up Loop	104					

Electric Token

Table A: List of Signal Boxes, Running Lines etc.

198

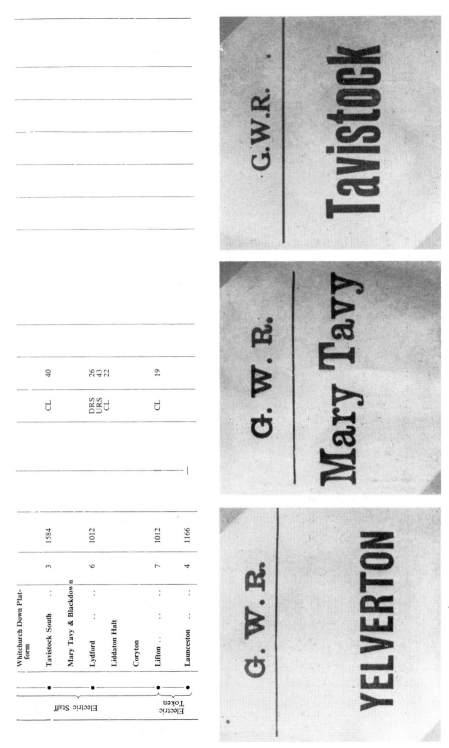

G.W.R. Tavistock

G.W.R. Mary Tavy

G.W.R. YELVERTON

Station				
Whitchurch Down Platform				
Tavistock South	3	1584	CL	40
Mary Tavy & Blackdown n				
Lydford	6	1012	DRS	26
			URS	43
			CL	22
Liddaton Halt				
Coryton				
Lifton	7	1012	CL	19
Launceston	4	1166		

Electric Staff

Electric Token

TABLE F.

PROPELLING TRAINS OR VEHICLES.

When trains or vehicles are being propelled in accordance with Rule 149 the undermentioned conditions must be complied with. The sections of line where propelling outside station limits is authorised are shown below.

When vehicles are propelled or gravitated within station limits on a running line or loop, the Guard, Shunter, or person in charge must, except in the case of the movement of freight vehicles in charge of a Guard or Shunter, ride in the leading or first suitable vehicle.

When propelling freight vehicles outside station limits a Guard's brake van must be the leading vehicle, unless otherwise indicated, and the Guard or Shunter must ride therein.

In the case of coaching stock vehicles or where authority is given to propel freight vehicle without a brake van leading the Guard or Shunter must ride in the leading suitable vehicle.

Drivers will not be relieved of responsibility for observing fixed signals, but the Guard, Shunter, or person in charge must keep a sharp lookout, warn any person who may be on or near the line, observe fixed signals and be prepared to give any necessary hand signal to the Driver. Drivers must keep a sharp look out and be prepared to act immediately upon any signal which may be given by the Guard, Shunter, or person in charge.

The speed must not exceed 20 m.p.h., and down inclines steeper than 1 in 200, through station platforms and over level crossings must not exceed 15 m.p.h. (This paragraph does not apply to Officers' Specials).

The engine whistle must be sounded when approaching stations and level crossings, also where there is not a good view of the line ahead.

Where the line is on a falling gradient a sufficient number of wagon brakes must be pinned down whenever there is a doubt as to whether the brake van will hold the train should it become divided, or where there is no brake van attached.

In all cases where coaching stock or fitted vehicles are authorised to be propelled, the automatic brake must be connected up and in use.

Vehicles conveying passengers must not be propelled under this arrangement except in the case of items marked " P " :—

From.	To.	Line.	Number of vehicles and Special conditions.
Tavistock Junction	**to Launceston**		
Tavistock South ...	Pitts Cleave Quarry Sidings	Single	Freight Vehicles not exceeding 20 wagons. Not applicable during the hours of darkness or during fog or falling snow. Instructions shown on page 124. See also Table S2.

TABLE S. 2.

TRAINS RETURNING FROM INTERMEDIATE SIDINGS OR STATIONS ON SINGLE LINES OF RAILWAY TO THE TOKEN OR STAFF STATION IN THE REAR.

The following is a list of places on single lines of railway worked on the Electric Token Block System or the Train Staff and Ticket system where trains requiring to proceed to intermediate sidings or stations only may return to the token station in the rear, subject to the modifications shown in the remarks column.

Unless otherwise shown, the instructions will apply only to trains not conveying passengers, and except where shown to the contrary, the trains must have an engine in front and a brake van in rear when proceeding to and returning from such intermediate siding or station.

When assisted in rear under this arrangement, the token must be transferred from one engine to another when necessary, by the Guard, so that it is always carried on the rear-most engine.

Should the Guard of a Freight, Ballast or Officers' Special train calling at an intermediate siding in a section require his train to return to the Token Station in rear instead of going through to the Token Station in advance he must obtain the permission of the Signalman before the train enters the section.

Siding from.	To.	Remarks.
TAVISTOCK JUNCTION	**TO LAUNCESTON.**	
Plym Bridge Platform ..	Marsh Mills ..	Rail motors conveying passengers and applies only on Bank Holidays and other days authorised by special notice.
Shaugh Bridge Platform ..	Bickleigh	Rail motors conveying passengers and applies only on Bank Holidays and other days authorised by special notice.
Pitts Cleave Quarry Siding	Tavistock South ..	Instructions shown on Page 124.

TABLE H 1.

WORKING OF FREIGHT VEHICLES WITHOUT A BRAKE VAN IN REAR.

Set out below is a list of places where Freight vehicles (in accordance with Rule 153(*b*)) may be worked without a brake van in rear.

One wagon of coal or stores for Signal Boxes and Stations, or the empty wagon in connection therewith, may be worked without a brake van between any two Signal Boxes, provided the Signal Boxes concerned are not more than one mile apart.

From.	To.	Line.	No. of vehicles and Special Conditions.
TAVISTOCK JUNCTION TO LAUNCESTON.			
Marsh Mills ..	Tavistock Junction	Up	Engine and not more than 15 vehicles. Before the train leaves Marsh Mills a proper understanding must be arrived at by the Signalmen at Marsh Mills and Tavistock Junction and the Trainmen. The engine must in all cases be at the Plymouth end.

TABLE J. 3.

SPECIAL INSTRUCTIONS FOR DESCENDING INCLINES.

DAINTON (EXCL.) TO PENZANCE.

TAVISTOCK JUNCTION TO LAUNCESTON.

BICKLEIGH TO MARSH MILLS.

Freight trains must not descend this incline at a higher speed than 20 miles per hour. Brakes must be picked up at Marsh Mills.

YELVERTON TO BICKLEIGH.

Freight trains must not descend this incline at a higher speed than 20 miles per hour.

YELVERTON TO HORRABRIDGE.

Freight trains must not descend this incline at a higher speed than 20 miles per hour. Trains must stop at Horrabridge to pick up brakes.

LYDFORD TO CORYTON.

Freight trains must not descend this incline at a higher speed than 20 miles per hour. Trains must stop at Coryton to pick up brakes.

TABLE E. 2.

LIST OF LEVEL CROSSINGS WHERE WHISTLE BOARDS ARE NOT PROVIDED BUT WHERE DRIVERS ARE REQUIRED TO SOUND ENGINE WHISTLES.

Name of Crossing and Mileage.		Crossing situated between.	Direction.
TAVISTOCK JUNCTION TO LAUNCESTON.			
Pitts Cleave	14 m. 17 ch.	Tavistock South and Mary Tavy ..	Down.

ASCENDING INCLINES—ASSISTING OF TRAINS.

Points between which Assistant Engines work.		Where only one Assistant Engine is employed.		Remarks.
From.	To.	Whether in front or rear.	Whether coupled or Not.	
TAVISTOCK JUNCTION TO LAUNCESTON				
Marsh Mills ..	Horrabridge ...	Front ...	—	Assisting engines must be placed in front of Down trains at Marsh Mills Station and assist to Horrabridge. The load of such trains must not exceed that for a train worked by two Class-A locomotives.
Tavistock South	Lydford ..	Rear ..	Uncoupled	Assistant engines must be placed behind Down Freight Trains at Tavistock South and push them thence to Lydford uncoupled. When such engines are going beyond Lydford they must be placed in front of the trains at that station.
Lifton	Lydford ..	Rear ..	Uncoupled	Assistant engines must be placed behind Up Freight Trains at Lifton and push them thence to Lydford uncoupled. When such engines are going beyond Lydford they must be placed in front of the trains at that station.

TABLE Z.

COUPLING AND UNCOUPLING OF ENGINES OF PASSENGER TRAINS.

Except where otherwise shown the following arrangements will apply to the coupling and uncoupling of engines in the Plymouth Traffic District.

Station.	Work performed by Fireman.	Work performed by Traffic Department.
Plymouth Millbay ..	Departure (Loaded or Empty) ..	Arrival and Shunting.
Launceston	Arrival and Departure	Shunting.

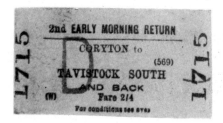

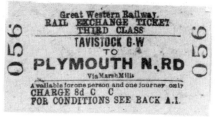

Delete heading **MARSH MILLS**—*continued* and *substitute*:

PLYMOUTH, TAVISTOCK JUNCTION TO MARSH MILLS

Add:

SHUNTING MOVEMENTS FROM TAVISTOCK JUNCTION YARD TO MARSH MILLS SIDINGS

The speed of movements over this siding must not exceed 5 m.p.h.

When vehicles are being propelled, the Shunter in charge of the movement must walk in front or ride on the leading or nearest most suitable vehicle.

All movements from the Marsh Mills direction must be stopped at the Tavistock Junction Yard stop lamp until told to proceed.

MESSRS. ENGLISH CLAYS LOVERING POCHIN AND CO. LTD., PRIVATE SIDINGS

Amend sixth paragraph under diagram to:

The telephone at points "C" connects with the Works Foreman's Office.

Pages 122 and 123

Delete **INWARDS TRAFFIC** and **OUTWARDS TRAFFIC** completely and *substitute*:

INWARDS TRAFFIC

1. Before a train leaves Marsh Mills, the Shunter must telephone the Works Foreman and obtain his assurance that:

(*a*) there are no wagons or cattle on the line between C and H, and any wagons between H and Y or Z are fully braked and scotched, and points H and G are set for the Shed Siding;

(*b*) any wagons in the loop are fully braked and scotched, the points set normal and the wheel stop at the Marsh Mills end is in position over the rail;

(*c*) any wagons in siding F are fully braked, the wheel stop is in position over the rail and the points are set towards G;

(*d*) the diesel locomotive is in the Shed Siding, clear of the line between C and H.

2. Having these assurances, the Shunter must unclip and reverse points C for the movement to come from A; after doing this he must so telephone the Head Shunter.

3. The Head Shunter may then authorize the movement to proceed towards X.

4. When vehicles are being propelled, the Head Shunter must walk in front or ride on the leading or nearest most suitable vehicle.

5. The speed of the movement must not exceed 5 m.p.h.

6. The train must be brought to a stand well to the rear of points G, after which the diesel locomotive may draw out wagons from the Shed Siding towards Y or Z, and when that movement comes to a stand and the wagons have been fully braked, the inwards wagons may be propelled beyond points G or H as the case may be, where they must be fully braked prior to the B.R. locomotive being detached and set back clear of those points to enable the inwards wagons to gravitate to or be positioned in the Shed Siding by the diesel locomotive.

7. The B.R. locomotive must not proceed beyond the notice board at X, and it must not enter the loop, sidings F and D, or the connections thereto.

8. Wagons may be propelled into siding F provided there are enough wagons attached so that the locomotive will not have to enter the siding or traverse the connection thereto.

OUTWARDS TRAFFIC

1. Outwards traffic is picked up at X or in the loop siding, and enough wagons must be attached so that the locomotive will not have to enter the siding or traverse its connection.

2. The standard incline instructions must be complied with so far as they apply, before descending the incline between X and B.

3. After the locomotive has passed points C, the Shunter must see that they are replaced, clipped and padlocked in the normal position.

4. The train must be stopped at points B for the Head Shunter to close them to allow the train to proceed.

5. Outwards traffic may be positioned between C and G.

6. E.C.L.P. and Co.'s employees are responsible for seeing that such wagons are fully braked and scotched.

7. Before unclipping points C to permit the B.R. locomotive to enter the sidings, the Shunter must ascertain the exact position of the wagons standing between C and G, and afterwards pilot the locomotive to the wagons.

If the diesel locomotive is not available to perform the shunting owing to failure or other cause, E.C.L.P. and Co. will give prior notice to the Marsh Mills Station Master who must arrange for the B.R. locomotive to carry out the work, subject to the restrictions shown in the above instructions. Any wagons to or from the shed siding via points G or H must be fully braked and scotched when left on the incline before the locomotive is detached.

Page 123

    Delete complete section: **HORRABRIDGE**

Page 124

    Delete completely.

Page 125

    Delete complete section: **LAUNCESTON**

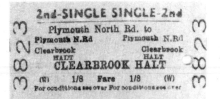

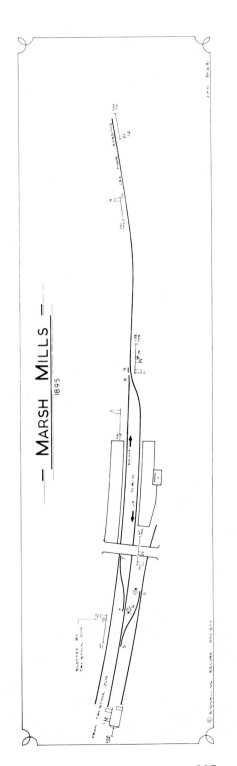

MARSH MILLS

1895

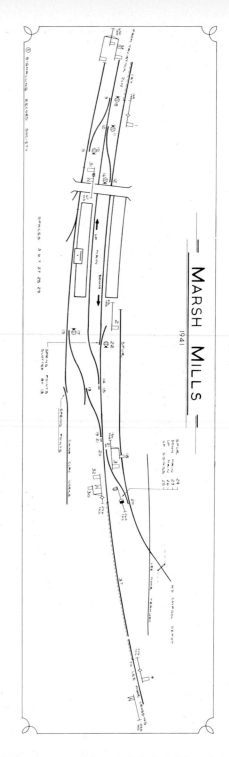

MARSH MILLS

1941

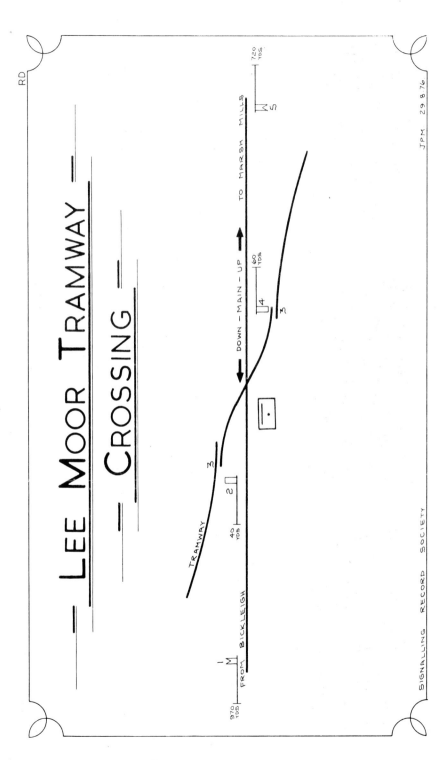

LEE MOOR TRAMWAY
CROSSING

RD

TO MARSH MILLS

DOWN - MAIN - UP

72.0 YDS

M 5

60 YDS

4

3

TRAMWAY

3

2

40 YDS

FROM BICKLEIGH

970 YDS

M 1

JPM 29.8.76

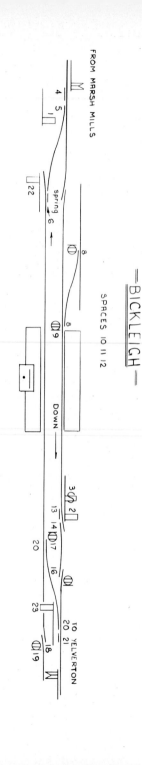

YELVERTON

1897

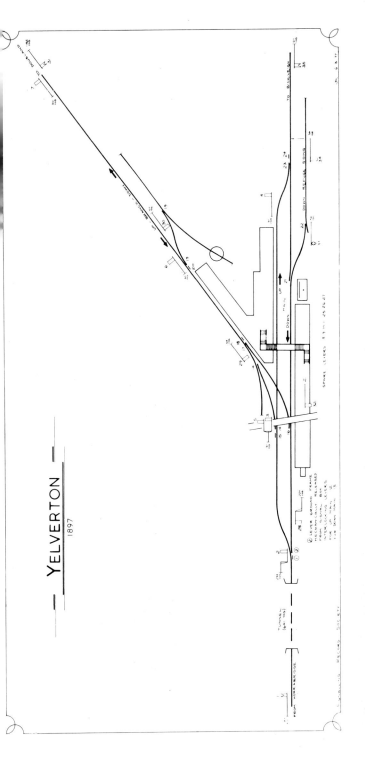

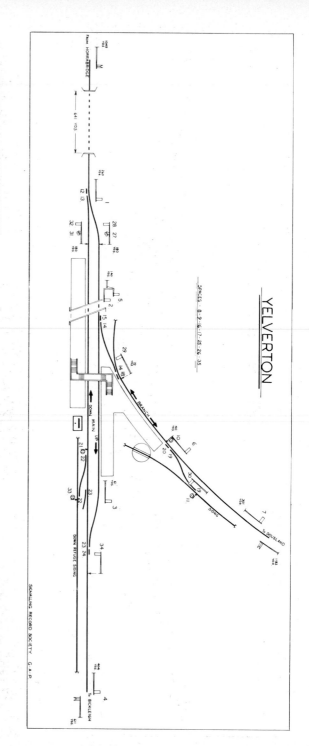

YELVERTON

SIGNALLING RECORD SOCIETY. G.A.P.

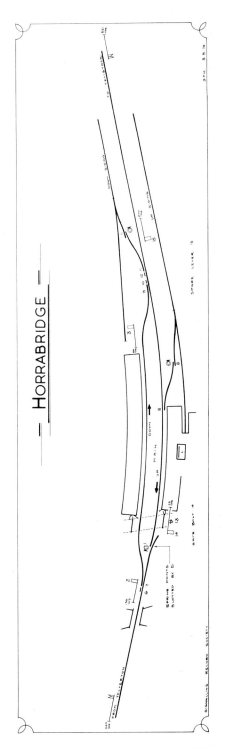

HORRABRIDGE

1736

2nd - **CHEAP DAY**
(7523)

Lidaaton Halt to
TAVISTOCK SOUTH
(W)
AND BACK
For conditions see over

1736

410

Great Western Railway
H.M. FORCES ON LEAVE
Via LIPTON TO
Third Class Fare
FOR CONDITI
SEE BACK
B.W.R.
N.D.

410

7396

Gt. Western Ry.   Gt. Western Ry
MARY TAVY   MARY TAVY
& BLACKDOWN   & BLACKDOWN
TO
TAVISTOCK G.W
(Tavistock G.W)
THIRD CLASS
3d Fare 3d C
(Tavistock.G.W.)   (Tavistock G W
FOR CONDITIONS SEE BACK A C

7396

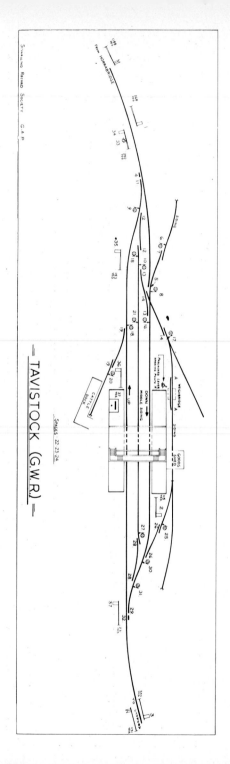

= TAVISTOCK (G.W.R.) =

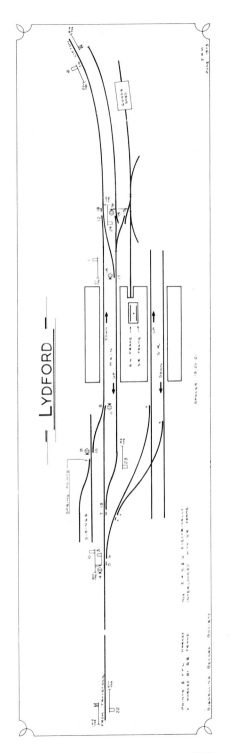

LYDFORD

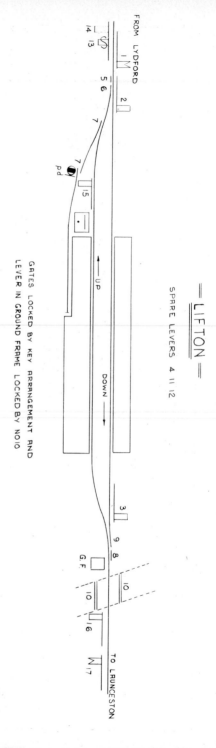

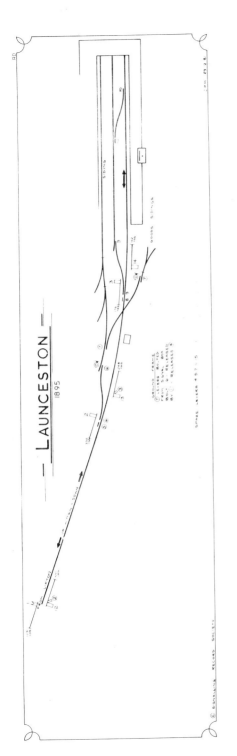

— LAUNCESTON —

1895

GOODS SIDING

SIDING

GROUND FRAME
(4 LEVERS) BOLTED
FROM S.BOX.
BOLT S. RELEASED
BY № 2. RELEASES 4

SPARE LEVERS 4 5 7 11 5

© SIGNALLING RECORD SOCIETY.

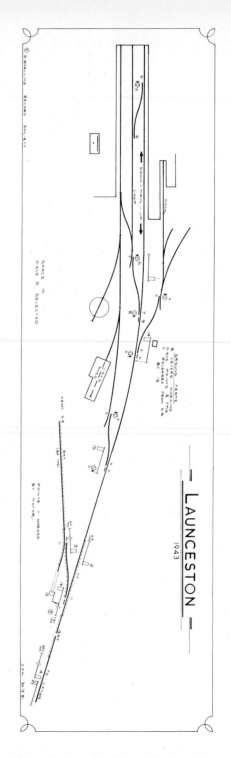

LAUNCESTON
1943

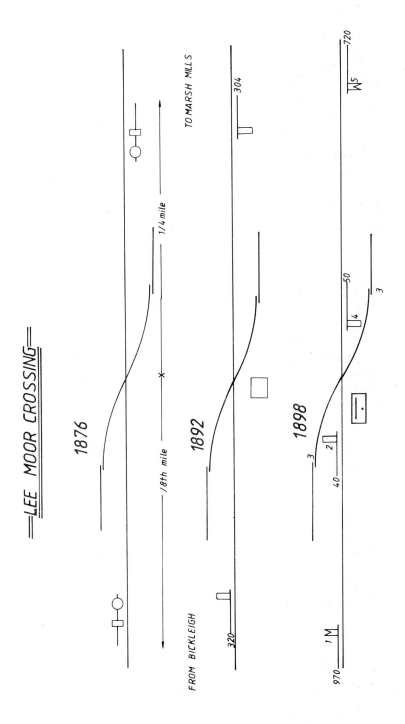

=LEE MOOR CROSSING=

1876

1892

1898

TO MARSH MILLS

FROM BICKLEIGH

1/4 mile

1/8th mile

304

320

50

4

3

2

3

40

720

5

M

1 M

970

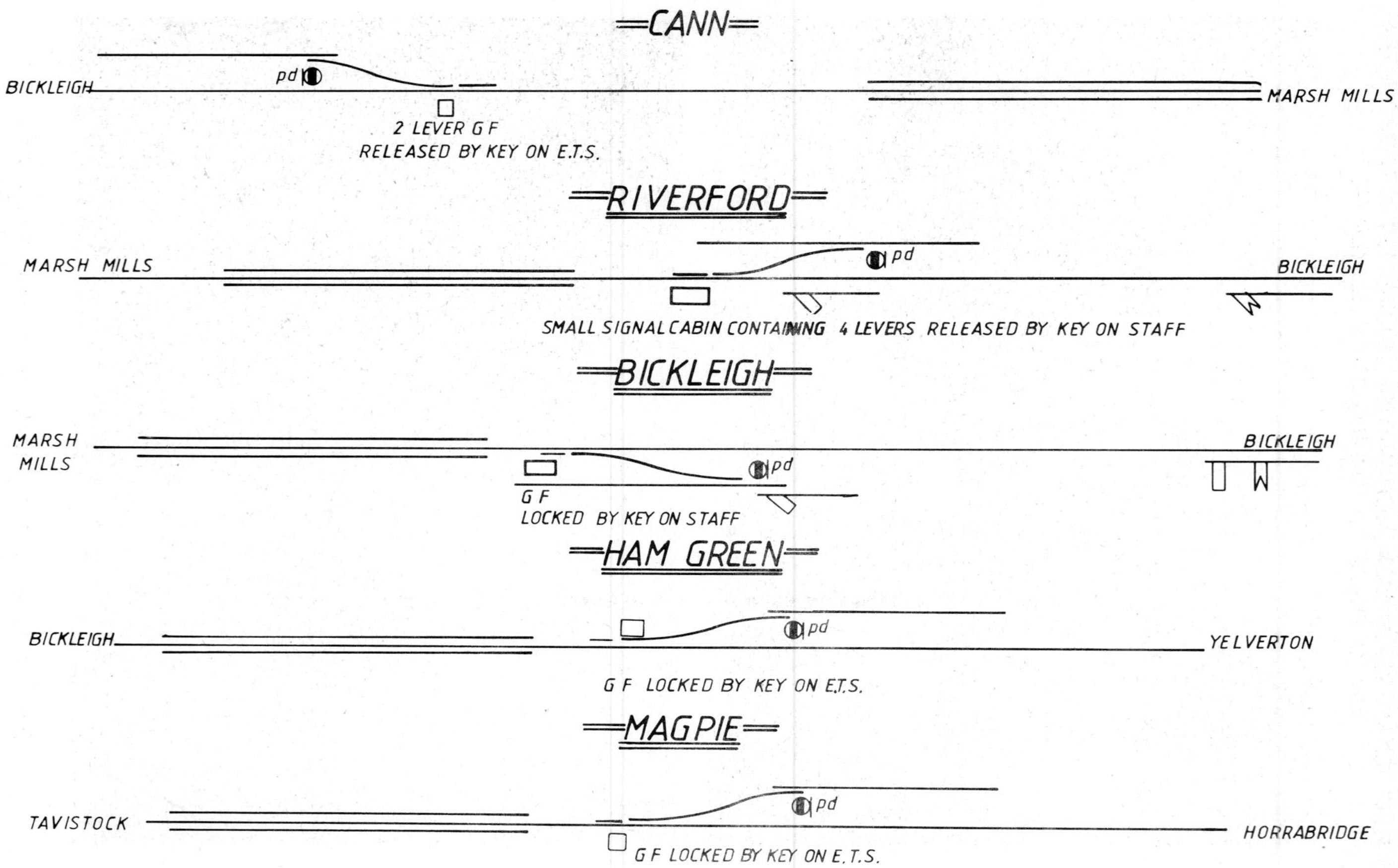

CANN

BICKLEIGH — MARSH MILLS

pd

2 LEVER G F
RELEASED BY KEY ON E.T.S.

RIVERFORD

MARSH MILLS — BICKLEIGH

pd

SMALL SIGNAL CABIN CONTAINING 4 LEVERS RELEASED BY KEY ON STAFF

BICKLEIGH

MARSH MILLS — BICKLEIGH

pd

G F
LOCKED BY KEY ON STAFF

HAM GREEN

BICKLEIGH — YELVERTON

pd

G F LOCKED BY KEY ON E.T.S.

MAGPIE

TAVISTOCK — HORRABRIDGE

pd

G F LOCKED BY KEY ON E.T.S.

Two studies of 0-6-0PT, No 6400 frozen to the rails with its train.
R.E. Taylor

A close up of No 6400's frozen motion.

A steam lance fed from what is believed to be No 6430, is being used by railway staff to free pointork.

R.E. Taylor

Two studies of No 6430 departing with No 6400 and the rescued Tavistock to Plymouth train.

R.E. Taylor

Two studies of what is believed to be, either No 4591 or 5564 arriving and departing with the rescued No 5568 and the Plymouth to Launceston train, stranded at Tavistock.
R.E. Taylor

Branch Demolition by Pitrail Ltd, April 1964.

Photos by Bernard Mills

Few photographs exist of the demolition of this much loved branch line, I think it is because enthusiasts 'hadn't the stomach' to witness and record such a sad occasion! However Bernard Mills was brave enough to attempt it and, thanks to him, a selection of photographs centered around the Horrabridge to Yelverton section, follow. they first appeared in his book on the line, 'The Branch', and were taken during 6 & 8 May 1964.

Below) The bridge over the A386 at Horrabridge shortly before its demolition c. April 1964. (Compare with scene top of page 95.)

a) Demolition train leaves Yelverton station for Horrabridge.

b) Contractors loco 'running light' near Harrobeer.

c-f) Scenes of activity taken in Horrabridge station during recovery operations.

a)

b)

c)

d)

e)

f)

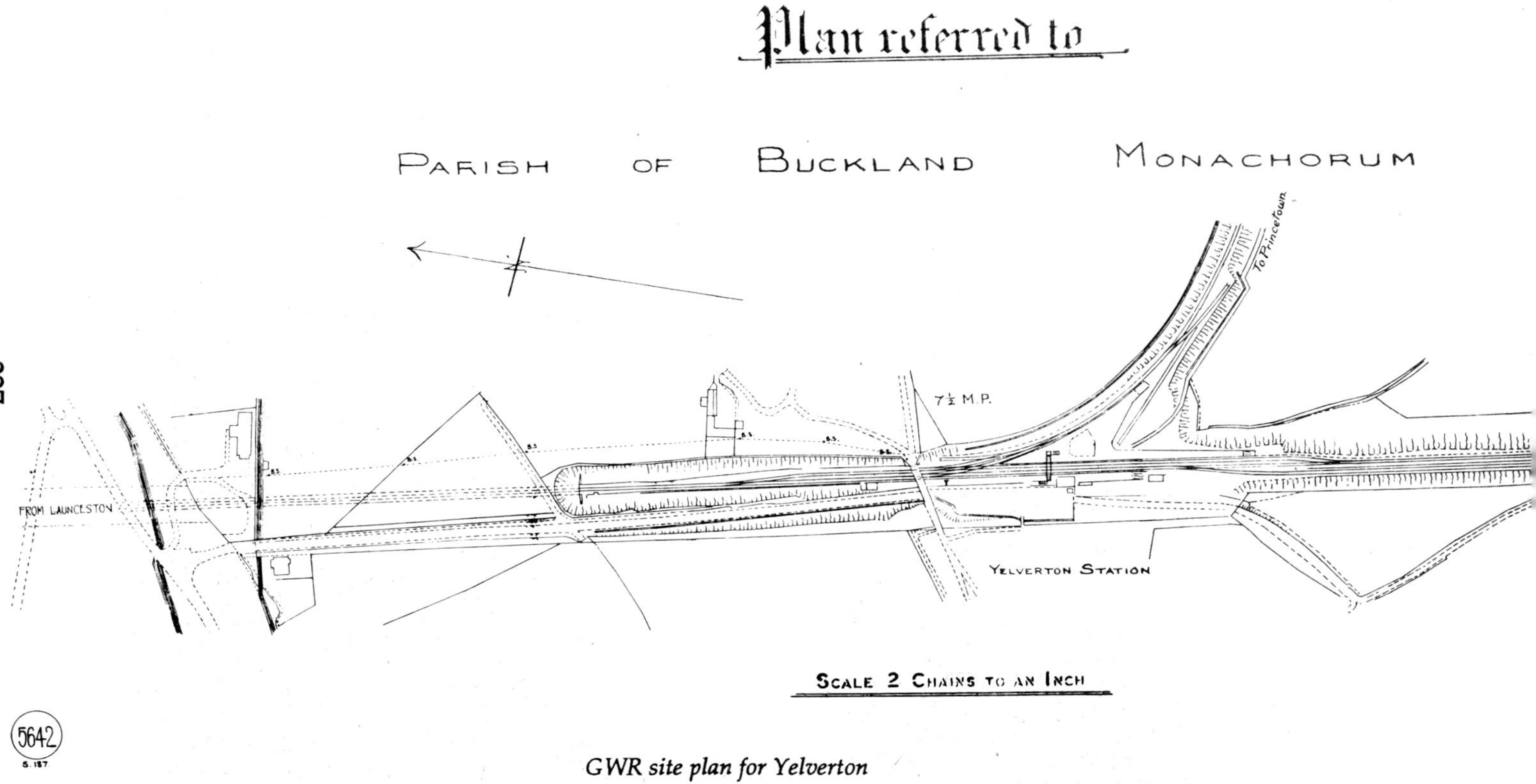

Plan referred to

Parish of Buckland Monachorum

To Princetown

7¼ M.P.

Yelverton Station

From Launceston

Scale 2 Chains to an Inch

GWR site plan for Yelverton

5642
6.157

227

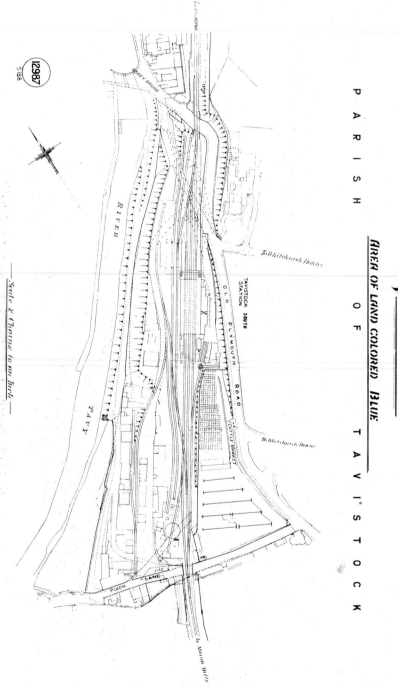

Plan referred to

AREA OF LAND COLORED BLUE

PARISH   OF   TAVISTOCK

12987

S¹⁸

GWR site plan for Tavistock (South)

Scale 2 Chains to an Inch

228

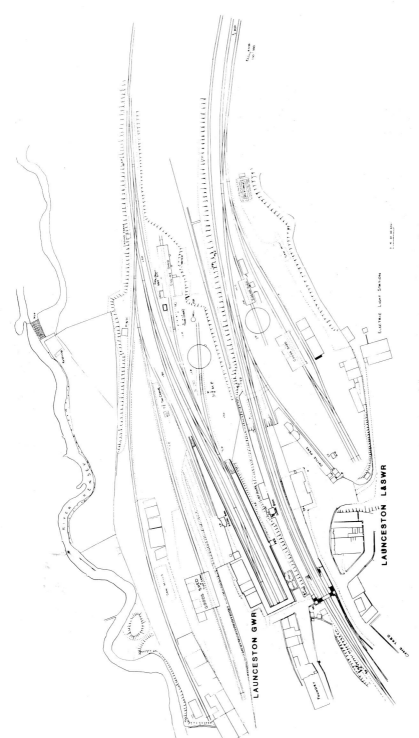

Joint Companies site plan for Launceston (Redrawn by d. Butler)

GWR station layout plan

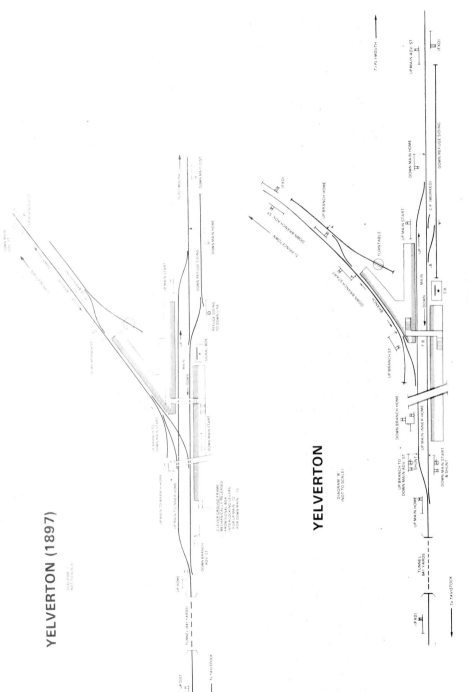

GWR station layout plans (Signalling)

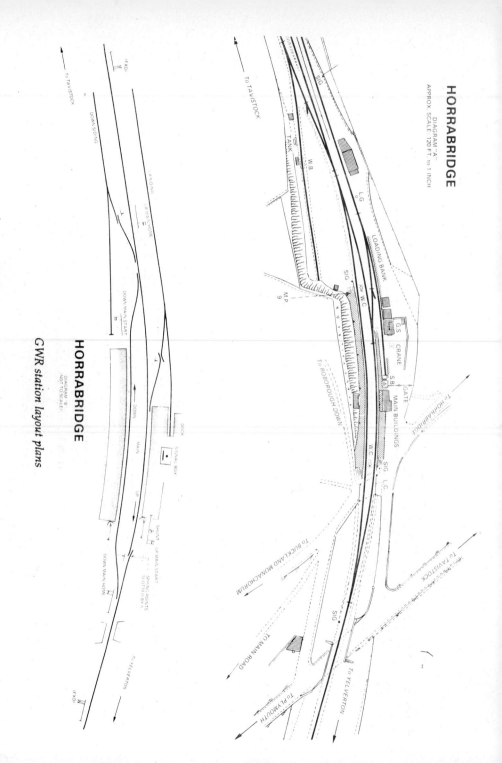

HORRABRIDGE

DIAGRAM "A"
APPROX. SCALE 120 FT. to 1 INCH

HORRABRIDGE

DIAGRAM B
(NOT TO SCALE)

GWR station layout plans

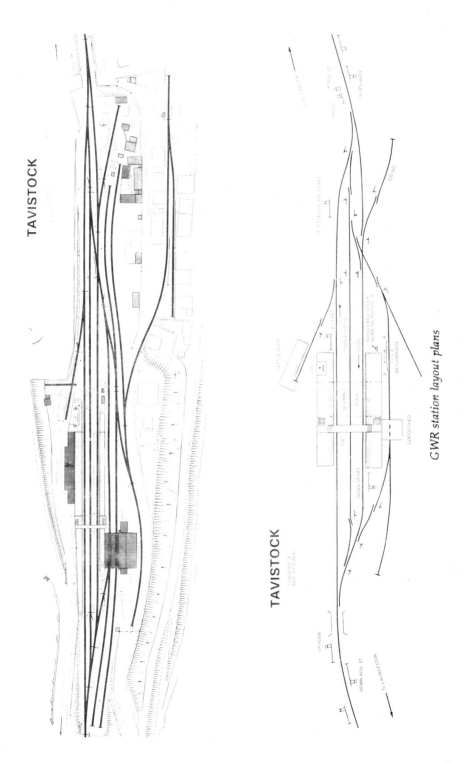

TAVISTOCK

TAVISTOCK

GWR station layout plans

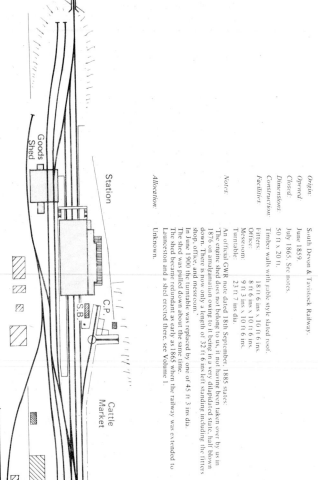

TAVISTOCK c. 1895

SD & TR station layout plan

TAVISTOCK

Origin:	South Devon & Tavistock Railway.
Opened:	June 1859.
Closed:	July 1865. See notes.
Dimensions:	50 ft x 20 ft.
Construction:	Timber walls with gable style slated roof.
Facilities:	
Fitters:	18 ft 6 ins x 10 ft 6 ins.
Office:	8 ft 6 ins x 10 ft 6 ins.
Messroom:	9 ft 3 ins x 10 ft 6 ins.
Turntable:	23 ft 7 ins dia.

Notes: An official GWR note dated 18th September, 1885 states: 'The engine shed does not belong to us, it not having been taken over by us in 1876 on amalgamation owing to it being in a very dilapidated state, half blown down. There is now only a length of 32 ft 6 ins left standing including the fitters shop, office, and messroom.'
In June 1900 the turntable was replaced by one of 45 ft 3 ins dia.
The shed was pulled down about the same time.
The shed became redundant as early as 1865 when the railway was extended to Launceston and a shed erected there, see Volume 1.

Allocation: Unknown.

Labels on plan: Goods Shed; Station; S.B.; C.P.; Cattle Market; Engine Shed; Fitters etc.

Scale: 0 50 100 ft.

1. Engine Shed
2. Fitters etc.

THE LAUNCESTON GOODS

Downalong the valley the smoke is rising
There where the green fields meet the woods
Chugging up through Coryton, struggling up to Liddaton
Working like a Trojan comes the Lan'son goods.

Upalong to Lydford the engine's climbing
Twenty heavy wagons and the "Toad" behind
Six wheels gripping, not a trace of slipping,
Steady in her progress as the weather's kind.

Oakenwood and larchwood, sycamore and hazel
Crowd upon the railway at every sudden bend
Torture in the autumn when the damp days shorten
Struggling up to Lydford at the long grade's end.

Standing on the steep path leading to the culvert
Tingling with excitement at the age of eight
Straining ears to listen, watching rails that glisten
I sense them all a-tremble from the goods train's weight.

Downalong the cutting there's a muffled shaking
Till at last the engine is clearly to be seen
Clank and hiss of piston and the words "GREAT WESTERN"
Clear upon the tank sides in gold on green.

Upalong to Lydford the train goes climbing
Worked by 4591 (or was it ninety-eight?)
She looks a little weary but her driver's wave is cheery
As she trundles slowly past me with the Lan'son freight.

T.W.E.R.

YELVERTON, 1967

The branch lines of Devon are dying and only
Prodigious embankments still show where they led
Their former trim stations stand silent and lonely
While Yelverton lies like a tomb of the dead

Right under the township the bore of the tunnel
Still shows where the railway to Horrabridge went
But no sturdy tank, showering sparks from its funnel
Emerges, its energy practically spent.

The red rhododendron has stretched its green fingers
Right over the curve of the Princetown branch line
Where somehow the ghost of the mixed train still lingers
Awaiting the "right away"—twenty to nine—

The waiting room structure most odd and polygonal
With big leather benches and polished oak wood
Has vanished and so has the curious signal
Which once beyond Yelverton's down platform stood

The flagstones succumb to the ragwort's invasion
The former trim roses revert to the wild
Round turntable site to the east of the station
A few tumbled rails are haphazardly piled.

The soft western evening shines golden and ochre
The raindrops yet glisten on heather still wet,
Can this be the junction where driver and stoker
Exchanged piercing whistles as three engines met?

T.W.E.R.

235

APPENDIX 1
STATION SITES ALONG THE
FORMER ROUTE, SUMMER 1989

1. Marsh Mills

a) Looking north showing the clay siding, level crossing and road to Coypool and shopping complex.

b) Looking south to Tavistock Junction showing overbridge to the original A38 road.

2. Plym Bridge Platform.

Looking north showing old platform foundations, gravel bunker and gradient post.

3. Bickleigh

The station master's house and platform edge are all that are visible here.

4. Shaugh Bridge Platform.

Now a foot and cycle pathway.

5. Clearbrook Halt.

The overbridge immediately north of the Halt site, the access to which, was just this side and to the right of the bridge. (Now sealed up).

6. Yelverton (Junction for Princetown).

a) Looking south out of the mouth of the tunnel.

b) Looking north towards the tunnel.

7. Horrabridge.

The site, looking towards Tavistock, from the level crossing. It is now obliterated by Westcon Agricultural Ltd. (Goods shed roof apex just visible, centre right.)

8. Whitchurch Down Platform.

Looking towards Yelverton.

9. Tavistock South.

Site taken over by Fire and Ambulance stations, and light industry.

10. Mary Tavy and Blackdown Halt.

The station master's house and trackbed now have become a fine rural residence and garden.

11. Lydford GWR/SR

The most densely overgrown site in terms of vegetation.

a) Looking towards Launceston the only sign is a pair of entry gateposts.

b) Looking towards Tavistock the houses backing onto the old station road are still in evidence.

12. Liddaton Halt.

The site of the former halt is to the r.h.s. of the picture, this side of the bridge, looking towards Lydford.

13. Coryton.

The most tastefully constructed residence of any line. It is the old station building rebuilt, extended and modernised.

14. Lifton.

The site here is completely obliterated by vast expansion of the Ambrosia Factory. Viewed at the former level crossing, looking towards Lydford, all that remains is the crossing keeper's house at the extreme left of the picture.

15. Launceston GWR/SR

Both stations are completely obliterated by a large industrial estate, lying in the valley below the town and castle.

Viewed from the north side of the site.

16. Plym Valley Railway site, Marsh Mills.

Three views of the site where restoration is taking place, albeit, slowly. There is still a lack of running track and usable loco's of a size suited to the branch and therefore as yet, no rides to the public are available.

G. W. R.

Mutley

G. W. R.

Bickleigh

1a

1b

2

3

4

5

6a   6b

7

9

11a

12

11b

13

14

15